T0065407

SICILIAN LIVES

BY DANILO DOLCI

TRANSLATED BY JUSTIN VITIELLO

(COLLABORATOR, MADELINE POLIDORO)

PANTHEON BOOKS   NEW YORK

SICILIAN LIVES

These works by Danilo Dolci were originally published in
the Italian language in the following publications:
Banditi a Partinico (1955); *Inchiesta a Palermo* (1956); *Spreco*
(1960); *Racconti siciliani* (1963); *Chi gioca solo* (1966);
Non esiste il silenzio (1974); and *Racconti siciliani* (1974).

Library of Congress Cataloging in Publication Data
Dolci, Danilo.
Sicilian lives.
1. Sicily—Social life and customs. 2. Sicily—
Social conditions. 3. Oral history. I. Title.
DG865.6.D64 945'.8 81-47538
ISBN 0-394-51536-6 AACR2
ISBN:978-0-394-74938-9 (pbk.)

Manufactured in the United States of America

144915995

CONTENTS

CONTENTS

FOREWORD

I have never met Danilo Dolci. I would count it a great honor to do so. He is a man who believes in poetry and action, a man who has devoted his life to an uncompromising struggle against injustice and poverty, yet who is tolerant. Perhaps most important of all, he does not believe in saviors, only in catalysts.

Without Dolci this book would not exist. Yet it is not his voice which speaks through it. It is a book of voices that he has assembled and encouraged to speak: the voices of impoverished peasants and fishermen from around the village of Trappeto and of the urban poor from the Sicilian capital of Palermo.

In recent years there have been many books which, using a tape recorder, have recorded and collected popular voices. Such a way of recording has become part of sociological research. Some of these books are valuable. But this one is in an altogether different category. Dolci, who kept a record of these conversations over a period of thirty years, had no sociological ambitions. And the women and men who talked with him were not talking to an investigator, not even to a well-meaning one. The quality of Dolci's life's work in Sicily is reflected in the stories of this book without a word being said by him. What are these stories like?

The few interviews with the rich and powerful, although forming an invaluable point of comparison, are of course different. I am talking of the poor, those exploited by the rich and powerful, telling the stories of *their* lives. They are graphic storytellers. This has nothing to do with literary ability. Many of them are illiterate. It has to do with a practice which predates literature.

In all preindustrial societies people have believed that living is a way of living a story. In this story one is always the protagonist and occasionally the teller, but the inventor of the story, the designer of the plot, is elsewhere. People who believe this, and who lead the story of their life in this way, are often natural storytellers. Just as, if they happen to be shepherds who spend a great deal of time alone, companioned only by animals and the spirit of the landscape, they are often natural poets: poetry being that form of language which addresses itself to that which is beyond speaking.

In many of the stories told in this book there is little or no hope. That is to say, there is no ground for hope in the events narrated. And yet they are never recitals of despair. Of bitterness, tragedy, injustice, hopelessness, yes. But of despair, no. How can one explain such a paradox? There is the inventor of the story and there is also the judge of the story. It is by no means clear that the two are the same. The distinction between them may be somewhat like that between the Devil and God.

This idea of an inventor and a judge of the story of one's life is closely connected with religion. Yet no religious formulation completely covers this belief. The belief arises in the face of an enigma, not in the face of a set of answers.

The stories are not recitals of despair because, despite all, the telling of them is an appeal for judgment. The judgment for which the appeal is made is a multiform one: it is human, social, moral, metaphysical. Ultimately it is an appeal for a judgment made by a being who is comparable to the teller, but who is more powerful, who has more opportunities, more time, more peace within which to judge. Who or what is this being? God, you will say. Perhaps. It can also be history, other people, the dead parents who brought one into the world, the children who may survive one, the coexistence of everything on the other side of time, the listener to the story. I cannot give the ontological answer. I want only to describe the spirit in which these stories have been told, and hence their essential character.

Dolci's role in the telling of these stories was a very special one. He was at the beginning of each story, in that he prompted it and then listened to it. And he was at the end of each story—

the very end—in that in some way he was, not the judge, but an agent, a trustworthy, understanding agent, of that which would judge.

Last year I and my family drove in our small Citroën 2cv. to Genoa. Just after the war the port area of this city had inspired me to make several paintings. Paintings made very much in the spirit of the early neorealist Italian films, such as *Open City, Bicycle Thieves* . . . "Let's go and see if we can find a pizzeria that I used to know," I said. We left the car and went on foot through the narrow streets which are still like ravines, and in which you can still buy and be sold just about anything. The pizzeria had disappeared, but we ate in another, rather more modern one.

We returned to the car and drove off. When we arrived at the house of the friends we were visiting, I unlocked the luggage compartment of the car to take out our suitcase. And it was then that I saw that my haversack had disappeared. It had been stolen whilst we were eating our pizza. It had contained an electric razor, a camera, a pair of binoculars, and a notebook. It was only the loss of the latter which really affected me. It was full of jottings for a story I was writing, and of theoretical notes about different forms of narrative. About the difference between bourgeois and popular narration, about how privilege or the lack of privilege gives a very different perspective to the narrating of events. Within half an hour the absurdity of either anger or regret became obvious to me. Occasionally the poor levy their own taxes in their own locale. And against this I was in no position to complain.

As you will learn from one of the stories here, it is quite possible that the band of two or three kids who opened the locked compartment of my car, skillfully, silently, and in full daylight, came from Palermo, on one of their professional tours of the mainland. As a result my notes on how *they* might tell the story of their sojourn in Genoa are no longer at hand!

Nevertheless I want to say something about their storytelling.

First, however, I want to emphasize that what I have to say is not the most important thing to be said. Dolci himself describes what the telling of such stories can do to the consciousness of those who have lived them. And this is more important. Nobody reading this book can fail to be struck by what the stories reveal about the intolerable conditions, flagrant injustice, and endemic violence imposed upon the lives of the tellers. What remains is the question how we, the relatively privileged, read such a book. The question how we translate these stories into our experience. For if we do not translate them, we shall read them only as exotica.

The annals of the poor. I choose the word poor deliberately. I might say: of landless peasants and of the lumpenproletariat. The word poor has a very long tradition to it, and it is necessary to recognize this tradition. And already we are hard up against the first problem. We have to recognize and respect this tradition, without, for one moment, falling into the revolting complacency which accepts poverty as an ordained component of the human condition. Personally I believe that Marxism, with its precise social and historical analysis, is an apprenticeship which the poor have already undergone or will undergo. Such an apprenticeship helps to train them to face the world as it is, and to contest it. Yet Marxism cannot draw a line under the centuries' experience of the poor and thus close the account, as if thereafter this experience were no more than an anomaly.

With modern means of production, and given a radical transformation of existing social relations, a world of plenty is today possible. Yet what we actually see, for the most part, is a world of unprecedentedly violent poverty. Everyone talks of this, but this talk does not usually even begin to eliminate the poverty. When it does—as in Mao's China or in the non-European republics of the Soviet Union—the improvement is hidden, at least in the minds of the West, under a barrage of political debate about other issues.

One could say that we are living the crisis of utopianism. The utopian vision of a just world of plenty nowhere accords with reality. It is not my task here to lay out what conclusions should be drawn from this impasse. What does need to be pointed out is that the crisis of utopianism has absolutely nothing to do with the poor as they live their own lives.

Their crises are much more immediate and material. There is no need to list them, for you are going to read some three hundred pages devoted to them. Likewise their hopes are both smaller and tougher, that is to say more persistent and longer-lasting. There have been educators, including revolutionary ones, who have explained this paradox of desperation and hope among the poor as the consequence of superstition and ignorance. But there are many systems of knowledge, and each one calls the other ignorant. The poor's over-all view of life is very evident in the pages that follow, but it is so far removed from the view that most of us have inherited that we risk not seeing its logic and coherence. And failing to see its logic and coherence, we risk being blind to its intellectual and moral courage.

First and foremost, life for the poor is an arena of struggle. Ceaseless, unremitting struggle in which only partial victories can ever be foreseen, and of those foreseen, only a fraction gained. Life is the arena, the stage, of this struggle; but not the struggle itself. That life is only a struggle for survival is a notion of nineteenth-century social and biological science. The poor could never allow themselves the luxury of such cynicism.

If life appears to them to be nothing but a struggle for survival, because they are living it and not merely investigating it, they conclude that life is a trial which, obscurely and terribly, must nevertheless have some other purpose. At the very least this purpose may be the grateful acceptance of repose at the end of the struggle. At the most, it may be that the eventual role of the poor will be to cleanse the world—at least temporarily—of evil.

And here it is worth remembering that this last occasional yet recurrent revolutionary vision was never utopian, for it was based, not upon a detailed vision of what would follow, but on a sense of the overwhelming justice of retrospective revenge!

The poor estimate that life is a trial: that pleasure is a gift and a mystery, perhaps the deepest mystery of all: that there are no final solutions: that all men are fallible: that events are more powerful than choices. The idea that life bestows a *right* to satisfaction and happiness is to them naive, and furthermore, because somewhere such an idea implies an unrealizable promise, profoundly dishonest.

Such a view accords with many thousands of years of varied human experience, but it is in direct opposition to the life-view of the privileged today in modern Europe and North America. And this opposition is part of the content of the most profound drama of our time.

It can be put very simply. On one hand an essentially tragic view of life; on the other hand a technocratic and optimistic view of life, which precludes the category of the tragic. And then, if we pass from theory to practice, the systematic oppression of those who have a tragic view by those who have a technocratic and optimistic one. Only the term "systematic oppression" is inadequate. For this oppression *is* tragedy.

It is necessary to say this, for it is not what the poor themselves are in a position to say. But once it is said, it is to their evidence that we should listen, and in listening something different will also become apparent.

To say that the poor are closer to reality than the rich is a cliché. And a somewhat patronizing one, in that it suggests that reality is coarse, material, brutal, physical. And it suggests that reality is thus opposed to the spiritual, from which the poor are mostly excluded. Yet the true antithesis of the real is the abstract.

What is remarkable in the stories and reflections that follow is their lack of abstraction. And in the interviews with the rich and the Mafiosi, what is remarkable is the opposite. In poor societies abstraction and tyranny go together; in rich societies it is indifference which usually goes with abstraction. Abstraction's capacity to ignore what is real (and the heart can abstract as well as the mind: unjustified jealousy, for example, is an abstraction) is undoubtedly where most evil begins.

Reality, as distinct from abstraction, is contradictory. Two-faced. (Is the limitation of the abstract the result of the fact that purely cerebral thought originates in only one of the two spheres of the brain?) The living of these stories has encouraged an acceptance of contradiction. From this acceptance comes truthfulness (an absence of simple self-justification), forgiveness, pity, humor, and—perhaps most notably of all—the capacity to reflect upon contradictions and their mystery. These reflections, unlike abstractions, are living thought.

> There's times I see the stars at night, especially when we're out for eels, and I get to thinking in my brain, "The world, is it really real?" Me, I can't believe that. If I get calm, I can believe in Jesus. Bad-mouth Jesus Christ and I'll kill you. But there's times I won't believe, not even in God: "If God really exists, why doesn't He give me a break and a job?"
>
> Then I remember I got kids, and don't hang myself. Still, there's times . . . When I can't find work, my head just spins . . .
>
> Skinning those frogs, I feel pity, but what can I do but kill them? I pity them but they got to die. This frog staring at me knows his time's come. There in my hand I'm telling him, he's got no doubt. How do I know it? Catching him by the legs before you apply the scissors, the frog pisses in your hand—like we'd do in the same fix—and more than once. That's why I know how he thinks.

Looking beneath the veil of reality I've learned that women and men are nothing but scarecrows or feathers blowing in the wind. Women are movable objects, and man is so weak, generically speaking, that he exposes himself like a peacock. Savage beast that he is, man in the presence of woman is like a newborn lamb.

If human beings had the slightest inkling of the secret, that we're only on this earth a fleeting moment, we'd cherish every day month and year a lot more. We'd see time flow past and our life with it, which is all the more reason to cherish it and help each other out, physically, and be at one in peace of mind.

Truthfulness, pity, humor, the capacity to reflect upon contradictions, yes, yes. But there is another contradiction: every woman tries to abolish poverty for her child, every man for himself or for his family. This struggle must become a vast social and political world struggle.

John Berger

PROLOGUE

Many Europeans think of America as an extension of New York City. Similarly, many Americans—and Milanese— think that all of Sicily, perhaps the whole Italian South, is Mafia.

I came here—to Trappeto, a village of peasants and fishermen on Castellammare Bay about thirty miles from Palermo—in 1952. Coming from the North, I knew I was totally ignorant. Looking all around me, I saw no streets, just mud and dust. Not a single drugstore—or sewer. The dialect didn't have a word for sewer. I started working with masons and peasants, who kindly, gently, taught me their trades. That way my spectacles were no longer a barrier. Every day, all day, as the handle of hoe or shovel burned the blisters deeper, I learned more than any book could teach me about this people's struggle to exist. After work I'd ask questions, trying to comprehend their reality. And I discovered that Sicilians were not what Northern Italians made them out to be. Those stereotypes—"bandits," "dirt-eaters," "savages"—were the products of racism.

Listening to the people one by one, understanding their language better and better, I began to write down our conversations. I realized that these painfully slow moments of radical self-expression were for them occasions to flower. I wrote quickly, respecting their syntax that needed no logical connectives, modifying only the most recondite words. Phrase upon phrase, the people's self-expression unraveled their inner life.

I couldn't write fast enough, and bit by bit I discovered that my note-taking was merely the occasion for these people to become more aware of their personal and cultural values. So I was tempted to tear up my reams of notes. But I found that after some of these encounters, during which we almost burned ourselves out trying to clarify too much, it was useful to review what we had said. That way we could study questions in greater depth, emend, add ("last time I was ashamed to tell you, but . . ."). Also, reading these notes or hearing them read aloud, other people might feel that their values were being expressed and perhaps be moved to express themselves in new ways.

All this left a deep mark in me. Their inner lives, their most intimate experiences, could be frightening, fascinating, or both at the very same moment. At the beginning of our work, these people, mute for centuries, uttered, literally, their first words. These initial tremors turned into waves of communication; then into an acceptance of responsibility for their future, at first on a personal level, next in groups, and finally in the whole area. And all that meant real development.

From our profession of ignorance a method was gradually born. While some of our encounters developed into lasting friendships, others led to democratic organizing and group action.* The individual and structural implications of this process, which became a useful method for people engaged in diverse activities in other parts of Italy and the world, led me to call it grass-roots consciousness- and conscience-raising (*autoanalisi popolare*).

In 1952 in Trappeto, wages for a working day of twelve or thirteen hours were $1.25 (a year later they rose to $1.50). Bread cost 30 cents a pound. That meant families whose fathers could find work—usually for three or four months a year—could afford four pounds of bread a day. Summers, on so-called half-time, a day's pay was 75 cents. Half-time meant eight hours.

The daily scenario went like this. At four A.M., when you still might see the lights of fishing boats in the bay, peasants who might have a small piece of land (maintained at exorbitant cost because the Mafia controlled irrigation) trudged to work. Around dawn the day laborers congregated in the main square, hands in pockets, feet planted. At their leisure the straw bosses would

* See *Non esiste il silenzio* (Turin: Einaudi, 1974) for documentation of this aspect of our work.

show up and choose whoever struck their fancy (or greased their palms) to work that day. If the day laborers were lucky and had connections, they'd be taken on for an olive- or grape-harvest season. During the morning, the square would fill up, with those left without a job that day and with Mafiosi and friends—government bureaucrats, landowners, the whole entourage—who would lounge around cafés getting rich by smiling.

In this postwar context, it was crucial to understand why many people had resorted to banditism, that phenomenon representing defiance of a system where the forces of law and order condoned Mafia violence. I was arrested during a strike we had organized to invent work.* Sent to Palermo's Ucciardone Prison, I developed a good friendship with a man who explained to me why he had become a bandit. Just married, he and his wife found a place on Madonna Street in Partinico. One evening he's home sitting at the table while his wife is making dinner. There's a knock at the door. She answers. It's a child, thin and gaunt: "My mother says soon as you strain the pasta could you leave us the broth, I mean the water? See, nobody at home's had anything to eat for three days, and she has to nurse the baby but the milk's stopped, so she wants to drink something to see if it gets the milk flowing." The woman sends the child home with some food and dishes out the macaroni. Suddenly she bursts into tears: "I don't feel like eating." The husband gets up from the table, embraces her, and goes off to join the bandits.

In this area (Partinico, Trappeto, Montelepre, a total of 33,000 inhabitants), the most bandit-ridden in Sicily, out of the 350 brigands, only one had two parents who had gotten through fourth grade. Among them, the bandits had about 650 years of schooling. Disregarding the quality of education, or lack thereof, they averaged less than a second-grade education. In contrast, they had spent a total of 3,000 years in jail. And arrests and trials were still in progress.

The government was spending $65,000 every month on police

* See *Esperienze e riflessioni* (Bari: Laterza, 1974) for relevant documentation on this "strike-in-reverse."

and jails in the area: more than $750,000 a year. Meanwhile, though they claimed to finance programs in community development, we'd never even seen a social worker. The area had 4,000 people who needed jobs to make it through the week, but our society provided nothing. It was chaos.

Not a single charitable institution had helped the families of imprisoned or dead fathers. The children, the real victims, were virtually condemned to illiteracy. For almost a decade (1945–1954), the State had intervened, spending over $12,500,000 of the public's money to jail and kill. But it had done nothing to put the water of the local river (the Jato) to any use. That meant $200 million worth of water had flowed out to sea. A project in which that water had been utilized and distributed democratically would have provided work, a living, for everybody in this area. That way there would have been no banditism. Such a phenomenon was rooted in despair.

The immediate creation of real jobs would solve many of our most serious problems. How else could the unemployed live? How else could the people of Palermo Province manage from day to day? In our work, we had concentrated on a small area of western Sicily. Now we branched out, studying conditions town by town, from the sea into the mountains. We gathered denunciations of intolerable situations, the research material urgently needed for a liberation struggle. It struck me that I was no longer simply serving the people with my pen. I was also expressing myself.

Naturally, outside the area where I lived and worked, it was more difficult to find people willing to tell their life stories. But I tried to win trust, develop real friendships. When I talked to new acquaintances, I never took notes. Only if they came to understand that they were real co-workers in a serious research project did we agree that it was vital to write down our conversations. Talking about your poverty and depression, about your deepest problems, is excruciatingly painful. But if you cannot excavate, thrash things out, reach a point where real dialogue takes place, you never get to the threshold of the solution.

I tried to excavate the city as well. I asked some friends in Palermo if they knew anyone willing and able to introduce me to its poorest neighborhoods. When they understood what I was looking for, they sent me to Gino Orlando, an unforgettable human being.

I met him in one of Palermo's slums. He was giving shaves in a back alley. As we began to talk, his intelligence and knowledge leaped out at me. We understood each other from the first, and our relationship led to profound research.* He'd had a real sense of direction already; now he had the occasion to clarify himself and focus his energies. Knowing Gino was invaluable for anyone trying to understand Palermo's cans of worms and nests of vipers. To this day, young scholars and activists seek him out for consultation† and for a vision of the people's essential needs that goes beyond party and union interests.

To deal with the complexities of Palermo, we needed, along with grass-roots analysis, facts and figures. We discovered, for instance, that in 1951 in Palermo Province (an area of almost 1,800 square miles, population 1,019,796), 69.1 percent of the people, desperate for work, were unemployed (compared with 52.3 percent in Milan). Yet official studies revealed that "job applications [in employment offices] cannot materialize on the basis of incentive to work if, as is verified by statistics, that incentive does not exist."‡ Even if any of the statistics were accurate, the real issue was their qualitative meaning: *who* was represented by these figures and *how* were they represented?

The aim of our work was not primarily to interpret sociological data but rather to mobilize concerned people in the province via self-awareness and analysis of their problems (the results of stigmatizing preconceptions) and to bring about social change. We had to break the vicious circle of poverty and depression at some point. Since Italy lacked a politically mature majority with

---

* For the results, see *Inchiesta a Palermo* (Turin: Einaudi, 1956).—*Translator's note*

† As I have every time I've gone to Palermo.—*Translator's note*

‡ See the Tremolloni Report, "Unemployment in Italy," published by the Italian National Bureau of Statistics.

a sense of democratic processes, and since the people didn't have precise instruments to do the kind of research vitally needed for well-planned and rapid development, the wheels had to be set in motion from the deepest furrows.

This process led us around 1960 to a most disturbing realization. In western Sicily, where in the face of the most widespread poverty, depression, illiteracy, and unemployment the Mafia was sinking its tenacious roots deeper and deeper, there was an incredible, literally absurd amount of waste everywhere, by everyone. On the simplest level, people threw a lot of things away. And consciously or not, we failed to use existing resources or to develop new ones. Nor did we evaluate potential resources. Meanwhile huge sums of money were squandered, frozen, or spent unwisely. Was waste innate in people? Or could we become aware of how to create an alternative: an organic way of life? Could we understand how time is being, a locus where we can create meaning, new values? In this area where development hardly existed or progressed haphazardly, reactively, at such a snail's pace that it was hard to perceive, could we find a working hypothesis whereby we could deal with waste? In a culture still bound by primitive technology, could we find ways and means to follow up on initiatives and to organize with a broad base? How could we best use our available natural and human resources? What, exactly, were the real obstacles to development in this area?

This spot is like many of the earth's orphans and vagabonds. Beneath the tattered rags, the wild head of hair, the scars, she's lovely. You can see how, given a chance to ripen, she could glow with intelligence, dignity, life. You can also imagine how she might go to seed, in pain and bitterness.

Traveling through western Sicily you see towns clustered, densely populated. Although there's virtually no industry in Partinico or Alcamo, the former has 27,000 inhabitants, the latter 40,000. In the countryside, you find a few isolated houses and abandoned fortresses, many of which serve as shelter for peasants and their livestock.

You sense in people's faces and movements the weight of the centuries, of the ancient tracks of Greeks, Romans, Arabs, Normans, Spaniards, French, Northern Italians, of all the people who've come, mostly via armed invasion.

The land along the coast tends to be divided into small landholdings. The desolate mountain interior is dominated by the heritage of feudalism. Vast tracts of land defy agrarian reform and make things easy for Mafiosi, heirs of the endangered species called aristocracy, to be masters of all they survey.

Spring doesn't exist. Summer seems to blaze without end—until the first rains of October bring some green. By Christmas, along the coast, the first almond trees are flowering in fields and citrus groves. The rains subside a few weeks after Easter, and except for the fields and rocky slopes where vines and olive trees have sunk their roots, the land is parched again.

To understand the complexity of this culture, you can't generalize. Sicily is as big as Switzerland. It has 4.5 million people (1 million more than Norway). Taormina is not Corleone. The Catania-Ragusa industrial belt is not Lampedusa's or today's Palma di Montechiaro. Enna, Caltanissetta, Agrigento, Trapani—each area is unique.

In the area where I'd been living and working for years, the courage and commitment of a few people began to bear fruit. The people's awareness had matured and they had, via nonviolent strategies, pressured the government to construct a large dam (the Jato) and irrigation system on the outskirts of Partinico.* In addition, they wanted to put the water to its best use and use it at a fair price. That is, they wanted democratic water, not the Mafia's. The next step, then, was organizing a peasant cooperative to distribute it democratically, thereby making the water a lever to change the politico-economic structure of the society.

An ancient proverb warns, "You play alone, you never lose." But years of struggle were now concentrated in a new and dangerous grass-roots analysis, a collective effort, that led, with the help of trials and tribunals, to a whole series of clarifications regarding

* See *Esperienze e riflessioni* for the history of this dam.

the misuses and abuses of power. We discovered that the host of political compromises which have led to Mafia control in postwar Sicily, a control initially aided and abetted by the American military and the OSS, can be attributed to four kinds of perpetrators of this classic client system: (1) opportunist politicians who, mostly during election campaigns, meet with whoever can get them votes, good contacts, clout—it's "you help me and I'll help you"; (2) politicians who coldly and calculatingly exploit the Mafia to get power and then work out all kinds of double-deals and double-crosses—while they are at the same time systematically exploited by the Mafia; (3) full-blooded Mafiosi who often succeed in getting elected to high offices (fortunately, they are in the minority); (4) young people who try to buck the system but eventually sell out.

The question still has to be asked: What are the local conditions that have made exploitation by the Mafia possible in the electoral process? In other words, how has the Mafia, in the postwar period, been able to have a hand in the governance of Italy, on local, provincial, regional, and even national and international levels? (And I'm not just alluding, in the latter case, to the heroin traffic, but to multinational dealings as well.)

If you look at Palermo, city and province, it's self-evident that the great majority are discontented, often chronically so. People are in mourning, embittered. The essential question, then, is, Why can't they act to become a new force, a new political majority? Why does the situation seem at first glance so irrational, so absurd? Is it because we can't put together all the pieces of our own inner puzzle? Or are we confronting an engine with stripped gears that forever grinds down? Determined as they are by a particular past, can present conditions be changed? If so, how? To what end?

Trying to understand these questions, we must undergo the slow and painful process of confronting what always seems to be the same old story, of pinpointing the real problems to be met head-on, and of opening ourselves up to new solutions. This apparently random movement will, however, result in a response based on past experience, our intuitions and aspirations, our authentic awareness and knowledge. It is in this context that we must try to find a thread of unity in our research to clarify all the difficulties of creating democratic structures of life in Palermo and its surrounding areas. Our instruments are primitive: naming, expressing ourselves, thinking.

Anywhere we go in this world, it is hard to evolve living structures in which we can communicate authentic needs and values and create a mutually productive life. Cancers, crises, violence, are endemic to every human community on this globe. But in the context of our aborting terrestrial city, we try in our work and in our books to provoke substantive, structural, organic change.

Of course, even a documentary study depends on your point of view. Other people might see and compose it differently. Whatever the case, readers have the luxury of reflecting. These pages don't give off any stench. You can leaf through them in a comfortable chair, between meals. A book speaks to your mind, not to your nose, eyes, ears, whole being. And after all, you can forget it. Reading, you don't risk slipping in the muck—or vomiting—as you do when you walk the streets of Palermo, Cammarata, Corleone, Palma di Montechiaro, Licata . . .

I've always been struck by how much most Sicilians desire truth. They are the real authors of this book. Speaking from their own experience about their concrete problems, they have succeeded in expressing something that is universally human. I am profoundly grateful to them—as anyone else should be if he or she, meditating on what they have spoken, seeks to conceive a new world.

Nowadays it's easy to find tales to read: Russian, American, Chinese. And in the particulars of a given time and place you can detect tracings of the universal. In this light, you can participate, empathize.

Time passes for Sicily, as it does for the rest of the world. Sometimes salaries increase—especially when people act on their own initiative, organize, grow stronger. Bit by bit, people change their skin and the way they cluster. And if you resist, patiently, day by day, and listen to the spirit rumbling strangely from the depths, you can recognize a voice, voices, that are yours as well.

These voices, however muted or choked, can have a unity. Or they can be a source from which life can unfold: the bursting and flowering of what struggles to be expressed. From primitive documents in which people faced urgent conflicts and tried to change their lives, I've gathered these voices without shaking loose the dust of the earth from which they spring. Perhaps they speak for all of us, in all our variations.

The world needs to see itself. Beyond distracting noises, it has to know itself via its most intimate voices.

Danilo Dolci

EGADI ISLANDS

N

San Vito Lo Capo
Gulf of Castellammare
Raisi Pr.
Terrasini
Cinisi
Carini
Arenella
Montelepre
Portella delle Genestre
Palermo
Giardinello
Monreale
Solunto
Trappeto
Partinico
Bagheria
Balestrate
Borgetto
GreekLake
Trapani
Madonna di Scala
Jato R.
PLAIN OF
THE GREEKS
Alcamo
Romitello
Jato
San Giuseppe Jato
Marineo
Termini Imerese
Segesta
ALCAMO MTS
Jato Dam
San Cipirello
PALERMO
Camporeale
Poggioreale
Roccamena
Roccabusambra
MADONIE MTS
Marsala
Salaparuta
Two R.
Arins
Corleone
Alia
Montevago
Contessa Entellina
Campofiorito
Prizzi
Cammarata
Valledolmo
Mazara del Vallo
Castelvetrano
Santa Margherita di Belice
Bisacquino
San Giovanni Gemini
Villalba
Mazara
Belice R.
Carboi Dam
Sambuca
Alessandria della Rocca
Mussomeli
Selinunte
ORANGE TREE PLAINS
Burgio
Menfi
Marinella R.
Lucca Sicula
Casteltermini
Sciacca
Caltabellotta
Calamonaci
CALTANISETTA
Ribera
AGRIGENTO
Canicattì
PANTELLERIA
LINOSA
Agrigento
Campobello di Licata
LAMPEDUSA
Palma di Montechiaro
Mediterranean Sea
Licata

SICILY

© A·Karl / J·Kemp 1981

LIPARI ISLANDS

Tyrrhenian
Sea

•Villafranca
•Messina

Sant'Agata
di Militello

•efalù

olizzi Generosa

•Sottana

•Petralia

Castellana
Sicula

•Alimena

Taormina•

MT. ETNA

CATANIA

•Acitrezzo

Catania•

•Enna
(Castrogiovanni)

•Caltanisetta

ENNA

•Piazza
Armerina

Strait of Messina

Ionian

Sea

•Caltagirone

•Gela

Syracuse•

Palazzolo•

Ragusa•

•Modica

Noto•

Miles
0 ___ 10 ___ 15
0 ___ 15
Kms.

THE
INDIGENOUS
CULTURE

1. ROSARIO

*We are in Spine Sante, Partinico's worst slum. Rosario, fifty-five,
is almost illiterate. Lean, very dark, with deep-set, sparkling eyes,
he is a jack-of-all-trades.*

There's five or six kinds of greens: wild ones, nobody grows
them, they sprout all by themselves.
You go out walking and what you find you pick—that's how
it's done. You get up in the morning, four, three, five, depends
on the season and where you go. You get up, go out into the
country, do six, seven miles, then plunge right into the fields
looking for greens. You go a ways because there's nothing along
the road—see, along that stretch they're full of dust or people
come by and pick them to make soup or the cows trample or
munch them. They're not in very good shape.

It'll take you two, three miles, maybe more, out there in the
fields. You fill one sack and that'll make about two hundred
bunches. Most times there's two of us, maybe three, even four, so
we get together to comb the whole area. Never know, you can
be down on your luck. Out there there's landowners will get on
us for trampling their grass—or else they'll tell you to move on
cause it's all the land they have.

When you go together you got to agree to pool all the greens
you pick and divide the money, then you can work together.
Otherwise, two guys working on their own'll start to let their
eyes wander. Each one'll try to fill his own sack with the best
greens. Let's say two of us are out there and you see a patch of
wild cabbage and run to get there first. If you don't, he will.
That's the way life goes: fill your sack or else. Because sometimes you go home empty. It's the same way with snails. If
you're in a hurry to get twelve, fifteen pounds, you got to beat
the other guy to it. You got to have a sharp eye and a quick hand.
Grab one, sizing up the next. Keep your eyes always peeled,
up ahead.

And you got to check if the greens are good. No worms, not even little ones. Take fennel, nowadays it's full of em. There's two kinds of wild fennel: the lowland and the mountain type. In the lowlands you can't eat them, they stink. They look alike but we know the difference, cause down below they lose their leaves come the season.

We got out walking and collect all the different greens together, the wild ones, you understand: chicory, wild cabbage, fennel, asparagus, beetroot, borage, sorb-thistle, all in bunches, we stuff em in the sack and when it's full up, we head back to town. When I get there my wife gets a tub of water. You need plenty of water to clean them, or else the middleman won't take them. You divide them up into equal bunches. When I sell to the middleman I get a nickel or four cents a bunch. I can sell them myself the next day, fifteen cents for two bunches, or a nickel apiece. But I'd lose two days with that extra day at the market. So I earn three or four bucks, sometimes five. But you got to give the middleman a gift, twenty bunches or so. This is your winter work, till March. Then we start to hoe the vineyards and you can't find anything in the bedding except a few strands of chicory and sorb-thistle.

You go out Sundays too, sometimes. If it's raining we decide to hunt for snails instead. If it rains when we're out there already picking greens, and the rain is light, we stay till we're soaked to the skin. You got to or else you don't eat that day, unless you buy on credit. Then you're out of cash to pay your debts.

There's twenty-five thousand of us in this town. Fifty pick greens as our trade. And the day laborers, when there's no work, they all go out picking to survive. The landowners pick em too.

Come March, the pickings are slim. For a hundred bunches you scrounge around all day. We go to Balata by bike, twenty-two miles, then we start walking. There's places haven't been picked cause the population's scarce and the season comes late. We leave our bikes along the road and climb the mountains with our sacks.

When our sacks are loaded we head for home. You get back

late, you're so tired you can't hardly bundle it up. So you fall
into bed and do it the next morning. It's the same story till April,
then the greens go all to seed. Nobody'll have em because they're
bitter. The only thing left is chicory, and a few stalks of borage.

To go for snails you get up at two or three at the latest. See,
you have to be there before it's light. They disappear at sunrise.
They just slink back into the ground, and there's no sign of em
the rest of the day. Sure, if it's cloudy, there's activity till eleven,
but then they disappear, won't come back for love or money.
Try the vineyards—no snails. They hoe them four, five times a
year. You got to look on fallow land, or where there's beans,
wheat, or clover. Near running water, that's where they are.
Mostly wherever you find dew. But with these new methods
nowadays, snails are dying off. They sprinkle all these salts,
ammonia, all kinds. You keep walking and there's not a one
in sight. Sure, in some parts they're thick as flies. But come snail
season, just about everybody's out there—hunters, peasants, everybody's got a basket—and come rainy season the kids get hungry
for snail stew. Let's say there's four or five kids in a family. The
mother says, "OK, go get us some stew meat." So they go out into
the country, get five or six pounds, come hell or high water, and
they got their stew.

Those of us in the trade, we have to sell them. It's our living.
There's three kinds of snails *Helix naticoides,* the plain old snail,
and the *Helix vermiculata.* These vermiculatas are the fattest
ones, but they're scarce, almost extinct. When there's a rainstorm,
the regular snails pop up. They push their horns out from between the rocks where they live all clumped together. See, snails
don't burrow in the ground, they clump together under a rock
or beside it and couple, mate, up against the rock. To sleep they
don't go underground, they just stick to the rock. We never
find them sleeping on the ground—not ever. They'll crawl into a
crack, let's say, on a bridge. No matter how tight, they'll clump
up together just like a fist. The first few stick in the crack, then
the rest stick to them in a bunch. We poke around with our
fingers, or a stick. We turn the stones over and shake em loose.

You won't find snails where there's just a couple of stones. You find them in big piles.

The regular snails are nicer for eating, but we eat the naticoides too, even raw. Say I go hunting for naticoides. I use a trowel to dig them up, but digging always cuts a few, so I clean those off and eat them. They stay under the rocks cause they like shade and where it's damp, or else in summer they'd fry what with the heat and the cracks in the earth. See, for six months they don't eat, the whole summer they sleep. Come March they start to curl up, all clumped together. Then they start to drool this slime. When the slime dries up, you get this thin white film. At first, it's like the skin of a baby onion. Then come April and the hot winds, it gets tough, almost as hard as the shell.

It's hard to hunt naticoides, though—the landowners don't want you around. We know all the good places here in the mountains, but there's always a Don Ciccio or two who says we ruin the grass for his cows. Come September, October, the first rains fall again, the ground gets wet, their coating softens up and the snails crawl out. Then the landowners don't complain.

Just when they crawl out, not eating yet, they're real sweet. Later they start to eat grass and get bitter. To sweeten em up you drop em in a pan or a bucket with a handful of bran. Two or three days and they're sweet again. But the regular snails are always sweet, they never get bitter.

Then there's the earthworms, the long kind. First they kill the snails, then they squirm in and eat them. They wriggle in, face to face, and the naticoides cringes back into the shell, but it can't go as far as the regular snail cause it's too fat so the earthworm catches it and eats it, naticoides or snails, whichever. Except in summer, when the naticoides is all shut tight and the snail sticks to the rock, and the worm can't travel much cause the ground's dry and hard, so it goes around the water and the dung-piles where the ground's softer because it's damp.

Lately, I went to Corleone to hunt for eels, and on the way we had to get the traps ready. You take earthworms, ten or twelve a trap, string em on a piece of fine wire and put the wire in the trap. When you have all the traps ready, you go down to the river and cast them along the shoals, all tied together. That same day the eels won't bite. So we sleep along the banks and next morning we get up and go our separate ways. Each one hauls in a trap—that is, if we're lucky and find them, or else we wade in to search for them, in the shoals or downstream. If they're gone, we go on home. But if we're lucky we find the traps with four or five, maybe six or seven eels. Or else nothing. These traps are made for the little ones, quarter-pound, at most a half. The bigger eels won't fit. But lately the eels are gone. They've been using poisons to catch em. And that kills the ones about to hatch.

When the water's down and not poisoned, we can catch them with forks too. I mean the kind you eat with. We tie the fork to a pole and stir up the pebbles—they bolt like lightning and we run till we spot them. If we lose sight of em we go and stir up the pebbles again, this time downstream, maybe ten yards. See, if they escape they always move with the current. You got to go in groups of two or three for eels. It's summer work. In winter there's floods.

Then there's the *Liguus fasciatus minor*—I mean the baby snails. They crawl around among the twigs and the brambles, and stick together in clumps. They come out in June, stay till July or August, depending on when it rains. After that what do you do? Well, the fatter ones come into season and they're all over the thorn bushes, they never dry up, they're right there on the tips of the thorns, that's their place. So you cook them shell and all, big or little, and suck on them and the meat just pops into your mouth.

That's the way we go, wherever the wind blows. What we find we take. The more you travel the better you get to know their habits. Let's take winter: they crawl around, poke out, see the sun, and burrow underground, eighth of an inch or so. And us, knowing the lay of the land, seeing this little mound of turned-up earth, we poke around and find him with his snout still out. See, he leaves a little hole and that gives him away. Or in some places they leave eggs, the size of rice grains but round. Look, they make love too, sticking to each other, just above ground. You can't tell who's the man and who's the woman. A few Septembers I've caught em in the act and took em apart to see what was what. And there's times four or five couples get together, just like that, all in a bunch. So in one throw you get eight or ten naticoides. It's a cinch.

Come March the new snails hatch, real little ones with skin so fine and shiny you can see right through it. Say I go out for a stroll and there's no snails in sight but I detect the slime on the ground, it's shiny so I follow the tracks or unearth it or find it in a clump—whatever, I got to find it. Winter nights they crawl all over.

How come we get up so early to be in the right place? To be ready to strike while they're still out. Maybe at night they can see us better but they're always on the alert, daytime too. If the wind blows they pull in their horns and stay put. Or if it's cold, same story. Heavy rains, no dice. They'll stay above ground, but curled up tight. With a slow rain they'll inch along. But if a breeze picks up they'll crawl back into their shells. A few drops of rain without a breeze, out they come again.

Then there's river crabs. What do you think they eat? Worms. When there's animals lying dead, the crabs go around and eat. You'll see thirty, maybe forty all over the carcass. They're river crabs, like the sea ones but not hairy. You can eat them too. Make a nice fresh soup, but there's not much meat, mostly shell. You can sink your teeth into something only in the months their pickings have been fat. Maybe it's the moon makes em lean or meaty, depending on the season.

Frogs eat worms too, just little ones. How do I know? When I skin them, the frogs that is, I take out all the innards and there's the gut where all the food goes and you see exactly what they eat: insects and everything else. Then there's the black river snake that lives on horned toads. They come to three-quarters, sometimes a whole pound. The snake'll spot the toad and stare him

down, fix him there with her eyes, freeze him, then take him
in one gulp.

How do frogs breed? We can verify it, skinning these frogs:
we catch a male and skin him, it's all there . . . What do I
mean? All right, first, before skinning, you take a look for the
stubble, the beard, just like we have. Then you do the skinning
and you realize frogs have balls, they're fully equipped just like
a man. Catch a female, you see it's the same story. Before skinning you check for the beard, but her chin's all smooth. Of course
when she's expecting, you detect it. Skinning her you might
find two bunches of eggs, you can almost count on it. You can
even tell the day she's expecting. Females, you know, deliver
twice. Grab em by the neck and turn em over, they drop the
eggs in your hand. But the second batch stays lodged, they're
not ready for at least a month.

To get the frogs ready for market, we snip off the head and
the legs, peel off the skin, take out the guts, and wash out the
piss. Then we break the legs to make them swell up. That way
the frog's cleaner and the thighs are nice and plump. Still, with
those broken legs, all skinned, no head or feet, pissed out, they
twitch. Two hours under water and we go sell them a buck a
pound. Daytime we catch em, and skin em overnight. If not,
six hours and they'd go bad.

Seeing this world of animals I start to think we're just like
them. If I want to eat somebody up I do it—or vice versa. Animals struggle just like us, with no escape.

There's times I see the stars at night, especially when we're
out for eels, and I get to thinking in my brain, "The world, is
it really real?" Me, I can't believe that. If I get calm, I can believe in Jesus. Bad-mouth Jesus Christ and I'll kill you. But there's
times I won't believe, not even in God. "If God really exists,
why doesn't He give me a break and a job?"

Then I remember I got kids, and don't hang myself. Still,
there's times . . . When I can't find work, my head just spins . . .

Skinning those frogs, I feel pity, but what can I do but kill
them? I pity them but they got to die. This frog staring at me

knows his time's come. There in my hand I'm telling him, he's got no doubt. How do I know it? Catching him by the legs before you apply the scissors, the frog pisses in your hand—like we'd do in the same fix—and more than once. That's why I know how he thinks. An animal, in the clutches of men, starts to tremble. I'll catch a bird in its nest; in my hand the breast is . . . a bell. It rings, they sense death. Like when you point a gun at a man. Snails are the same. Animals have brains. They think, too. They think, no kidding. They have their own way of doing things. Every creature thinks about death.

Land an eel, and before you cut off its head to pluck out its guts, it opens its mouth, gasps, snaps at you, with those fine sharp teeth. Out of water, it thrashes till it's dazed silly, all out of breath. And you slit from head to tail and clean out the piss and the guts.

Skinning frogs, we all sit around the basket. My wife does the skinning, one cousin snips off the heads, the other the feet, and I clean out the guts and the piss and break the legs. And we start up a game, just to pass the time. The guillotiner gets thirty years—he's the killer. My wife, twenty or so—she's the castrator. The other cousin about twenty for mutilation, and me a life sentence because I started the whole tragedy going. It's all a trial with the accused and the judge.

Cut off a frog's head, put it on the table, look it in the eyes: they're alive. It's like looking at a painting that's staring back at you. Cut off all the heads, it's a slaughterhouse.

First time it was so awful, I can't begin to tell you . . . but . . . last year I killed three hundred pounds' worth. Now when I'm not careful and let one slip away I get so crazy I grab it, bite off its head, or smash it on the ground. People who take things all for themselves, not giving a damn if the rest of us croak, should dream sometimes about baskets full of frogs' heads, rows of em, eyes of people who die for the rich men's sins.

I'm skilled in this trade, that's how I earn a living. But I'm real good at any trade I dedicate myself to. Since I was eight, after second grade, I lived as best I could. Thank God, to this day I've never had to deal with the law. The bread I bring home to my family comes from clean honest sweat.

It's tougher than office work. It takes a lot of thinking. Today one place, tomorrow another. You got to study at night. I've always done it for love, but I'll be damned if I want a job that racks my brains like this. Give me a steady job: up in the morning and out, regular hours on the site. Look, I don't want to beat my brains out. I can learn to be useful in this world. I have some intelligence, I can learn and improve. Sure, first off I'll be slow, but give me ten, fifteen days I can pick up just about anything. Since I'm back from the army, five years, I've been a day laborer: first year, three months; second year, four months; third, six months; fourth, three months; fifth, five months. Otherwise it's been in the country: they call us "green-flickers."

Since I was seventeen, nineteen, I've gone out hunting for coal and charcoal. I'd go out into the hills where they burned wood to clear the land. Seeing it was burned out and there was nobody around and they'd hauled off all the coal, we'd go up there with a sharp stick and dig around—the ground was soft enough after being burned—and look for the good pieces they'd missed. We could get twenty, twenty-five pounds per kid. If not, we'd go down by the tracks and gather coal. Virgin or half-burnt, thirty, forty pounds. When the locomotive goes by it always lets some drop. And sometimes at the stations the stokers throw out the odd pieces—burnt or not. The charred pieces are good for the tinsmiths—they don't give off smoke—and the virgin stuff blacksmiths will buy for hot coal.

Nowadays we go collect lead. The cops have target practice. Have you ever heard that ringing in your ears? May, from dawn to dusk, they're shooting. Just imagine the taxpayers' money, while we go without work or anything else. You can find a few shells outside, but you can bet you've got to dig and scrounge around in the dirt. Sure there's plenty of lead, but it's like shrapnel. They'll shoot maybe forty rounds. First we dig where there's holes. If not, we just scrounge around. We dig with a trowel, in rows, together, leaving no stones unturned. We collect scraps of aluminum too, from the hand grenades. We rake in the capsules they forget and leave. That's the way we gather what we try to sell.

So we earn our living. It's the only way we know to turn lead to gold. Wind's got to come into church, but not so much that it blows out the candles and sweeps away the altars.

2. LEONARDO

He is about eighteen, totally illiterate. We talk in sight of his
flock in the Madonie Mountains, which bound Palermo Province.

When I was little, I played out in the alley, that's all. What else could I do? I hired myself out at thirteen. My father was a shepherd, first I worked with him. When you watch over animals all year round, you get to know them.

First my father did it alone, then I tended to those animals with him. At San Giorgio they didn't want to let me milk because I did it with too much love and care. I always milked that way. See, if you pinch their udders to start with, they don't let you milk no more. You got to be careful not to scratch them. When you milk them, each one's different. Some are wild and others are tamer. There's some with real good teats and others all cock-eyed. Some are harder and others just ripe for milking. They won't go near a lot of other folk. Me, they'll let hug em.

I can't count, but I can tell from a distance if one's missing. I look real close till I know. I know them all in person. There's this one's mother, here's that one's lamb. Don't matter how many, I know em all. I been with sheep, a hundred, maybe two. Come sunset the boss'd count em. He knew the exact amount. Me, I watch them, I'm always on their track, combing them out, petting them, gathering beans to feed them. They come right up to me. I love them and they love me.

They don't got names. If I call em, they turn and come back. When a ewe's going to drop a lamb, I figure it all out, cause her teats swell and she don't eat. Then she'll sprawl on the ground, and her water'll break. And she bleats. If everything goes OK, she'll stop bleating. If not, I go to her, make her comfortable, and help her deliver with my own two hands. First the feet come out, then the nose, and the mother keeps licking to dry it off. When it's born, the mother jumps up. About a quarter of an hour and the lamb gets up too. It starts to suckle. I saw lambing the first time with my father, and I lent a hand and learned to deliver sheep.

The virgins are the ones that still haven't given birth yet; we call em "ewes" when they have lambs. Goats who still don't have kids are called "kids," if they have one they're called "nannies." After that they're just plain "goats."

Kids are different, they don't tag along with their mothers unless they're too scrawny. They'll stray from her after a month, the ones you raise—the others you slaughter before that. Unless they get a whipping they never stick with the nanny. They'll nurse at daybreak and then at dusk, that's when you can keep em in the barn. Otherwise they like to run free, they always try to get loose. Trouble is, then they don't get enough to eat. Their umbilical cord dries up all by itself.

They're beautiful animals. I pasture them where you find the best grass. If there's nothing to eat they complain. Come noon, they huddle together and try to give each other shade. Later, they scatter all over the place.

Do I know about towns? Well, I been in Castellana and Alimena. And money? We never touch the stuff.

Sheep die off the minute they eat certain flowers and wild berries, so you got to send the goats out into the fields first. They eat everything and don't die. Nothing hurts em. After that the sheep can pasture, they won't die cause the flowers and berries are gone.

To pass time I make dummies out of clay and throw rocks at them. When shepherds have pipes, they play. But I don't. I don't know how to make one. I make dummies or just pile up rocks as a target. I get what I need from the road. All us shepherds do it.

The stars? I seen em, I don't know what they are. They're like pictures of the Lord. See, in pictures of the Lord there's stars. They're sort of like eyes, who knows? The moon is the Madonna. So I heard, and I'll say so too. I pray to them. When it's cold I say to the sun, "Come forth." When it's too hot I say, "Refresh us."

If it's cold I say, "Warmth, come," so it will. When it's dark I call on the moon. I love the moon and the sun. If it's cold and the sun comes out, it's good. If it's dark and the moon shines, that's good too, so you can see where you walk. I pray to the stars too, "Come forth." I like the stars, just looking at them. They're beautiful.

The things I like best are having a nice time, going into town and having a nice time. When I go in for a day, I see Momma, my brothers, Poppa, all my aunts and uncles. I like animals, and working too. You get good at your trade. You sow, reap, and eat.

There's times I pray for good weather in winter or to keep the storms from coming in their season. I pray to the Lord: "Hey, Lord, keep the weather going good." I mean I talk to Him.

It's the wind makes it cold. What's the wind? The grass sways back and forth, that's the wind. If it's cold you pray to the sun to make it warm so the animals get on better. My mother taught me how to pray for sun, my father too. All us shepherds pray to the sun for warmth and to the moon for light when it's dark.

The sea, yeah, I've heard about that. We stay up here all year long. The world's a sea, but I don't know what the sea is. That's the way the world is. I've heard the other guys say that. A sea of troubles, they say.

Clouds I've seen, but I don't know what they are. They travel when there's wind.

Being as we have a house and work, we're in this world. You eat. We're in this world to work. To eat. To work. I don't know nothing.

Men get old, just like everything: humans and animals. It's the sun never ages.

3. BASTIANO

We're near his home in Capparrini. Almost illiterate, he is fifty-five or so and shows traces of once having been robust. He is still active in masonry and land reform.

We waste all our manure in this town. People haul it out of the stables and dump it all over the place. Wherever you go you find it piled up, manure all around town. They come in trucks from Partinico, Alcamo, Mazara, just for our dung. They even come from Palermo. We dump it all over town in big heaps. We don't take stock in things, we just throw it all in these heaps: rocks, bones, even our own garbage. Depending on the wind, disease spreads in the town. Flies breed in that manure and swarm around when there's no wind and they bite you and everybody starts to feel like it's the mange. Fact is, with all the stench typhus spreads, the kids get real sick, and the whole place stinks because the sewers empty out at the edge of town, where lots of folk live.

The dungheap ferments all by itself, it smokes, and come the rains, the good part washes away. Then they'll burn the dung till it's nothing but ashes. And the women, they make bread at home, and they take all the ashes and coals that's left and douse it with water and carry it in a basket and throw it on the manure piles. It's habit. Then guess what happens. They haven't doused the coals enough, so they start to get hot again, and all the manure burns up. Call it carelessness or just plain ignorance, whatever, it all burns for two or three days, and the smoke and the stench fill the town, going wherever the wind blows. And you breathe it all in . . . So they do us a big favor, these people who cart away our dung. At least they clean up the town some. But it's all wasted, the piss, everything. See, during the war they sent me to Germany and I saw them collect animal piss in ditches, and a man drove these oxen around, hitched up to this big gadget like a wheel, and they pumped it into this sprinkler system and that way they watered all the fields, and the grass grew so tall and thick you could hardly cut it with your sickle. But us, we got five donkey carts in the whole town: Pietrino Pizzo's, Gioacchino Messina's, Spadaro's, and Roccolo's. And Francesco's.

The land around here can't be developed. There's just no water. It's all a desert from the lake on the Plain of the Greeks along the left branch of the Belice. The farms and orchards just die because there's no irrigation. All those thousands of acres are wasted, from the outlets of Greek Lake down to Menfi. All it takes is for the government to build a dam on the Bruca. Why don't they do it? All the tests they did came out good. I know cause I worked on that project. There's plenty of mountain springs, and the water never stops. Come heavy rains in winter, the river gushes down and the current's so strong a boat can't cross. It pours down from all over the place: on the left bank it comes from the Ficuzza forests, San Giuseppe Jato, and the mountain springs around Corleone, Prizzi, Campofiorito, Contessa Entellina. On the right bank it rushes down in hundreds of streams that flow together and branch out from the hills of Camporeale and Roccamena all the way down to Menfi. It pours and there's no dam. It floods the land near the river and erodes. It carries off all the good soil. First it tunnels way in under, then the land gives way. Fact is, eight miles from here, the rush of water made a new river all by itself and took lots of good new land with it and left nothing but rocks where it used to run. Of course, you never know where a new river will settle. The earth keeps shifting. See, the sand still hasn't settled, so it dissolves with the current and the river just keeps on getting wider. Canebrakes spring up, or you try to plant vineyards but the water washes them away before the year is up. And it never stops. It just keeps on spreading. Meanwhile you start terracing the hills. You don't know what's in store for you down in the valley. Then all your topsoil starts eroding. What you plowed is now all gullies, they're so deep you can't even cross em. Nobody told us to plow crisscross, instead of up and down.

If they'd build a dam on the Bruca, the whole valley below Poggioreale and Salaparuta as far as Menfi, it'd all be beautiful farmland. Greenery and fresh air, with orange trees. Land costing five thousand dollars at the going rate would be worth four or five times that much. It could be all full of trees, lemon blossoms, oranges, like you see around Palermo. I'm just a master mason, don't know much about farming, but my father's a wholesale dealer in citrus fruit at Palermo. I've got this vision of houses among the trees, bees among the flowers, the joy of fruit getting ripe, children running around eating it. You know now our fruit comes from Naples. You can hardly afford it and sometimes it's all shriveled up. Same as the salad we get. It comes from the city after the dogs snub it.

Those steep slopes up in the mountains should be woods, almond groves—the paste you get from them is good for sweets—and if you know how to plant and terrace on some of the other slopes, you can have a vineyard or two. Then down below, with a dam, everything could change for the better. You could have one cooperative farm from Roccamena to Menfi, stretching for fifty miles. Besides, there'd be electricity. And the women would have work too, with the vegetables. Industry would flourish. It'd all be one big garden. And pasture land with cows you couldn't count. With all the grass that could grow below the lemon trees, you could pasture a thousand head or more and still fill the hay bags, and it'd rain milk. Toward where the river winds to the sea, forty, fifty miles, everybody would have a nice piece of land with two or three animals and milk right there at home. And the women could take care of things around the house and the men could work out in the fields. The women would cut grass, bag the hay, feed the cows, milk em and wash em down. We'd have pigs, pigeons, chickens. Life would be like morning sunshine, beautiful, new for the womenfolk too. Then they'd build roads for cars and buses. All that land wouldn't be wasted just on grain and clover. After the harvest, there wouldn't be all those miles of desert. It wouldn't be all shepherds and cowherds looking for a little green grass and grazing their animals on the stubble. No more cows scattered and pawing the dust. See, now they just wander around with their calves, dying of thirst cause the stubble's too dry. Morning to night, it's that same feeling in the throat. In the heat of a summer day, the flies attack em right under the tail and bite. The cow flips her tail and starts to run, she don't know what else to do, and the cowherd starts to chase her with a stick. The men go around on horseback, with bandannas tucked under their caps and draped down over their necks. The heat even stops the goats. They look up and around and forget about eating.

There's a few patches of green along the riverbanks. Being there's no other water, animals and shepherds all drink from the river. Now and then you see somebody hunting for frogs and eels. Come evening the cows feed on a little hay and blades of prickly pear bushes—if you can find em. Their udders are all dried up. Every day they give less and less milk, and the milk's not much good anyway. Winter milk is fine, good for making cheese too, but in summer it comes out almost like powder. It's too coarse and tastes sour.

With all that heat, the earth breaks into crevices wider than your arms can stretch. It dries up and crumbles away. And the cows and mules go with it. They'll even break a leg. And the earth is scorched, it's on fire, and everything's the color of gold, it shimmers over the stubble, and the air is suffocating. It's all moving waves of heat, for months and miles, that's the way it is. No plants or trees, just desert. It stares you down. You walk and maybe glimpse a little green patch of cotton and feast your eyes and that cools you off, or a stretch of vineyard along the state road and your eyes drink it up. The mules and horses huddle together to find some shade, and the shepherds hide under their huge straw hats to keep from getting sunstroke. The horses go snout to tail and try to flick off the flies. The dogs' tongues hang out arm's length. They go through hell.

We could transform this whole valley. It could be a sight to see, orchards and gardens. It gets narrow, but then it widens out where the two branches of the Belice meet—at Two Arms, it's four or five miles wide . . . But what can one man do alone? A peasant can't channel all the winter springs. Or make a dam. Nobody can built a dam without help. That's the government's job. They got the cash, they should spend it on us instead of catering to rich folk. Do you know where we get our food? Potatoes from Naples, beans from Turin, peaches from Naples, pears and apples from Upper Italy, Stella Brand milk from Lodi, butter from Milan, eggs from Belgium and Holland.

With a dam on the Bruca, this land would yield everything. Reap and you would sow. It's deadly hot here. Without water, it all dries up. But them surveys and soundings are all done. All it takes now is the government spending some money. With the dam we can produce millions. I talked it over with the surveyors. The people, they don't understand. Without water, this land's a waste. It's all used for one crop, and if it fails they shrug their shoulders. They don't use dung cause it's dirty. They don't plant grapes cause the neighbors steal em. One year you clear stones from the land, and next year there's a new tenant. Forget about fruit trees. "I got to leave, so why should I leave anything for anybody? After all, I did all the work."

There's another problem. Some folks have forty acres they leave fallow, or they rent out just a plot or two. If everybody sowed all the land they owned, the rest of us could work for them come harvest time. Then the seeds would give fruit.

The other thing is young people. They need real technical training. Just look at the labor force from eighteen to twenty-five. There could be real good programs to qualify them. As of now they're just left on their own, without training or the hope of a job, so they just give up and stand around in the squares or play cards in the bars. Early in the morning, if you take the bus for work, you see them hanging around, gambling for a cup of coffee.

When the harvest's over you're usually jobless. So you wander all around town. We call it café-hopping. You just sit and if you're broke, you just watch the cards fall. You joke around to pass the time. One, two, three hours go by. You squirm in your chair, and when you're tired of sitting, you go around talking politics—about how you'd like to line em all up in front of the firing squad. Then you sit down again and gamble for a cup of coffee or an ice-cream cone. It all depends on the season. Then you go back home and the wife is grumbling, there's nothing to eat, words fly. "How can we live on bread with onions and oil? Can't we afford a few tomatoes?" So what do you do? Nothing. You go back to the bar. If you have some spare change, you gamble. If not, you just watch. "You blew that trick, you should of thrown the king, the ace, the trump." "Mind your own goddamn business." "I'll say what I goddamn please." And fights break out. Cards fly, but mostly words. "You bum you, go ahead, just sit on your ass, what do you know about work?" Luckily there's always some peacemaker to make everybody shake hands. (God bless him.) And the bartender'll say, "Come on now, boys, I'll lose my license." And he'll sit down and watch, because he's broke too. For months it's the same twenty or thirty or even a hundred people, just sitting around the bar. Or they go to the Peasant's League. And do nothing. It's the same old tune. Then back to the square for a stroll.

We all want to change this way of life. But where do we start? For me the only real intelligent escape is hunting. See, the doctors and lawyers, the educated folk, they're eager to go out with you. That way you learn a lot of things, like how to speak correctly.

Kids eight, ten years old watch over the sheep and cows, but it rains and they get drenched. They stay out there all alone the whole day and get so caked with mud they can hardly drag their feet. They start real young and get corns and walk funny after that. At Roccamena we're poor in everything but corns. The kids look like little old men. Weatherbeaten, downtrodden, hunched over from all that work. You can't tell if they're old men, kids, or dwarfs. You could guess my son is twelve or thereabouts, but the rest of them, you never know. Their fathers can't feed em so they just wear out.

Here kids don't even know what the sea's all about. They only see it from Lord's Rock. Sure, the ornery ones go down to have rock fights or duel with prickly-pear stalks or steal almonds. But they don't really see the sea. It's just fifty miles away as the crow flies, but it's a waste for these kids, and for us too. Like it wasn't even there. And the kids just hang out in the street. They're all dirty and most of em hardly ever take a bath. Maybe a mother or two'll dip em in the washtub about once a season. This year the town had a raffle to send fifteen kids to the beach for a vacation. They made out tickets with all the kids' names and drew lots. It was just like the lottery, gambling with the children as stakes. And what about the schools? Well, teachers can take what you call travel leave, with allowances. Besides, they always come late to school, no earlier than nine. Then they have breakfast, and the kids sit and watch these gentlemen eat their pastries right in front of them, just taking their sweet time and doing whatever they damn please and taking off the minute time is up. And they rotate teachers in the middle of the year and the kids don't know who their teacher will be half the time. That's the way it goes year to year in all the towns roundabout. The kids never get a year's worth of education. They don't get enough of nothing, not even fresh air. Even that's wasted. They live in one room with fathers, mothers, sisters, brothers, the mule, the goat, the chickens. Lots of em don't even have light. It's shameful.

The book down at the employment office is like one big cemetery, with all those X's us illiterates make. We can't understand all their bureaucratic proceedings, so we get taken right and left. We're like plants that don't give much fruit in the first place, but you strip em anyway. Like when the grub attacks the beans, it sucks all the juices and gets nice and fat, and the beans die off.

Election time I worked at the polls. I directed voters to the booths: "Turn right, turn left." I had to teach a lot of people the difference between left and right, and some of them still made mistakes. People have no idea what political parties are. They don't understand all these platforms and programs. A few of us have trust in the parties of the Left because a poor person can go talk to one of their representatives and be treated like a brother. The other parties just ignore you, even the Fascists. Sure, you could talk to Mussolini in those days, but now his followers are too uppity. The worst are the Christian Democrats. Their Christ is just a gadget to bedazzle poor ignorant people who get hooked on the idea of Jesus. Fact it, while we starve, the Christian Democracy keeps nursing its nice fat bank accounts with good investments.

A lot of women vote against their husbands on the sly—see, they let themselves be fooled by the priest. The women are even more ignorant than the men. At least we get around a bit. The women always stay at home. Fact is, come election day, some guys'll lock their wives and daughters in the house. Just before the elections, the priest gets the women of the Fraternity of the Immaculate Conception and Christ Crucified to go from door to door telling people how to vote. These women go around pissing and moaning that if the Enemy wins there'll be no more family honor and no fathers to provide for the wives and kids. That's the way they divide and conquer families in Sicily. And if they can't ruin your family, their lay associates will terrorize you by getting at your animals. It's all envy, jealousy, hate.

Here it's impossible to get a community organization off the ground. See, people just don't trust each other. Besides, we're all too poor. Let's say I'm in business with a couple of friends and I have a few thousand to invest. But the trouble is I'm always worrying about my partners robbing me or getting the best piece of the pie. So I stick with them wherever they do new business, but then I decide to invest on the side, just for my own profit. And being alone the odds are I'll lose. Take shipping oranges to the Continent. You have to be in ten different places at once, work with people you don't trust, and try to do it all alone. You waste all your time, money, and energy. Everybody's like that here. They look out for their own interests and not the interests of the group. Nobody understands that's the way to destroy communal enterprise. We waste our whole life that way, because we don't get together and organize.

If the people would work together and really concentrate on

what had to be done for the good of the community, Sicily
would be a horn of plenty for everybody. But just to start, we'd
have to be honest. When you're honest with your fellow men,
everything works out.

But now, it's complete chaos. They send peasants from San
Giuseppe Jato to work in Capparrini—sixty miles away. And
peasants from Roccamena are assigned to work the land at
DeSisa and San Giuseppe. Some farmers are assigned to land so
far away that they waste two days of the work week just getting
there. Let's say they send me to Marcanzotta, I have to go by
way of Monreale, especially during winter when the shortcuts
aren't passable. That means traveling, let's see, twenty, plus seven,
plus how much? About fifty miles all total. When you get there
the animals are so tired you can't get em to pull the plow. You
got to let em rest and start the next day. The allocations of land
got all messed up, and some land is so far away peasants can't
even get there. You know all it takes is talking to the peasants:
things would be straightened out.

It's complete chaos and all our energies go to waste. Take Capparrini down in the valley, or any of the towns that were built up
after the war: Saladino and Aquila, DeSisa (that's near San
Cipirello), Marcanzotta (that's beyond Camporeale), Modichella
(toward the Alcamo Mountains), La Pietra (just past Camporeale). They all need water and light. Their roads are like ours,
half finished. And now construction's at a standstill. Everything's
just left on the sites. Us, we have no idea why.

I've gone all over looking for work. That's how I know about
this stuff. Sure, they spent millions in construction, just the way
they did during Fascism. But nobody can afford to move in, so
everybody comes and steals—a door, a window, the roof tiles,
everything. To build a house on your own, all you need is the
mortar and the nails. All these new homes are abandoned. All the
material is sitting there for the taking. The stones are all cut to
size, but they just sit on the ground. Contractors come back and
haul them away to start up new jobs.

4. SANTO

Over sixty, semiliterate, he has struggled as a tenant farmer and trade unionist most of his life. We are talking out in the fields where he works.

The Túdia estate's just this side of the border, Palermo Province. By inheritance it belonged to a certain nobleman named G., four thousand acres worth. After a while he rented out half to Counselor-at-Law D. and half to another nobleman, P. For a while all they had to their name was packsaddles. Then they got us.

Us tenant farmers sweat blood for every acre. For every ten acres of beans or wheat, we paid a share to keep candles lit forever in church, a share for the upkeep of the paths, and one for the overseer. Then there was the gift you gave to the clerk hired to deliver the product to the owner, and the special gift for the police.

These straw huts were built when we were little by tenant farmers. Then the owner "requested" a contribution of a dozen chickens per year as "rent." And lots of times, when he'd spend the night at Túdia, he also "requested" the farmers' women, and they'd go wait on him hand and foot.

At first there were about two hundred farmers. Come dawn, around four, they'd all gather at the threshing floor and the doors'd open up there on the balcony, and they'd have to back off, accustomed as they were to the boss's habit of taking his morning piss. I got my witnesses: Giuseppe B., Antonio T., Francesco M., Mario P., dozens of peasants. If one of them had done it, it would have been a scandal.

Don Eugenio kept peacocks with the hens. The duke of S. did too, in his patio, because they're "grand" and give the place a proper fancy look. Come time to divide the produce, it was all up to the farmer (it still is, you know) to go to the owner's place and settle accounts on seed and other items. And it'd often happen that the farmer would protest an unfair settlement and the owner'd jump up and say, "Tough luck, see you later." To milk us even more, the heirs of D. have bought up the whole estate and go right on making us farmers pay through the nose.

Come '41 I started work at Túdia. I had a farmhouse and kept six head of cattle, and me and the owner, Cesare D., we came to an agreement how much the stock was worth and how we'd go shares. But after a few months, when we got down to brass tacks, I had to accept his estimate or else he said I'd have to take my animals and get off his land. Being I had no possibility of pasturing anywhere else, I had to give in.

Next spring, come the time we had to portion out the fodder, he wanted a higher percentage and I wouldn't give in—this time the law was backing me up. The friction with the owners all started then and there. One fine day I get the eviction notice dumped right in my lap. I come home and find my wife all flustered. "Look what the owner just sent us." I didn't know where to turn cause I still had no idea what unions were all about, but talking to people they informed me that at Petralia Sottana there was this party that could give me instructions how to defend myself. One day I take the mare and go off to Petralia, six-and-a-half hours away. Getting there I inquired who was in charge of this party and who could give me some information. Now then, this miller's son, a young student, hears my story and sends me to Doctor B., and I set right out. The doctor wasn't in, he was making visits in the slums, so I waited about two hours. Then he arrived, polite as could be. He didn't recall my face but what could he do for me? I told him all about the notice I received and he says, "For the moment, stay put, let them send their shock troops. I'll write to Palermo to find out exactly how to proceed." He took down my address, we shook hands, and I headed back toward Túdia.

The twenty-eighth of June I'm on my way to Petralia Sottana for Saint Peter's Fair. In town I notice some proclamations all signed by Gullo, minister of agriculture, concerning the distribution of products. (See, I made it through the fifth grade so I could read them.) Back in Túdia I held a meeting with all the tenant farmers, explaining that there was this new law, made for everybody. I put up some of the posters I took with me. They said the products got divided sixty-forty. Just a bit before the end of harvest time, the owner, who never bothered himself before about how long it took us to thresh, he comes over to Túdia and orders us to get a move on. Not too many farmers were ready to start, see, they'd hardly winnowed as yet, but the owner, he wanted to use the old distribution system.

The farmers said no. He threatened that the police would lock them all up if they didn't agree to the percentages he wanted. These farmers came to me with the farmers from the estate of L. and I started to feel real encouraged. To be on the safe side, I went to Petralia along with these farmers. We made the trip on horseback, thirteen hours in all, and a couple of comrades came with us, Giovanni Neglia and this student. We set out late and spent the night at Fontanelle, on the mountaintop where there's this shelter, and I was struck to see that young student bedded down with the rest of us on the ground with nothing but straw to cover him. What made him do such a thing? I was really moved like I am even now every time I hear from him.

Next day the farmer working the land up there offers us some milk, and that way we felt good and headed down toward the estate. It was a big meeting, with some three hundred peasants and tenant farmers. I got there last, and when I did, the peasants informed me that the comrades down there'd already gone ahead to see the owner. But while they were waiting they started to grumble and argue cause they remembered all those times the leaders sold out and rubbed elbows with the powers that be. Everybody was afraid it'd be the same old story. I cooled them off saying you had to trust em, they were men of conscience, decent guys, they'd defend the working class and couldn't be bribed.

I start to make my way through the crowd. The owner sees me coming and meets me on the stairs, stretching out his hand all buddy-buddy, patting me on the back, whispering, "Santo, let's be real men!" Inside there's the [police] sergeant and his men and the comrades: "Listen, your boss is willing to take fifty percent of the harvest and give you all the rest. Right now talks are going on between Minister Gullo and our own Commissioner Aldisio, so if we don't settle now, we'll have to wait for their decision." I said, "Comrades, this gentleman here can wait to divide the produce. He's got thousands and thousands in the bank. But our stakes are too high, we need that little more just to provide for our families."

Then he says to me (the owner, I mean), "Don't you boys trust me?" I said, "No," never again, because it happened, and not just once, that come distribution he'd cart off a little extra, saying he'd owe it to me. Of course, then I'd have to make a few visits to his farm and there'd always be excuses like he couldn't find the key to the storage barn or he was just too busy today. Four miles there and back, I'd crawl home, feeling like I was begging.

He says to me, "Did you get the notice?" I says, "Yeah. By the way, would you be so kind to explain, with these gentlemen present, why you sent me the notice?" He says, "You're a good boy, but we can't work anything out." "I'm sorry I can't give you satisfaction. Santo S. stays at Túdia as long as the law allows it. Remember, we don't have to sleep in the same bed."

I took off just then, and he rushes out onto the balcony and right there in front of all those peasants says we'll distribute everything on the usual terms, and after the agreement between Aldisio and Gullo, if he owed us anything, he'd come across with it. I asked to speak: "We'll do just fine splitting it up sixty-forty, and anyway we don't have too much to divide right now. We still have most of it left to thresh." He says no deal. I says, OK, we won't split anything and we'll stop threshing unless we all sign an agreement that the law will be respected.

Now it's got to be confessed, I'm ashamed to admit it, everybody gave in to his threats . . .

When we staged a general strike in '47, the people lost all their patience with the taxes they had to pay the Farm Surplus Bureau. So they broke into their offices and set fire to the records. I go there to keep the peace and see that nothing happens, but they arrest twenty-one of us and pack us off to jail. Eighteen months in the coop. Eighteen months with the family stranded in the countryside. Then the trial and appeal pending on a four-month sentence. While I was in jail the owner terrorized my family: eviction threats and promises he'd give them a grand if they'd agree to get out. My wife refused.

The year after, it all starts with the hay. The new boss is Don Vittorio. Always with the same old story come distribution time. Never any respect for the law. So the farmers' battle begins all over. We finished picking some beans, so we asked for the legal distribution. Like a broken record, he wouldn't agree. So I asked the provincial union leaders to intervene and while I was filing a complaint with Comrade Totò A. from Caltanissetta, my son called and told me the owner'd brought in men from Modica to pick the rest of the beans and stack the grain for threshing. I get back to Túdia and I'm informed they have a paddy wagon all ready. Next day Comrade Totò A. comes to Túdia and quick all us farmers hold a meeting and Sergeant A. comes up with his boys and tells the comrade to disband the meeting, he's breaking the law. The comrade says, "Officer, be so kind as to back off and leave our meeting alone. If I'm breaking the law, go get a warrant for my arrest."

Half-an-hour later the meeting's still going strong and the police commissioner shows up with a paddy wagon full of cops. He's all high and mighty but I invite him over anyhow. My comrade told him, "Look, it's not that we don't want to settle. We know you won't enforce *all* the laws, but at least we can apply a few of them."

July thirteenth we started out at four in the morning to meet with the powers that be at the courthouse. But they didn't bother to show up. When we came back empty-handed the peasants were still waiting, losing all their patience. And Don Vittorio just happens to pass by with the police sergeant in his fancy new Fiat. He calls me up to him and says under his breath, "Take the share you want, let the other guys fend for themselves." I said I'd wait till the others had their fair share. Then he got all high and mighty, but I talked back: "You're on your high horse here cause you've got certain officers of the law in your saddlebags, and instead of enforcing the law, they act in your interests." They drove off, and I went back to join the farmers.

Soon after I spot the boss's driver coming back with that Fiat, and he stops and tells me the sergeant wants to talk to me. I says, "I'm not obliged to go, you know, but I got a clear conscience, so I'll come along." When we get there the owner invites us into his office, and it's the same old story all over. The cook interrupts, saying dinner's ready. I was all set to leave, but the owner stops me: "If you'd dine with me, it'd be my pleasure." I accept and he insists on playing the big host: "Have some more, Santo. Drink up! Us, we're good friends." He's playing the jolly back-slapper— "Let's talk, man to man"—trying to con me with good food and drink. Me, I want to laugh in his face. I just wasn't used to being treated like that. Fact is, many a time when he had farmhands cart chickpeas and beans from one storage barn to another, he wouldn't stoop to giving em a glass of water.

"Have some more, Santo. Drink up. You know I'm very fond of you." He winks. "Be a good boy now, don't disappoint your family. Go ahead, take a hundred percent, I won't say a word. And if that's not enough, you can take some of their share." I was careful not to drink any wine, I wouldn't fall into the trap. While we were eating, his secretary took down what we said and typed it out like a contract. Right after dinner we went back into the office and the owner signed and handed it to me. I wouldn't sign. The sergeant tries to strongarm me: "At least have the courtesy to read it." So I did, then threw it back on the table right under the owner's nose. The sergeant jumps up and shows off his authority: "So you won't sign?" "No, can you make me?" "I hereby authorize the owner to take four witnesses and confiscate one hundred percent of the produce and store it in his barns." I started to leave, but they insisted, "Wait, go in the car." "Thanks, I have my own two feet."

I find the peasants still assembled. The boss's lackey was there already to get the stuff put into sacks. Right at the state road junction the sergeant's giving orders and lining up his men. Soon as everybody's stationed he asks me, "Mr. S., do you have a permit for this demonstration?" "Yes, it's called the Law of the Republic of Italy." Then, peasants and all, we go to the threshing floor and there's the lackey with nine sacks full of beans. I ask him, "Who authorized you to fill the sacks?" He doesn't answer. I call my son Giuseppe: "Get some sacks; here we distribute things according to law." Soon as we finished dividing the first load, the police sergeant leaves the threshing floor and gets stationed on the state road. The owner'd gone to the commissioner already. That's where he found out we'd gone ahead and divided things sixty-forty, in the presence of witnesses.

Around eight in the evening, the commissioner arrives on the scene with a paddy wagon full of cops. We were in the farmhouse, singing. The accordion was playing. They raided us and hauled off fourteen of us. Meanwhile they confiscated the beans. They took us to the Resuttana Station. The day after, we wound up in the Polizzi Generosa Jail. That evening this judge interrogated us and two days later we were in the Termini Imerese Prison. Eight days later we were released, provisionally. Then there was a trial and we were acquitted.

Eight days after the verdict we went ahead with the distribution of the grain. Same old story: twenty-eight days in jail. A new trial. Acquittal on circumstantial evidence. But while I was in custody they saw their chance and by their own accounting they hauled off a ton and a half of my grain and stored it in their barns.

Finally, one year, we got it divided sixty-forty. But just that one year. See, I'm all alone. I'm too weak, too exhausted, too alone. We'd hold meetings and I'd go into a cold sweat. I'd keep saying, "Watch out, wise up, or they'll lock us up. I'll be the first to go." And they'd assure me the struggle would go on, even if just one of us was left. But many a time that show of force, all those cops, would scare the pants off them and they'd go tell the boss, "It's Santo. Get him out of the way, *he's* the instigator."

And they bring him baskets of eggs so he'll forgive and forget. See, it's not that people are unawares. But talk to any one of them, face to face, they'll tell you, "There just isn't no unity." "You understand the problem, join me, there'll be two of us, come on. Unity doesn't fall from heaven." And they'll say, "I never stop believing in unity, but when I look over my shoulder, there's not enough of us, I feel like I'm alone. And the cops keep on saying every day how you're an outside agitator."

Just five miles from here they killed Epifanio Li Puma—the Mafia from the estate, that is—but according to the law the peasants occupied that land.

THE
PARASITE
CULTURES

5. THE HONORABLE CALÒ

He relaxes in his easy chair. We are in his Palermo office.
Sixty, originally from Caltanissetta, he is a typical product of
the Mafia-client system. During the 1964 elections in Trappeto
(population somewhat more than 1,000), he collected 400 votes—
without being known personally. He is a dangerous man. Two
years after this interview, while he was undersecretary of the
National Ministry of Health, we denounced him for his direct
political connections with the Mafia. He is "Honorable" only
because he's been elected to Parliament.

Generically speaking, affluent society has transcended any need for grass-roots organization. Consider this fact: there will always be a lumpenproletariat, in addition to the so-called people, but nowadays we're dealing with a hyper-evolved power structure. Naturally, here we're in Sicily: hyper-evolution is yet to come. Let's face up to it, even the lesser nobility is still not in tune with the times. They're as recalcitrant as the lumpens.

I'm saying there's hardly a free institution in all of Sicily. Please, don't count the unions. Take the Farm Owners' Association as a case in point: nobody's there to participate in the political process. They just want economic aid, or manure.

If you ask me, we should wipe them all out. Let's go from Left to Right: the Labor Federation is totally infiltrated by Reds; the Workers' Union tries to enlist believers with anarcho-socialist tendencies; the Confederation of Trade Unions has God on its side but is full of politicking; the National Federation of Labor Unions still thinks Mussolini will be resurrected; and so on and so forth. But listen, the unions have no business in politics. They're all rotten to the core, the whole barrel of them. Without education and schooling, they've never reached maturity.

Now me, I believe in cooperatives, I founded them by the dozens. But in practice, they've all flopped.

What about religious societies? Now that's significant. See, if your parents inculcate Catholic beliefs in you, that makes you a Catholic. The conviction comes from tradition, but here there's no tradition of free institutions. The only thing that really works in Sicily is a system based on connections, and political muscle.

Ninety percent of our party politics is based on promises. The Christian Democrats tell you, "We pledge this," and the Communists say, "We pledge that," and the other parties swear they'll do the rest. Look, they all pay lip service to what they think you want to hear. And of course, if one party talks a good line, you check it out and maybe join. But if they don't have a real power base to be able to come across, you switch sides. You swap parties like they were trading cards. If you don't get instant satisfaction, you move to another camp. See, everybody's hard up. Hyperevolution would free us from these fetters of hardship, but we've got a long way to go.

You can talk all about the agrarian problem around Palermo, but it's the same story for Agrigento, Caltanissetta, Enna, parts north of Ragusa, upper Catania Province—I mean all of central Sicily. They all have one thing in common: backwardness, and that comes from feudalism. It's not a result of the large landholding system. No, it's their tendency to depend economically on a single crop, and that's a trend toward poverty. You call it underdevelopment. Even if they could, they don't irrigate, and there's no knowledge of how to use fertilizer. It's just a vicious circle.

Man's mentality, like the economy, is feudal. I mean individualistic, anarchical, absolutely lacking in the spirit of association. You ask me why? On those huge estates, man is isolated. These are all my own original theories, you understand. There's no integration into the social structures. The only coherent unit is the family. Sure, it's their natural instinct to cluster together in towns, but they never manage to materialize this instinct in viable organizations.

This isolation is universal in the private sector. They're suspicious about joining any sort of group. It goes like this: "If I join a union, a party, any organization, what kind of guarantees can they give me that they're watching out for my interests?"

I'm independent of power blocs and lobbies. As you can surmise, I have grass-roots connections. I know everybody in the front offices of the province, in all its influential organizations: the Farm Owners' Association, the Confederation of Trade Unions, and the Christian Fraternity of Italian Workers. I have official ties with all these groups. They send me directives and requests.

Then there's my open-door policy. You want something, it doesn't matter how or when, the Honorable Calò is always approachable. He never asks to see the color of your flag. For me, all voters are created equal. You could honestly say my constituency's like a rainbow. Just come to me, I understand your needs. I can give you a lift. I know how to lend an ear, and all I have to say is, "You know I care."

I read all my mail personally. I do all the sorting myself and tell my secretaries exactly how to respond.

My constituency consists of peasants, farm owners, a few masons, and artisans too. But mostly I attract the peasants. They come to me in swarms, giving me a landslide of 81,000 votes. Then you have to add another 80,000 who promise me their vote but don't come across. Whether they vote for me or not, they have their pitch all prepared: "I voted for you, so let's see what you can do for me."

I never miss a chance to speak at a party demonstration or a Farm Owners' gathering. During election campaigns I must hit at least 150 spots. Three public appearances a day, plus private sessions. That's why they call me the Campaign Bomber. Even in the off-season, I hold at least one meeting per week. I do the whole speaking circuit: here today, tomorrow in Palermo, the day after in Bari, and then it's on to Rome.

6. SONIA ALLIATA OF THE HOUSE OF SALAPARUTA

She receives me in her villa at Bagheria, the fashionable Palermo suburb. Sixty-five, alert, she is the last true princess of a house whose name is now known best on the labels of wine bottles. Though a member of a decaying, still parasitic class, she is always the lady: elegant and down-to-earth.

I f I may say so, in the ambience of the aristocracy, the individual is isolated and dedicates himself only to the immediate family.

We aristocrats don't reside in the country any longer. Oh, some, like Princess Paternò and myself, will have their villas out here in Bagheria, but after all we're only eight miles from Palermo.

I don't mean to say that in the past we were altruists, but naturally we were wealthy. We could afford to be the hosts for balls and festivals, and that way the aristocracy was a cohesive class. As you can appreciate, it was money, and not any spirit of cooperation, that brought nobles together. Deep in our hearts we trusted only our most intimate relatives, our own children and grandchildren. Otherwise we kept a proper distance, even from our cousins. What we held most dear was the glory of our own house: our coat of arms. I'm finally convinced that it's always been so: your wealth inevitably means the poverty of others.

In these times, there are very few festive occasions to celebrate; the arrangements are simply too costly. But one can still go to the Opera. You see, showing off one's jewels and being the envy of everyone is one of the few pleasures we have left. I must confess the truth, it is still a pleasure for me to hear people say that as long as the princess lives, the House of Villafranca Salaparuta is invested with a certain dignity, and that even in modern times it has kept its luster and maintained its decorum.

The nobility is dying. We are in the twilight of the gods. Once we were truly divine. The greatest geniuses, from Michelangelo to Leonardo, were all our subjects, for we are a chosen people. And yet today we are curiosities, like museums, where one can come and browse. We are taking our last gasp, and our children are no longer princes and princesses, in the financial or moral sense. Of course, I am old and unable to change, so I stay attached to the past.

There's still a link, however invisible, that binds us all together: our sense of honor and pride in being of the nobility. A racehorse should never stoop to drawing a cart. A man of learning, I believe he was a philosopher, once said that it takes several generations before the carthorse loses its golden mane. How can we forget overnight all those centuries of refinement?

Today we are being swallowed up by materialism. One searches in vain for genuine expressions of the spirit. Of course we instinctively defend certain values, yet we have not translated this instinct into organized forms of action. It is truly the twilight of the gods. We have even lost our reactionary spirit. Our coins are virtually out of currency. We have nothing left to prize but our resistance to the vulgarity that is creeping up upon us.

Naturally one must remember the distinction between the truly grand families and the lesser nobility. I mean the hierarchy of barons, counts, etcetera. But today there are barons worth as much as princes. Everything is a matter of money. Even in aristocratic circles, the wealthiest have the most prestige, and those who have gone bankrupt are virtual outcasts. Once, all the peasants voted for their lord. Every prince commanded his own province. Why, the House of Villafranca alone had forty estates. And naturally we had our senators. Everyone depended on us for his survival. You vote for whoever holds your breadbasket.

Nowadays the people are better off than we are. Poverty really doesn't exist. If you are poor, that simply means you are lazy. Some of my very best acquaintances, generals' wives, duchesses, princesses, can no longer afford to have maids, because these people want too much money or think such work is beneath them. And these high-ranking families are left to manage with the service of one or two menials, causing the close ties between aristocrats and the people to be severed for good. We have no more peasants or servants.

Once we had a beautiful relationship with them. For generations they served us with devotion. For five generations our gardener came from the same family. The father would pass on his skills to the son. And you know, indentured servants still prefer to work for a lord. They are humiliated less by accepting a pittance than by working for the bourgeois class. They despise working for their equals—just listen to them: "If I have to serve, let me serve a lord." You understand, they still have an inkling of our superiority. And we treat them with familiarity, as gentlemen, while the bourgeois lords it over them in all his vulgarity.

It grieves me to see the people make progress because their gain is by nature my loss. Of course I realize, intellectually, that such things are inevitable. I only wish it would happen more gradually. *Natura abhorret saltum:* rapid change does more harm than good.

We had a parental relationship with them. "May Your Excellency bless me," they would say, and many say it still. You see, they were happy with their estate in life. They felt protected like a child feels with its father and mother. They flocked to us in multitudes . . . But that's all in the past. The sun is setting. The bourgeois class knows nothing of that loving-kindness that characterized the upper nobility.

Of course, I don't want to paint the picture too bright. We did keep them in their place and naturally maintained the proper distance. For example, I love dogs. I take them to the veterinarian for checkups, feed them, and even cry when they pass away. But dogs will always be dogs. We never cherished the illusion that the people could change their station in life. Peasants were meant to be peasants, forever. Personally I beg to differ, but I'm something of an iconoclast along these lines. I can recognize that the world is changing. Yet deep in my heart I am pained, like all of us who must lose. Please, try to understand this and pardon us a bit.

Our society should be ruthless in stamping out lawbreakers. We should abolish the secret ballot. Every man should have the courage to choose publicly and a sense of loyalty to his choice. Everyone must fight for his ideals, instead of bandying them about. Voters should be required to pass an examination proving they have these basic qualifications: proper upbringing, sound mind, fundamental awareness of sociopolitical problems, and common sense.

The great once welcomed geniuses at their courts and gave them splendid banquets. It makes me want to weep. Wherever you look nowadays, there are nothing but fools: all those beatniks with their god-awful music and art. But pause for a moment and look at my roses. Aren't they a joy to behold? One must remember the spiritual goods, the pure love of beauty.

Fortunately, there's one thing left to keep us in touch. Twenty-four of us can get together to play canasta. Mind you, it's not for the money. On the contrary, it's a game that requires real intelligence and revives our competitive spirit. One day, it's at the Marquise X's, the next day at Countess Y's. It's an innocent pastime, a trifle, I'd say. Whatever value we derive from it is purely superficial. But I play every afternoon. What else would you have me do?

7. PEPPE VOLPE, KNIGHT OF THE ORDERS OF...

Self-made man and opportunist par excellence *in politics, he is fifty-five, still full of that perverse energy and spirit that characterizes many of his fellow Fascists (past and present). I meet him at our Center for Research and Initiatives at Menfi.*

Given the present state of affairs, the people are against the Belice Dam and the water and they use it only because the consortiums say, "Take it or leave it, you pay." Still, almost nobody uses the water, and if it wasn't for all these threats, it'd all go down the drain. Naturally the big landowners—take my associate, Baron Planeta—had to give in to the water first. Then some peasants followed suit. But when you talk dollars and cents, the peasant's only aspiration is owning his own land and farming it the way he darn well pleases. He doesn't like to be told what to do, so to really help him you have to take him in hand—or by the throat. See, the peasant is nearsighted. He seeks instant gratification, as I'll demonstrate throughout the course of my history. Everybody talks about "The People" because you can't get into power without their votes, but once politicians get in, they go deaf, dumb, and blind to the people's needs. The common man is left stranded, but that's not all his fault.

When I give speeches, I start off by saying I got my degree with a hoe. I beg their pardon if my grammar "ain't so good." That gets them on my side, hook, line, and sinker.

The cooperatives are gasping for a lease on life, but mine's the first in all of western Sicily. We've received countless contributions from the region, the State, and the Emergency Fund for the South. Nobody rakes it in like me. About two months before an election, the deaf, dumb, and blind have their senses restored by a miracle. They find the right words and angles. I know them all, these politicians, and how to untie their purse strings. I've been in every party. I've worn shirts of every color, and got the peasants to do likewise. I'm a man who knows how to be grateful, and my kind of gratitude cuts to the core of the peasants' hearts.

At this moment in history, I'm biding my time. But sooner or later I'll make my move again, and make it click. It's like being a general, you have to know when to retreat and when to counterattack. At this stage I'm in my fiscal retreat: the resale of surplus tobacco I've engineered with the Honorable Abisso. Every morning at five A.M., when the masons and carpenters set out for work and the peasants head for the fields, my wife is out there to sell them tobacco at fabulous discounts. That way they're happy and grateful. My strength lies in my poverty.

The agrarian reform law is like an ice-cream cone. You pay for it, have it wrapped up to take home, and it's all melted when you get there. There's too many people running the show, too many debates, counterarguments, directives, services. All the money is pocketed by the bureaucrats, and there's nothing left for the peasants. With all these departments and decisions, nothing ever happens and they let the people go all to hell.

Back during the Heroic Period, the greatest of our leaders came to witness my achievements and pay their respects: the minister of public works, Luigi Razza, who fell on a mission over Africa; the Honorable Amilcare Rossi, president of the Blue Ribbon Beer Corporation (that was in '32); and Terruzzi and Starace, whom I honored duly with a mass demonstration right here in this very square. Starace was a stalwart, dead-serious type. Then there was Farinacci; he was quicker on the draw, a real revolutionary. Both of them were congenial too, they had poise and verve. We got along just fine. We had parades on horseback, speeches, banquets. Seeing all these murderers and thieves go scot-free nowadays, people still vote for the Old Way. If The Man [Mussolini] was still alive, he'd win in a landslide.

Now I'll account things in their proper order:

Peppe Volpe, born in Menfi, the ninth of September 1887, one hundred percent farmhand. In those days the people were starving to death, and a real sense of cooperative organization just got into my blood. Menfi was surrounded by abandoned and badly cultivated estates. But there was plenty of farmhands, and as I say, they were starving to death. The labor force consisted of eighty percent day laborers and twenty percent tenant farmers. When there was work, they'd do it, so to speak, for beans. They were all in the same boat, but nobody got together to talk about it. They were happy being slaves.

For three hundred years the family of Prince Fabrizio Pignatelli had all the property that stretched from the sea up to the Castle and then farther on up to the plateau, bordered by the Genovese estate. When the people started to riot against their conditions, the owners started to take the census. (You know, a census tax is still paid to the prince.) One problem was the nobles spent all their time between Rome and Naples; they had no idea where their property ended, or began, and everything was left to the overseers. All the children went around with the clothes God gave them at birth, and the older kids were always barefoot. They'd beg, "God bless Your Lordship." "May I kiss your hand?" They called the aristocrats "Master" all their lives. But in practice the overseers were the bosses, and so the Mafia started to evolve.

I investigated the people's living conditions, but they got scared we all might wind up in jail. So I took a new course of action. I got the idea from Colaianni. He'd set up the "Mother Earth Cooperative" at Castrogiovanni. So I did him one better at Menfi, and called the cooperative "Colaianni." I'd sell it this way: "If we're united we can use the law for our own good and then the politicians will get smart and make the laws stick; but if we're not together, then . . ." Fact is, it was young people who joined me—the older folk were afraid. Eighty strong, all but three under eighteen.

I launched the cooperative November 24, 1912; 1913 started to prove me right. If you're not united, you're sheep, herded by party heads. But if you're in a big group, candidates come looking for you. They "just happen to drop by" at local branches of the cooperative. Then it's them who need us. As you remember, the government in those days granted universal suffrage and we voted on a one-candidate-per-party ticket. There were four parties on the slate. Fact is, the cooperative supported the youngest and least rich of the four: Attorney Abisso, who was with the party in power. He paid us visits and made lots of good speeches, and the twenty-fifth of October of '13, the cooperative delivered six hundred votes to Angelo Abisso, who was elected to the Parliament. Even after the elections, the cooperative managed to keep the Menfi deputy and ward bosses under our control.

I have a brain that's finely tuned to the times. Even though most of our members went off to war in '15—of course I was the first to enlist—we managed to make ends meet between '13 and '18 by requesting monthly dues of about a dime apiece. And people started to join our ranks because they felt they could be proud of their cooperative. The landowners couldn't use the police against us any more because we had political power and the deputy was at our disposal. Abisso would always say, "I'd rather have your six hundred shock troops than those thousands of middle-of-the-roaders."

The eleventh of October 1916, I incurred two wounds on the Sangrato del Merna River, one to the chest and one to the forearm. After being treated for a year or so, I got a government pension. By then it was 1918. Back in Menfi, I resurrected our institution, and created another cooperative, this time for consumers.

In 1919, they enacted the national law for a veterans' public works program, and I took it upon myself to apply to the government for the expropriation of the Fiore estate. That's just outside of town. That amounted to twelve hundred acres, which once they were expropriated were let out to the Colaianni Cooperative on two years' worth of credit. The Palermo aristocracy put up a real fight against me because we were becoming the nemesis of rich Sicilian landowners.

Well, the land was close to town and there was a surplus of farmhands, so we broke the estate up into acre lots and distributed them to six hundred Peasant Veterans. But knowing peasant psychology, I kept 166 acres of drained swampland as common property of the cooperative. Remember, the peasant is nearsighted. He wants instant gratification. Unless you keep a carrot hanging in front of his nose, he'll just pay the set price for his own land and never funnel the profits back into the organization that got him the land in the first place.

At any rate, the peasants were bubbling with joy for what the cooperative did for them, and we were in the driver's seat politically. In 1920, we supported Abisso and won all thirty town council seats (majority and minority). Come '23, he became a Fascist and so did we. We got on the Black Bandwagon. We combed this province with our billy clubs. Let me tell you, we busted a lot of leftist balls. In all modesty, we made history. We'd be the first to intervene in political confrontations. We'd beat the fear of God into those devils and get the people's endorsement. Our job was to wipe out the opposition. Parties didn't matter anyhow. Our job was to get our candidate elected with clubs, pitchforks, whatever we had on hand. In fact, come '24, he was a shoo-in on the Fascist slate. Then in '28, he was named Senator-for-Life, and we became hard-core Fascists for good. Our political thrust, our meetings, our propaganda, it was all orthodox, get me? On the up-and-up, especially when voting went out of style. I mean we were in the right, follow me? That's how things worked in their totality.

Saturdays we'd hold our meetings and I'd proclaim, "Before our cooperative started to march forward, you were like gypsies selling copper pots on cowpaths. And now . . ." Our membership skyrocketed from eighty to eight hundred. Abisso would tell us, "Before Fascism, as the husband was setting out for his day's work in the fields, the wife would warn him not to put up a fight if somebody was stealing the animals, or else he'd never make it back home. Even children had to be afraid to walk the streets. Now, there's peace and quiet." See, the people accepted Fascism because it got rid of a lot of bums and sent the crooks into exile.

Let's take one step backwards. In '21, they passed the Solchi-

Falcioni Law that allotted land left barren or just abused. That time I applied to take over the Greater Bertolino, that was the estate of the Baroness Aroni de Lazzarini. Fact is, we were granted a thousand acres and I rented out shares of twelve acres each to seventy different families. It was quite a show to engineer. The peasants flocked to our assemblies to get their ID cards. You know, land is their blood. They followed us like crusaders. Here I was, a farmhand, raising them almost to the moral level of landowners, and they were carrying my banner. Now they had political power, moral gratification, and more to eat. By '22 the land was all ours and we turned the shareholders into men of property.

When Fascism arrived, being as we were veterans we manned the battlefronts, singing all their anthems about love of country and war. It was "All Praise to Fascist Youth" and the song the shock troopers sung: "Fight! Fight! Fight!"—ha! ha!—"Oh, Fight! Fight! Fight!"—it was invigorating, let me tell you. Of course, it could just as easily have been "Let the people march forth" or "The Internationale"—ha! ha!—but the idea this time was "Fight! Fight! Fight! Fascist Youth is always Right!"

Fascism was a total way of life. When you'd write a letter, instead of closing with "Warmest Regards," you'd say "Fascist Regards" or "Heartiest Partiness."

We'd take out bank loans to buy our fertilizer at the end of the summer, and by the time we had to buy choice wheat and cotton seed, we'd have the loan paid up. The peasants rushed to join us—they had a competition going. There were never any problems. The cooperative amassed, along totalitarian lines, a full supply of all our products: wool, cotton, everything. Its head, me, was on the board of directors of the Bank of Sicily for Aid to Agriculture. I lasted fifteen years.

We come now to '42. Remember, I'd started as an errand boy, but due to all my triumphs from '20 on up till '46, I was in the driver's seat politically. Except the podestà, you know, the mayor, who I was pushing myself for praetor, I mean regional deputy, had me sent into internment. See, there'd been a shortage of foodstuffs. Everything had to be rationed. Mothers of who knows how many kids had to go hunt up spare pennies for a little sack of grain and have it ground on the sly. Then the podestà decided that the subsidies given to the families of veterans would be suspended. Since one word from me would have mobilized all of Menfi for any damn party or regime, the people came to me to have the subsidies reinstated. Now, being a Good Fascist and backing the podestà for praetor, I couldn't support any resistance to his power, because that would mean going against Fascism. So instead I sent a telegram to the Chief of State and got the subsidies reinstated just like that.

But one day the podestà was having his coffee at the Italy Bar and a bunch of women walked in. "Ah-ha! That beer may cool off your balls, but you're on the hot seat. Yeah, we know what you're up to, selling surplus grain at seven-fifty a sheaf and letting us go hungry!" See, he was selling it on the black market.

Well, the Strong Arm of the Law began investigating, and the podestà figured I had turned against him. I just sat tight that August of '42, confident the authorities couldn't hang a thing on me. But after five inquests at Menfi, they denounced me with the following accusations: "Dangerous and irresponsible behavior, slander of a public official, demagogical tendencies." The evening of September thirtieth, during a session of the Internment Committee, the praetor duly warned me. He said I'd become too powerful, like a Panepinto or an Alongi, and that one nod from me could start a revolution in Menfi and beyond. It was so serious, he reiterated, that the podestà couldn't even show his face in town. In conclusion, I got two years.

Well, I did exactly four days. They dispatched my release before I got to the camp. But technically I'd been a political prisoner. From a logical standpoint, I wasn't a Good Fascist any more. So the podestà leveled more accusations at me, but they didn't hold water, and in the meantime Sicily was occupied by the Allies.

Dammit, I wanted political revenge. Look, in '20 Italy was painted all Red and I'd been the diamond in the rough. I never forfeited my allegiance to the forces of the Right, that is, the bourgeoisie; and then they had me interned—and unjustly, to add insult to injury. So in '44, as a fitting reaction, I launched a leftist campaign. Right here in this very square where you and me are sitting. You can't imagine how jam-packed it was. I mustered enough support that, in twenty-four hours, I was another Lenin. In fact we set up a trade union right there and then, with an affiliated local section of the Communist Party, and in the elections of 1946, we beat the United Front of the Right. It was a rout—by five hundred votes—and we stormed City Hall. Then we triumphed again in June of '46, for the Constituent Assembly. It was always our cooperative in the forefront of the political struggle.

In '45 I dissolved the old council and created the post of city manager. I was the first ever to be elected. But it got into some people's heads to horn in on my constituency, all that I'd developed over forty-five years. So they started to politicize and set up another cooperative in terms of ideologies. Look, I didn't give a good goddamn if we were Christian Democrat or Communist; the main thing was the way I personalized the cooperative. But they tried to phase me out with ideologies, so I had to make an agreement with Prince Pignatelli's overseer. He had faith in me, and I trounced my enemies. I had to do it that way to show my competitors I was smarter than they were on all fronts. See, at that point there was a split in the Party. Li Causi was leading the opposition, and between me and Bilello, in the confrontation, our guys had to choose Bilello. Let's face it, he was a hardliner his whole career. And me, I was just an extemporaneous Commie who'd joined the Party in retaliation. Bilello got the nod, so I went to see the Prince.

Meanwhile thirty-five of our cooperative's cows got stolen, so we rented out some of our spare land as pasture. That way the Sickle moved in on us. But I can document for you how, as cooperatives come and go, theirs was a complete flop. The whole horde of em, hard-core Red, they thought they could fool me and take me for a ride. But it was the other way around, see:

hosts of other politicos came running to court my favor. The Honorable Borsellino, a Christian Democrat, worked real hard to win me over. Well, I was faithful to the interests of the cooperative, and besides they needed my leadership, so I had to go with the party in power. That meant I had to strike at the Sickle's sore point: they weren't legally registered. Presto chango, their license got revoked and their land fell into the hands of the Colaianni Cooperative. At that point we chose Commander Antonio Papa as our head (he was ex–police chief). Then, I was again elected president of our board of directors.

I took a new approach to politics. I had my constituency vote for the Christian Democrats. Since the people were still behind me, it all slipped through the Communists' fingers. When times got hard I sold my own shares and took out loans on my mortgage: just to save the cooperative.

The Christian Democrats were extending their sphere of influence, and Borsellino was becoming an institution. He was all right. At first he'd try to persuade you, but then he'd listen to reason. When you got him votes, he'd cooperate. You see, we took possession of this land that we used to manage for Prince Pignatelli and we got it for a total of $226,000, payable with a Bank of Sicily loan of $170,000. It all involved 170 families, and instead of the normal rate, the peasants paid 2.5 percent interest. It was all arranged under the auspices of Borsellino. He was with the party in power.

I sponsored a project for the construction of modest farmhouses on each and every lot, one building every two acres. I got the project approved, but the funds were late in arriving, so I had the expenditures covered by the special National Pool (pool of money, you understand). That way I instituted my own particular administrative mechanism. I sent seventy promissory notes to certain individuals in Palermo and got back seventy pledges real quick. See, I'd always been nice to them, and they knew the cooperative was backing them with votes. Then I had these seventy shareholders delegate me as head of this new contracting firm. It was all done on the up-and-up at the notary's.

That way I could dispose of the promissory notes as I saw fit, to build the houses. Anyway I needed credit references at the banks. I managed to open a current account worth $25,000 in titles, with the anticipation of another $25,000 in deposits, and so on. It all meshed and the wheels started turning and slap! we had our 170 houses. Plus we built roads by dipping into the Emergency Fund for the South.

Let me clue you in—it was complicated. I can't count all the letters I dictated to our attorneys and secretaries (always reminding them to correct the grammar); but they can't complain, I made them landowners too. Still, there was the danger of far-sightedness, so always acting in the peasants' interests, we had them pay for these shares to keep the cooperative's strong arm in there. That way the founding members, who became small landowners around the First War, could make sure their children would keep that land and make it grow after the Second War.

But this enterprise wasn't so simple. Sure, it meant the redistribution of two thousand acres, but it also had undercurrents. The owners of the large estates saw the writing on the wall, and that scared the pants off them. They started to send me threatening letters. They even tried to bribe me (though in public they grinned and bore it, and sold at our price). Yeah, I received anonymous threats to shut me up and stop me from applying for the expropriations. But think about it like this: flesh that dies a natural death gets burned and thrown on the heap, but flesh that's butchered gets eaten. Which means, nothing scares me. I'll die protecting the people's interests.

So the anonymous letters stopped. The Mafia and the rich finally got the message: "Volpe doesn't act out of hate, or for personal revenge. Everything he does is based on love for his class." They haven't killed me because I'm too shrewd. During Fascism and after, the Mafia was afraid of me. I was too strong in politics and in the hearts of the peasants, who would fight for me at any price. See, a man with real intelligence can kill his enemies *politically*. Through my career Menfi's whole economy's been transformed and you can't mess with that.

But as the years flew by, the cooperative was getting in worse and worse shape, economically speaking. We tried to launch this scheme of acquiring $180,000 worth of farm machinery as part of a package deal including 1,400 acres priced at $750,000. But the Bank of Sicily stopped me cold—all for political motives. It was like driving at ninety miles an hour and having your brakes lock on you. You're as good as DOA. Let me tell you what their motives were: that little ingroup of the powers that be, I mean the Christian Democrats, they wanted the cooperative's land for themselves. In October of '57, they held a historic meeting with our members, engineering a vote of no confidence against our board. On the spot I made my declaration: "You don't deserve me as your leader. I'm handing in my resignation."

Then, I laid low. You know, it's my belief that a politician has to be an artist. An actor. You've got to play the fool sometimes to get your audience's sympathy, or play dead to let things cool down. Then there's times for the cloak-and-dagger and the sawed-off shotgun. For me the time is ripe to wait in the wings till the right moment to come back on the scene.

Given my constitution, if the Communists took over, it wouldn't much matter. See, I'm so far above them in my love for the people, they could never top me. Anyway, as I've manifested to you, I've been with all the parties in power to put the will of the people and their law into action.

When I left the cooperative it had a debt of $350,000: $250,000, maybe more, for the acquisition of machinery, and the rest with the Bank of Sicily. Don't forget, the cooperative's assets total $750,000, but at this moment in time it can't shell out a nickel because the regional administrators of agricultural and labor programs haven't figured out a way to get it running again. A leader of the Agrigento Agrarian Consortium came to me seeking advice as to how to surmount the crisis. I told him, "Surgery won't work; you need a master brush-stroke." It's all a matter of administrative flair.

Now that I'm gone, the cooperative's good as dead. The only property it has left is 176 acres of the Fiore estate and 100 acres at Casenuove. Sure, without any of them college professors by my side, I made a few mistakes. But through my enterprising ventures I got respect from the intellectuals. Fact is, they've exploited me to get into power. All my opponents say the same thing about me: "As far as his ability and integrity, we've got nothing to criticize. His only problem is the people who work for him." Like I said, we couldn't find enough mechanics to keep the machinery in good running order and the threshing machines would get all fouled up. It'd all break down and we'd have to go into debt to get new machinery. But you have to skim over the petty details and take an overview of my achievements: just add up all the acres of land I gave the peasants. And my achievements are not just economic, they're social too. You have to look at the total picture. It's like war. Sure, there's the dead, the prisoners, the wounded. It's the same story come the threshing campaign: some sacks get filled and delivered, others get robbed or swapped, you read me.

They say I've done special favors for my relatives. Come on now, legally, I don't even have any. I'm a foundling. But my stepfather took a liking to me and adopted me legally—so I wouldn't have to do military service. That was when I was nineteen. Then the court discovered my real identity: son of a blind beggar, Volpe, Francesco—mother unknown. Come the Great War we were all mobilized anyway—us only children like everybody else. But this name of mine, that could of gone down into oblivion if not ignominy, I've made famous in Menfi, in the province, in Sicily, and even up there in Rome. And it's all due to my enterprising exploits—for which, by the way, I've been decorated three times. I'm Knight of the Crown of Italy, Knight of the Republic, and Commander of the Order of Liberté (that's French). It's not that I'm bragging, I just want you to have all the documentation. Sure, you give a break or two to the friends who are faithful to you, come fair or foul. OK, I looked out for them, they were like blood-brothers to me, but . . .

Yeah, it's in our blood. Here we all look out for our own interests. They jump on the cooperative bandwagon only to land their own property. Then they mind their own business. That's as far as cooperativism goes here. At any rate, the opposition's always warning them: "Haven't you heard about cooperatives? Watch out, it's all a front for collectivism. And you know how that winds up. Get out quick or they'll drown you too." The rich are threatened by the cooperative because it makes the people free. We don't have to go begging any more.

Our cooperative is the first and finest in the province. A few more came after that. But still, nobody has what I had: flair, that certain stroke of genius.

8. SALVATORE VILARDO

*We are in a Palermo bar. Once a soccer player himself, now a
promoter, he has a scarlet face and a pronounced wheeze. There
is something shady about him. (In fact, he will soon be arrested
for various illegal practices.)*

You can draw crowds up to 35,000 and keep them riveted to
their seats two whole hours. Everybody gets into the spirit,
it's like they all form part of one single body, an organism
possessed in a fit of love for their team. That's what unites
all in one mass. For two hours there are no class distinctions. If
one of their heroes blows an easy shot, a five-star general gets
just as pissed as any day laborer. A chief justice pouts like a
little kid or screams insults at the ref. A bank executive flies
off the handle and a street cleaner has to calm him down. All
it takes is a goal for the judge and the worker to embrace and
spill tears of joy in common. I remember this high-ranking
bureaucrat, he was probably a holy terror at the office, but he'd
come three hours in advance and wait in line like a lamb just
to get a good seat. Well, the first time he came with his package,
we thought it was the lunch he packed to eat before game time.
But as soon as the ref blew the opening whistle, he unwrapped
the package and it was salt, and he sprinkled it all around to
protect us against the jinx. For two hours all social distinctions
disappear, everybody forgets what and who they are. They're all
united, with one face. Everybody in the stadium forgets his own
identity and fuses into the mass. Even the guards forget they're
policemen. They jump up and down if the team is winning, and
if things are going bad they get in brawls too. Every Sunday we
have to change the guards, or else they get to be real fanatics
and forget that they're on duty.

When things go bad for the team, it rains cats and dogs on
the ref: curses, oranges, lemons, bottles. When we clear the field

after a game, we collect shoes, lighters, umbrellas, coins tied up in kerchiefs.

Until 1930 the crowd was mostly male, but now the percentage of women is up to twenty-five percent, and they're usually the most rabid. If they're not, they come anyway, just to be on display.

The stadium unites them, but then they go back home to their private lives and separate walks of life. Monday they're like strangers again. Yesterday they were blood-brothers, equals, but today the bureaucrat and the day laborer don't even recognize each other on the street. Within the confines of the stadium, there's unity in competition and in discussion of the technical angles of the sport. But here in Palermo all attempts to make the sport a microcosm for concrete social action fusing diverse individuals and social classes have always been doomed to failure.

During a game these classes galvanize. You get two hours worth of social homogenization. But the minute the game is over, the high tension dissolves and it's back to the normal voltage. People are themselves again, all isolated. With the upper classes it's like the game never happened, but the hoi polloi are still charged up. They never stop talking about this and that play. They're still ecstatic, and it's so contagious that converts are made just from hearing about the play-by-play action. It becomes a passion—or if you want, an epidemic. By Thursday, maybe they wind down, but Saturday they plug back in and charge up. Sunday the tension mounts to new peaks.

Beyond any shadow of a doubt, the sport, as a meeting of the masses, promotes social dynamics in Palermo. But in the poorer neighborhoods like the Capo or Ballarò, the repercussions go deeper. The involvement of the disadvantaged is more intense. They're totally captivated. Even if disagreements flare up, sociability is kindled. In wealthier neighborhoods you find appreciation for the sport, but along these upper-class lines, it's mostly dilettantism. They look for good excuses to live out their fantasies and make spectacles of themselves. Or else they'll exploit this "spontaneous show of enthusiasm" for political ends. Just look at the history of their support of soccer. Their promoters disappear from behind the scenes if their political goals aren't achieved. (I mean votes for the party your stars endorse.)

Soccer's definitely our most popular sport. Under Sicilian law, it's the only sport that's officially subsidized. Of course, we have a highly developed equestrian awareness. The Favorita Park Race Track is one of the most ancient in all of Italy. Naturally this passion has evolved from our intimate relationship with horses, in the city as well as in the country. More often than not they sleep with us in our homes. Here, from time immemorial, even before tracks were built, we've had races in the smallest of villages. For eighty years or more, winning horses have been immortalized, and the aristocracy has always indulged in the snobbery of steeplechasing. No festival is complete without a race. For centuries, horses have been the belles of the balls.

Then there's cycling, but it's in bad shape. You see, soccer and the horses are funded by the State, by legalized betting, but cycling hasn't managed to get a boost from the government. At first it mobilized the masses, but now it's on the downswing. Other sports don't have much muscle. Like tennis, it's all for the snoots. The people couldn't give a damn.

The internal dynamics of the soccer team is complicated. You have mule drivers and college graduates playing together, so what with their backgrounds and outlooks being different, inequalities, frictions, and resentments crop up. You always have to worry about the other guy vying for your position. This is where the coach comes in. See, it's his job to train sound minds as well as bodies. He irons out differences, boosts morale, and inculcates momentum by making the players feel they're World Cup material. He's got to make them real champs, whether they really are or not. Of course, nowadays what drives the pros onward and upward isn't the medals or the scholarships to go on with their studies. It's the tournament winnings, green and crinkly.

The coach drills the players in the fundamentals and teaches them all the latest techniques. But above all, he has to mold his squad into a perfect unit. You've got to understand, it's this togetherness that makes the team stronger. They've got to jell and filter out all individualism. Even a superstar can foul things up and disrupt the coach's game plan. Basically, soccer's a team sport.

There's two categories of spectators: eighty percent are fans, twenty percent are connoisseurs. Connoisseurs get engrossed in the beauty of the game for its own sake. They'll even applaud the opposing team for a play showing technical skill and group spirit. On the other hand, the fans get much more excited when their hero makes a brilliant play, even if it disrupts the team. But the percentage of more discriminating fans is slowly on the rise.

All over the city, wherever the action is, you find people gathered to talk about soccer. The bars, cafés, even the markets, they all become community-action centers. Soccer is their cultural and moral life. They form squads of their own and delegate leaders for their cheering sections at the stadium. If there's an enemy goal and morale gets low, it's the leader's job to talk it up and get the people to chant in unison so the team's spirit of unity will be restored. "Hip! Hip! Hooray!" they'll shout, trying to get the team to bounce back. In my opinion, this idea of strength in unity on the field carries over into private family life as well.

Our society hand-picks the team members. We organize the club where sportspeople can meet with fans and interested parties. We also charter buses for away-games and, collectively speaking, keep spirits high for our favorite team.

There's no other phenomenon in this whole city that can bring so many people together with so much interest. By comparison, even the Festival of Saint Rosalia is poorly attended. People just go to eat ice cream, listen to a Te Deum or two, and watch the fireworks. Once, maybe twice a year there are attractions, where ten or fifteen thousand take part in the procession, but that's an isolated event, without a lasting effect. I'd call it folklore. There's no concrete results. It doesn't create any kind of group consciousness. Once the party's over, there's no tomorrow. You can't even compare it to soccer. If you want to see real mass unity and organization, go to the stadium and study the stands, the toilets, the parking lots. One of our Sundays will make you a new man. It hits you like a strong country wine. You have a purpose in life, higher goals. You're part of a multitude swarming to the stadium with the immediate goal of victory that day and the ultimate goal of moving into first place. That's right, the standings, that's the people's first passion. They dream night and day of being at the top.

What far-reaching effects does Saint Rosalia leave in this city? Miles and miles of garbage, piles of snail and pumpkinseed shells, that's all. She can't compete. Our methods and objectives are completely in tune or maybe ahead of the times. She's just too antiquated. To challenge us she'd have to develop a more forward look.

In a city like Palermo, it's not just those 35,000 who show and see it all live. No, there's at least another 200,000 followers who play the pool. Let me stress that's legalized gambling. They read the sporting news every day and get really involved in heated debates. Just think of it, little old ladies, seventy, maybe more, they don't even know what the word "soccer" means, but they'd croak before missing the weekly pool. That's the way we've hooked the aged on soccer. Otherwise they'd just be oblivious. We know how to reach all ages and sexes, that's why we're on the upsurge. Plus we've remodernized the stadium twice, and it's still got to grow because we still can't supply all the seats the public demands. Talks are in progress to redesign the stadium for 80,000 spectators.

The masses go to relax, drown their sorrows, forget about the bills they have to pay on Monday. All of us have to blow off some steam. There's people who fast for days to be able to buy a ticket. Once the spectator's got the bug, he can identify. Watching a good athlete is like a holy communion. There's a mystical union with the athlete, it's sort of like having a woman. She's a beauty, she gives you pleasure, OK. But if you love her to boot, it's real passion.

When Palermo has a losing streak, a lot of people mourn and fast. The wife'll shove the pasta under the man's nose and he'll throw it out the window. Last Sunday there was another casualty, due to heart attack. But all it takes is one goal and the heavens are full of ovations, hats, jackets, shoes. The people embrace. It's a thrill of thrills, a spectacle that gets you right here. You see what I mean. Sure, it's an ongoing struggle, a constant tension. But we need a goal to achieve in life, and the games keep us going because they're played in series. The divisional standings are always on our minds. They're not ephemeral like Saint Rosalia. One game lost today leads to disastrous consequences for the whole year to come. Still, it may not be the end of the world. You can't give up. You have to take the long-term, philosophical view. The world wasn't created in one day. It takes endless striving to have victory in the palm of your hands and never fall out of the first division. What I mean is, it's an eternal battle.

9. A PARISH PRIEST

Thirty-five or so, he is one of the most educated and socially committed priests in this area. We walk through the poor coastal town of Balestrate, location of his parish. He ruminates.

It fell to me to encourage the day laborers to organize a cooperative, but here mistrust is a pestilence. Everybody suspects his brother of covetousness. The elderly remember all those errant experiments in the past.

Another problem is our relative lack of social conscience. Oh, perhaps it's a deficiency, a retardation, rather than a lack. We need people devoted to their fellow creatures. There's a generation gap as well. The old still cherish the sayings and proverbs that reinforce solitary activity and mutual distrust. The young feel a greater need for community.

We could promote a sense of unity by inculcating those edicts promulgated by the Curia regarding the liturgy and the Church. Herein, the congregation is heralded as the community. The family of the diocese guides the parish family and both are subsumed in Mother Church. Naturally we have to sensitize Christians to the genuine meaning of charity, understood on the grand scale, as it was in the early days of our Faith.

The ways are many whereby we can foster a sense of community: liturgical innovation, the use of Italian instead of Latin during the mass, the populace's choral participation in the mass (by the way, in accordance with recent edicts I've changed the position of the altar so I can face the people), and a real dialogue between the priest and the congregation.

In my parish everybody's baptized, except one child of six months. If we define practicing Catholics as those united in the Spirit, then ninety percent are Catholic. But if you judge only from those who come to Church and Confession, the percentage drops to thirty, and that depends on the season. Everybody comes to processions, Good Friday and Corpus Christi. Christmas,

Easter, and Saint Lucy's and Saint Joseph's Days, they also draw crowds. Especially Easter, with all its ritual.

As for groups, we have four branches of Catholic Action: boys, girls, men, and women. Each group takes its own initiative, studying the official edicts and spreading the word, so to speak, in the community. The women go out into the countryside to inculcate in isolated families a sense of our cardinal principles. This year, it's the concept of grace and the taking of the sacraments. Next year it will be the liturgy and the parish as community guided by faith, prayer, and charity. People give of themselves as best they can. We utilize every body and soul. They circulate our printed matter and xeroxes. The young people rally support with megaphones. They inculcate beliefs through slogans. I try to get the adults to do it too. You see, we also have to improve our public image.

Everybody should be granted the right to work close to home. No one wants to go to Northern Italy or Germany or America, but fifty percent have to. Emigration is a blight upon the land. Integral Christian communities are a rare blessing, but on the other hand we can't hope for a collective society. That's Communist. People must always be free to express their individual personalities. To create a socioeconomic community is not within our power. We inculcate cardinal principles. In the social doctrine of the Church there are tenets forewarning that damage to the property of others is a mortal sin.

The parish is spiritual father of the union of all the faithful. Thus, it promotes social and cultural progress. I try to motivate students to work for the Faith. Otherwise they'd hang around doing nothing. Inculcating principles in those near and far, the parish priest prods all his children to know themselves as brothers in Christ and as God's creatures.

There's a group of Evangelists at large and I've tried to ferret them out. But they're not really a threat, at least for now.

In his domain, the parish priest has the right and the duty to attend to everything. His presence is felt everywhere.

10. THE CARDINAL

*I thought it would be useful to have a meeting with Cardinal
Ernesto Ruffini, the most powerful prelate in Sicily. Some of his
credentials: Doctor of Philosophy, Professor of Holy Scriptures,
Official Censor (1924), Archbishop of Palermo (1945), Cardinal
(since 1946), Knight of the Great Cross (since 1963), a great
admirer and friend of Generalissimo Francisco Franco, and a
strong candidate for the papacy in his lifetime.*

*I phoned his office and asked for his secretary. They summoned
him. I asked for an appointment with the cardinal, explaining
that I'd like to know his views on democratic structures of life in
Palermo. The secretary erupted in benevolent laughter: "So
you're the Danilo Dolci! Please call back at eleven. Ask for
Don Luigi."*

*I called punctually and got an appointment for five p.m. that
day at the Episcopal (once Royal) Palace. The cardinal received
me with extreme graciousness and cordiality. He launched into a
soliloquy that lasted about an hour. I am not authorized to
quote him.*

*I had prepared a list of questions I wanted to use at relevant
moments during our conversation: What do you think of
democratic structures of life in Palermo? In your view, what are
the obstacles to democratic organizing? How would you like
Palermo to be? In the city and the province, what are our most
pressing needs? What do we have to develop? How do you
conceive of your role in the development of Palermo today? How
do you run your meetings with priests and seminarians?*

*During the conversation, His Very Reverent Eminence hardly
glanced at my list. "As you know, we are on opposite sides of the
trench." He parried my questions with a beatific smile. His
thrust: "I have grave responsibilities. Punch once said that the
only free men in the realm were he, the most humble of men,*

*and the king. The rest of us are caught somewhere in the middle.
We have to watch where we tread . . . I think conscientious
objection is folly. The individual should always assume that
established powers are wiser than he. Therefore a single national
party would be auspicious . . . What do I think about
nonviolence? Naturally we oppose war, but as the Ancients have
taught us, 'If you want peace, prepare for war.' "*

*The following excerpts from the Pastoral Letters (disseminated
between 1947 and 1964 by the Episcopal Palace to the "blessèd
flock") were not direct answers to my questions. But read
attentively, they spread the message, shed the official light.*

A uthority comes from God.

It is revealed that the Church *sui generis* is a hierarchical
society created perfect from its inception. Let modern democ-
racies founder in search of equality. The Church is structured
from the top.

Ergo, we make a scholastic distinction between ecclesiastical
authority and the laity. It behooves the former to instruct and
govern; the latter is disciple and subject.

Our Savior does not seek succor for the members of His
Mystical Body *out of need* but *out of His infinite clemency and
ineffable worth.*

Saint Ignatius of Antioch says, "Whoever acts unbeknownst to
the Bishop, serves the Devil."

How imperfect is the faithfuls' knowledge of their Catechism!

How infamous was that French Revolution!

How we labor to instruct our children in their Catechism!
We begin in elementary school, where all the children are gathered and properly disciplined. In accordance with the teachers,
the great majority of whom are paragons of the enlightened
Christian life, we can reap the greatest rewards by preparing the
children for the Sacraments of Confession, Communion, and
Confirmation.

Saint Pius X teaches, "The priest is to the common, upright
man as heaven is to earth."

Democracy, at its best, is justly and properly Christian. However, it tends to degenerate when it arouses in certain environments the strange impulse to organize the Church democratically. Confronting the Church, other elements claim complete independence in the social and political spheres. These specters nowadays are diffusive and they underhandedly advance the argument that the temporal and the eternal are separate. Furthermore, we deplore repeated attempts on the part of our flock to associate with individuals hostile to Church and Religion merely for the immediate gratification of social betterment.

To collaborate beneficially with the Hierarchy, laymen must be docile, candid, and obedient to their Shepherds.

When Jesus admonished that we *render unto Caesar what is Caesar's and unto God what is God's,* he was revealing the separateness of two universal orders. But he also inculcated in us a sense that spiritual values prevail over the material. Said teaching establishes the superiority of the eternal and the subordination of the temporal.

The Church founded by Jesus Christ is one and supreme. The Church Fathers saw it prefigured in Noah's Ark, the only means of salvation from the Universal Flood.

The Doctrine of Christ is one and supreme. The Apostles and their successors are to promulgate it. He who believes is saved; he who does not accept it is damned. Baptized, we become Christians. Baptism is one and supreme. The multitudes unite in the social body under one single authority: the sacred hierararchy presided over by Peter, to whom all obedience is due.

In recent decades, scattered attempts have been made to promote the union of Sister Churches—the Anglican, the Greek Orthodox, the Roman—under the aegis of a compromise with official dogma and with the Pope's jurisdiction. But that will never come to pass. The Faith could never wander about in rags, for she is the unassailable bulwark of the One Religion. The way to preordained union is one and one alone: obedience to the Holy Apostolic See consecrated by those Princely Apostles, Peter and Paul, and submission to its teachings and governance.

The decline of nationalism (which had erected high walls of

divisiveness) and the ever-pressing need of a power that guides and sustains will reveal to our dear sisters the way that leads to Rome.

The priest, albeit a man, must not consort with other men, for he must be, in Christ, the Mediator and Advocate of the Almighty. Baptism, by which we are embraced by the Lord our Shepherd, is most inculcating. At the Gates of the Temple, the priest receives the child, who asks to be purged of original sin. With great solemnity he asks the child, "What do you seek in the Lord's Tabernacle?" "The Faith!" the godparents respond for the infant. And the Holy Minister, rapt by such wisdom, requests a further confession: "Why do you seek the Faith? What does Faith reward?" "Eternal life!" The newborn child has no more sublime wish. Newly arrived on this earth, his soul aspires to transcend the heavens and be assured eternal light. "If you seek life eternal," the priest continues, "obey the Ten Commandments."

The Venerable Pontiff admonishes us, "The sacred right of private property is the cornerstone of social order." *Sui generis,* this right is the rock and the fulfillment of the dignity of the human person. It is the bastion of family stability. It ennobles our labors and increases production.

Man does not live by bread alone. On the contrary, wealth is the cause of petty concerns, endless anxieties. For the moribund destined to leave his large estates to squandering heirs, it is a bitter void.

By all appearances, some Christians nowadays have an inferiority complex. They deem faith worthwhile in their private life, but not valid enough for society as a whole. Therefore they may behave in practice as if the social doctrine of the Catholic Church, to be brought up to date, to be perfected in accordance with the needs of our times, should be integrated with other, dubious doctrines.

11. DON GENCO

His full name is Genco Russo (famous in the olive-oil and meat industries). At sixty, he is still one of the most powerful Mafia bosses in all of Sicily. We meet at his home in Mussomeli, heart of Mafia country. He is gracious, almost obsequious, but always paternal. He chooses every word with caution and design.

I was born this way. Acting without ulterior motives. It doesn't matter who you are, ask me a favor, I do it. That's my nature. Human nature. We're made that way. It's fellow feeling. You could say it's my whole temperament, my character. People can identify with me. Don't be surprised to see me among sheep, mules, threshing machines. Why is it they all flock to me?

A man'll come to me: "I have a bone to pick with X, could you help me out?" I get ahold of X, here or at his place, it's all a matter of diplomacy. We make peace.

Look, I'm not trying to toot my own horn, let's be perfectly clear. You've come all this way to see me, so I'm just being hospitable. I've never been guilty of vanity or ambition.

I have open arms for every size and shape.

What about politics? Only if I can do good. There's nothing in it for me. I don't have my finger in anybody's pie.

Do I respect priests? Absolutely. I respect religion. I mean the Holy Roman Catholic kind. What you are I respect. You can judge from my sense of courtesy.

Other people and their habits aren't my concern. The only thing that matters is how my temperament works, and my way of thinking.

Are things going well here as is? Nowadays, agriculture's going rotten. To develop we need roads, water, stable prices. Meanwhile, here you have me. After all, you're my guest. Come ask me a favor, it's said and done. I can't say no. It doesn't matter who you are, how hard the job. I can't resist. I have to meet your need head-on. It must be a higher power. I'm obliged to help other people.

I'm made that way. I know my fruitful nature and how to multiply it. But I repeat, don't ask me. Ask the people I help. And the police.

It's my life, Mr. Danilo. I can't change it. Gratitude and friendship are won according to disposition. There are times you do expect reciprocity.

Live life one way, you get results. They multiply, too. Come to me, I do you a favor, just the way I do for your enemy. That's how it's done. It's habit. So the circle where my name is known keeps swelling.

That's the story. You have to realize I'm not putting on airs. Please don't imagine I'm bragging.

People seek advice about how to vote. They feel it's a duty to show their gratitude. You see, they're confused and want to be sure to reciprocate.

Take tomorrow, for example. I'll drop everything, my threshing machines, animals, my own business, and run off to Agrigento to recommend that a certain person pass an exam.

VICIOUS CIRCLES

12. ROSARIA

She is sixty, a woman of the old school: a passive, candid peasant conditioned by her religion and by her frustrated desire to become a nun. We are in Cammarata at her house, which sits precariously over a landslide.

The beginning of it all was they made me get married. It wasn't our idea, we didn't really love each other. See, an aunt of ours was the first owner of this property: she needed somebody to help her around the house and in the fields. I suited her fine. My husband-to-be was a soldier at that point. He was my momma's brother. I didn't want to get married. See, I was all set to go and be a nun. My father loved me so, he didn't ever want to lose me, but I was all set to go into the convent. Poppa said, "I'll take you to the station, all right . . . You get on that train and I'll jump under it and the kids'll be all in your hands." He didn't want me to be a nun. He was afraid of never seeing me again. Get married, he let me go do that. So as not to disobey my father, I stayed tied to the family. There were nine of us, I did all the housework. Momma was always sick in bed.

My father went to see my future father-in-law: "What do I do with Rosaria? She's itching to be a sister." They were right under a picture of the Ecce Homo. My grandfather kneeled down and kissed his own hand: "Don't worry, the day'll come she'll be Cola's bride." At that point he was still a soldier. "How're we going to do that?" my father asked. "Just wait and see, we'll arrange it."

I didn't know anything about these plans, but out of obedience to my father, I gave up on being a nun. So Grandma and Grandpa started off by bringing me special things to eat. They'd say, "Enjoy it." I'd say, *"She's* your daughter, feed *her"* (I meant my mother). I'd get a touch irked and try to refuse.

The time my mother went for a stay in the country I was left all alone with the family. Grandpa'd come everyday with a gift.

One day he brought me a pair of shoes. I refused just like that. But when he saw I was getting so fed up I might say yes, he sent word to Cola not to make any other plans because Rosaria would be his, come hell or high water. Then Cola came home on leave. I saw what was cooking so I kept my distance. He dropped by one morning. All my brothers came to call me. "How come you wasn't there to welcome him?" If I'd of cared for him one bit, I'd of gone running, but I didn't. Then my father comes and takes me by the arm: "I won't have it said Uncle Cola visited and we didn't make him feel at home." Well, he just about drags me into the sitting room. Cola's there already. My father and him embrace and he comes up to me. I kiss his hand like you do with uncles. He saw I was stand-offish, so he turned to his father: "There's nothing in what you wrote me. There's nothing doing with her." "Just give her a few meaningful looks, you'll see." He goes back and sits in his chair and starts looking, nodding too. All I did was turn away and hide my face in my hands—like this. Then he jumped up and said to my father, "Zu Turi, I ask for your blessing." (See, my poppa was his godfather.)

Next morning my grandpa shows up, hopping mad: "I see how ungrateful you are. Uncle Cola came to see you and you rejected his love and affection." "My love and affection I give only to God. People on this earth are flies to me."

He came back from the army and got discharged. Then they all got down to business again. This time it was my father: "Rosaria, I have to tell you this, I'm obliged. Uncle Cola's going to have you, no two ways about it. You'll be set up just fine. There's plenty of property and your aunt's leaving everything to Cola and you. Sure there's complications. Your aunt's getting old. It'll take some patience to cater to her whims, but you'll manage just fine." (It was a lie.) "I don't want all these complications." "Come on, don't be an idiot. What's so complicated about a gold mine?"

They went right ahead with the wedding plans. My aunt kept saying, "Go be a nun and you get a nightgown, a tablecloth, and sheets. Come live with me and help me out, I'll leave you all my land." Finally I figured it out: I was trapped. I gave in but I felt so miserable. One Saturday we went to the Town Hall. Next day we got married. I was still in my house dress when the wedding guests came to get me. We had a wonderful ceremony.

We got back from church, my aunt was waiting outside. Everybody remembers what she said: "In this house, you'll bear an iron cross and it will weigh you down forever." They still tell me, "It's true, your cross was too heavy to bear."

Right from the start we were like strangers. Take the Feast of Saint Joseph. We were all at home; he says to our aunt, "I'm going out." "Aren't you taking Rosaria to the festivities?" "I'll give her time to get ready and come back and pick her up. You" —(he meant me)—"put on your silk dress."

I waited, going from window to window to look out for him. He never showed up. It got dark and I was still waiting. He returned late at night and we went out. They were sweeping up. It made me sad. We just didn't love each other.

A couple of years went by like that. Then one of our uncles got to hate us. He was wanting the property. So he went to Casteltermini and looked up a sorcerer. They must of brewed up something cause he came back and approached this woman who worked on my land: "Would you do me a favor and bring this wheel of cheese to my niece? See, I want to send them this gift because I have a debt to pay them." I see her coming with this big wheel of cheese. It was a beauty, twelve, fifteen pounds, with spices, but the gift was a trap our uncle set.

I decided to keep the cheese in a big pot, to keep it fresh, right? And I put the pot behind the clock, near the cupboard. Then I piled six plates on top of the pot. When I went for some cheese I found all the plates broken. I turned to my sister, who was living with me: "Take all the cheese you want, but why'd you break the plates?" "I didn't break no plates and didn't take the cheese neither." So I hid it somewhere else, with a big stone on top. When I sent for some cheese, the stone was gone. That wheel of cheese was bewitched!

Then I recalled the year before that. Four bales of hay were missing. We'd tried to guess who it could be. A woman who divined that sort of thing had me summoned: "You're on the wrong track. Beware: disaster awaits you." "Is there any way around it?" "Yes, there's still time. Bring a dollar to my room. We'll work on sidestepping this disaster." I told my aunt all about it: "The hay doesn't matter, disaster awaits us." "You've always got to be careful and not be a fool. Take everything people offer you with your left hand, eat nothing, throw it all away with that hand. This way we save a dollar." I obeyed because my aunt was the boss.

So after a while, here's this cheese, the ruin of our family, the land, us people too. They even cast a spell on my husband. He started taking a real liking to that sister of mine, she was seven, and he proclaimed around town that the child would be his wife, not me. Our uncle saw the time was ripe to mess things up for us, so he went around asking the neighbors, "How are Cola and Rosaria getting along?" They gossiped and he was tickled pink. For him our poison was his pleasure.

Things got blacker and blacker everyday. My husband kept on abusing me, worse than a dog. People saw how he fawned on my baby sister and they treated me like a dog. I was pregnant, expecting come Saint Joseph's. People were amazed seeing my sister out in the countryside and me stuck at home. They'd tell me how my husband pawed that little girl. At first I couldn't believe it, but everybody knew it. Then a young lady, the judge's sister, convinced me. Well, I went into labor and sent word for help. My sister and my husband came for three days, then rushed back to the countryside. I was left alone with my baby boy. Two weeks later I went out to lend a hand. I should of taken a shotgun.

One night my husband hears a voice. It was his dead mother. "Cola, wake up! Go to Menaca"—that was our land. "Behold the disaster!" He couldn't go back to sleep. Well, it was the beginning of April and around seven-thirty or eight, a young man came by: "Can I pick wild fennel on your land?" "Sure, come on." (My husband wanted company.) A ways out of town the boy takes the high road and my husband heads down toward our house. He gets to our property and sees these cracks so deep two men could stand inside, one on the other's shoulders. The boy comes running toward the house, shouting, scared stiff. My husband leaves the mule at the house and goes with him. When they get into the fields, there's this holy terror, cracks as wide as a highway, the earth moving, trees getting swallowed, the mountain, the animals, all kinds of snakes, everything going down. My husband's desperate, but he decides to salvage the wood, so he sends the boy back to me with word to get a team of men to come help him cut the lumber. I was sick in bed with the flu. The boy pokes his head in: "It's a disaster! A landslide's taking everything with it!" I sent him along and he rounded up eight men. But they took advantage of our misfortune. My husband was all in a daze, just sitting there staring right at the edge. So they put their heads together and decided to stay away from the landslide but take all the lumber they could cut. My husband was a holy terror to behold. One man propped himself against a rock and started chopping, and man rock and tree moved like they were on a belt and all the while my husband just gaped. Then all of a sudden he had a vision, and that night he took *The Book of the Five Hundred* to the mountain and deciphered the meaning divined in his fellow men's actions.

The men kept working to save the lumber, and my husband shouted orders: "Load it up, take it to my place." But they all dumped it on their own property. From one minute to the next the house looked like it was about to collapse, the landslide was moving so fast. We'd put a lot into that land. We had a reservoir ten yards by ten, and medlars, figs, cherries, peaches, all kinds of fruit trees. In twenty-four hours it was all sunk, gone, and the house was a wreck. With all those cracks around it, it's a miracle it's still standing. It's in the center of the first piece of property and the landslide keeps working its way under and it looks like it'll be gone soon too. Palm Sunday my husband takes four master carpenters to save the roof tiles. Before starting work he kneels and raises his eyes to heaven: "Lord Jesus, I pray for your grace. At least save the house. I'll build you a chapel to Saint Francis tomorrow." His faith was so fervent that he sent everybody home without the tiles and the few trees still standing, but the landslide wouldn't stop. The rocks kept tumbling down. My husband would stay there and sleep right in the house. How did he do that? With his faith. Before going to bed, he'd just cross himself. Then my father got worried about the danger: "Come stay at my farmhouse or else one day we'll have to dig you out from the rockpile."

The Feast of Jesus the Nazarene was coming up. The sorcerers sent for me. They knew the whole story. It was one of them who'd told me about the cheese and the disaster in the first place. She told me to get a new piece of cheese, it didn't have to be as big, but it needed all those spices, and bring her a black hen and three yards of red ribbon. I started to hunt around and dig everything up. She wanted holy water too, from seven churches, and she dropped some medicine in it and it turned the color of wine, and she said it was the blood of Jesus Christ. Then my husband had to drink a whole quart, at midnight, at the point the landslide had reached, holding the bottle in one hand and sprinkling the extra blood with the other and chanting, "In the name of God, I curse you. Begone from my land." At midnight he had to walk around and sprinkle the blood all over the landslide. He was terrified, but he emptied the bottle. The landslide wouldn't stop. He had to jump from stone to stone. Finally things calmed down. Next day the rocks stood still and the landslide stopped. That time.

My husband was all in a turmoil. He made himself a pair of clogs, let his hair and beard grow so long he looked like Saint Onofrius, and wandered around stopping everybody who passed by, just ranting and raving about the Gospels. It was that spell made him crazy. He'd tell people, to be a Christian you had to obey the Gospels. Then he'd check to see if the holy water was still working to stop the landslide. I started to worry about his peace of mind. He kept preaching instead of eating. He just fed on words, and I had pity on him so I asked a neighbor to take him on for the harvest. "Please hire my husband. If other folk eat, maybe he will too." The man said OK.

Well, he worked just fine with the other men come harvest time. He did more work than a man eating three meals a day, and all he ate was breadcrust soaked in water. He'd work and proclaim the word of God. The man who hired him came to me: "It hurts me to see your husband. He works more than a guy on a full stomach, but he won't eat. That bothers me." So he decided to let him go.

I decided to see the father confessor: "Let him starve out there in the country, he'll come back." I had two small children plus the baby. The priest told me to go and visit a bit more. We went, kids and all. He was at the edge of the landslide. His hair and beard were even longer. I called "Coooo-la" and told the kids to do the same. "Poppa! Poppa!" He was bent over, washing. He stood up and looked around. "Momma, who's that? Where's Poppa?" We stopped and waited. He finished washing up and went and got a sickle and started waving it and shouting he'd cut off our heads. It wasn't him, it was the devil making him do it. It had to be the spell they put on him and the earth. He rushed right past us and disappeared up the road. I wanted to leave, but I couldn't. "Being I came all this way, I'll cook him up some pasta." I went toward the house, but what with the house in that shape and him possessed, I was frightened. I wasn't sure he'd come back, but I cooked for him anyway. He came and gave it to the dog. He couldn't think straight. The evil spirits were preying on his mind.

People were talking. My father, too. "Let him beat his brains out. Let him croak. He's abandoned you and the children." But I knew what was wrong with him. It was still the week of Jesus the Nazarene and I kept watching over him. The doctors wouldn't even see him. Fact is, they drew up some papers to put him away, but the sorcerers came around and I went to see them. They were experts in all sorts of spells. "Yes, we can cure your husband, but you have to do as we say." They asked three hundred and fifty dollars. "I don't have that kind of money." They wanted proof that I cared for my husband. "You can borrow it." I went around trying to scrape it up, but it was nowhere to be found. They were testing me to see if I loved my husband. I was desperate so I said to the storekeeper, "Look, advance me the sum for twelve acres' worth of beans and I'll pay you back come the harvest." He offered me five dollars and I had no choice but to take it to them: "What are we supposed to do with this? Buy bird seed?" I started to cry and beg for mercy: "Just trust me and cure him. We'll pay you back." "We trust you, sure, but we have to eat too." The way they insisted, I had no hope. Sure he'd abused me, but I still couldn't hate him. Sometimes he'd come home and bang his head against the gate. He wouldn't bash his brains out, but it still made me heartsick. He wasn't my uncle or my husband any more. He was just a sick child.

Well, the sorcerers wouldn't budge without payment, so I kept bringing them gifts, a silk spread or a hand-woven rug. "This is my pride and joy. I'll even sign credit notes." Or, "Take a piece of my land, please." "Let's see if you love your husband. Are you prepared to sign a pact with the blood from your own veins?" I agreed. "It must be signed by all of us alone at midnight." Eleven-thirty, quarter to twelve, I went there. They were staying at Don Ciccio's Inn. At midnight on the dot they led me into this little room. There was a lamp on the table with a ledger. "Stretch out your hand." They slit this vein here, dipped the pen in my blood, and had me sign for my husband's cure. They did me a favor and let me bring my brother for support, though he and my father had a shotgun loaded and wanted to put my husband away for good—in a grave out in that countryside. See, if somebody keeps doing people harm and they kill him, we say, "Good riddance to bad rubbish."

The sorcerer embraces my child: "Today your father refuses to recognize you. The time will come when you will be his pride and joy." He turns to my brother: "He's done no harm, seek no revenge. He's laden with spirits, the bullets would pass through his body without wounding him. Now go home and collect a handful of dust and bring it back here. I'll give you living proof here and now that your husband's been cured." All this time my husband was in bed, sound asleep. I rush home and find a pile of hair on the floor. He had shaved. I was so happy I was scared.

Was he cured? I looked for him upstairs. He was washing up: "Rosaria, get me a clean pair of underwear. I have to go to mass." He got dressed. He was making sense, talking about lumber. Some people came by and he made a deal. Seeing our little one barefoot, he bought shoes for him on our way to church. In the square, people stared. After mass, he said to the children, "Today you all get a treat. Choose whatever you want." One picked out a whistle, another got a harmonica. Around noon, he said to me, "I'm exhausted. I feel like I've been sick. I forgot to get you the ice cream." It was all from the battle with the evil spirits.

All my five children worked real hard along with us, but they saw how living off the land skins you alive, fleeces you like they do with animals, and it's all up and down, the terrain too, and there's nothing but taxes and debts. So two of them got so fed up they went to be Jesuits, at Bagheria. One was seventeen, the other nineteen. That was six years ago. They both got through third grade by burning the oil till late at night. Then they got sick and tired of this rotten life and all these taxes, and the one who's still a Jesuit tried anything to get out of it, except he didn't know where else to go. Then he heard about this seminary and said to his brother-in-law, "Work, work, work, and what do you have to show? I can't even treat myself to an ice-cream cone. What if I go and study with the Jesuits?" I heard about it too: "Joy to the World." I went to talk to the priest. "Be content, Rosaria, rejoice, God is calling your sons. Don't dare deny their will." "I wish they'd all decide to do it." And there, they did just fine. It was eat, drink, and pray to God. Now one's in Messina, living in peace, doing real fine. The other left the seminary and went to live with my brother. He did the military for eighteen months; then the bishop of Prato found him a position in Florence.

When the weather's mean and it rains too much, we pray to all the saints and ring bells to break the spell. The priests know how to exorcise the dragon's tail (that means the twisters). When the weather's dry they carry the Lord outdoors to make it rain. The people are always excited about seeing Him. They flock to His processions too. And we weep and the men wear crowns of thorns and the women wear the rosary. The young folk are ashamed. They don't have the discipline and won't do flagellation, but even nowadays we weep for miracles. We shout out and weep, "Have mercy on us, Lord Jesus, give us this day our daily bread." Then we sing out, "Father, forgive us, have mercy, long live the cross."

We pray for bread and beans. All our trials and tribulations are for bread. Some years diseases come, grub and mildew, and we always pray to the Lord, forty hours on end. Two years ago, they put Jesus the Nazarene outside and before you knew it it was raining. Years back it rained so much He got soaking wet. Our Jesus is the color of coffee. Once they painted Him white, like flesh, and the next day He was black again like He is now. The almightiness of God is great. Of all the crucifixes, the greatest is Jesus the Nazarene. When somebody's sick and dying, they light a candle in His Crown of Thorns so that that person'll heal. Filippone's son was sick. They gave him up for dead, but they lit a candle and he came out fine. The father'd promised his house as a vow.

Jesus the Nazarene likes fireworks. One year they didn't have them, and to punish us Jesus the Nazarene sent maggots all in a row right up to the high altar where the firecrackers were supposed to be. Another time it was slugs. They crawled up to the altar too. Then there was whistling hail, and so it came to pass. If the animals get sick, they take them to the blacksmith and he washes their feet with copper sulphate solution. One cow of mine was so sick its tongue hung out and it just kept slobbering. We washed her down with copper sulphate and alum, adding some honey, and she healed. A mule had a belly-ache and an old man taught us to make a little cross of tare-grass. I waved it three times around a stone, every time touching the mule's haunches with the cross and reciting a Pater, Ave, Gloria. That animal turned out just fine too. Then again to heal a sick animal, you can use the nightgown of a woman who's had twins. It all goes away if you rub the gown on the animal's legs. Aunt Francesca had twins twice and she keeps her gowns for her animals' stomach-aches. Other folk use shots. If your first child's male, you get some wolfskin and make a little pair of shoes, and when he starts to wear clothes you have him wear the shoes three days and three nights and that way he gets powers to rid the animals' pains just by straddling their haunches. Of course, the wolfskin comes from somewhere far away.

When the worms crawl out of children's mouths, you take one, wash it, roast it, mash it up fine, and give them three doses in their coffee. No more worms. We all have these worms. That's what keeps us alive. That's the way the Lord makes us. They eat inside us. When you feel weak in the morning, it's that the worms have been eating. When we eat, they go to sleep and we don't feel weak any more.

We're God-fearing people. Decent girls stay indoors and talk from the balcony. Their fiancés visit from ten till midnight, or maybe one or two. She talks from up there. He stays in the street. If you don't give in and come down, you're a good girl. If you do, you'll never get married. That's our law. If a stranger passes by, you hush up and go inside and watch to see if the coast is clear. Girls are like rabbits: when it's quiet you come out to eat; hear something, you run back into the hole. Three years back my son was courting his girl at Cammarata. She lived on the top floor. Well, he got a stiff neck. That happens a lot. On Sundays the girl goes with her chaperone. The boy can walk near her, five or six paces away. Everybody does it this way. Of course, the men in church never look at the priest. They're always watching their fiancées. But my son and his girl are much more serious and proper. In public, they never even look at each other.

If the men have to work some Sundays, they'll go to two or three masses another Sunday—to keep accounts straight. Yesterday my son heard three-and-a-half. The men stand with their hands in their pockets, or more often with their arms folded. Sometimes they go to extra masses in advance—to stock up, you understand.

Over the years we replanted: summer and winter and Japanese medlars, cherry trees, all kinds of peach trees, lemons, mandarines, prickly pears, vineyards. We irrigated, and up to two years ago the trees looked like they would drink from the heavens. Then the landslide started up above us, where these people had some vineyards. Bit by bit it traveled down. My husband kept saying, "Let's hope we're saved." Some folks said the spirits were still around and we better lock them back up, but I was out of cash. The landslide reached the Cozzo di Ciummu and forked out. It hit our land and three years now it's still traveling and everything's gone. The first one came like a flood, this one takes everything with it bit by bit. It's more than fifty yards wide, and in front of the house the earth is about thirty yards high. The house is suspended in midair, just hanging, but my husband insists on staying. He's still trying to stop the landslide with faith. You stay there and you hear the rocks crash. You jump up, hardly able to sleep, just listening for it to rumble so you can get out on time. Him and my sons sleep with their eyes wide open, shaking in their boots. I mean it, they go to bed all dressed and if there's a noise . . .

The landslide shifts and can take away stones that've been there as long as you can recall. My husband has the rosary. He recites prayers all the time. He knows the *Prisoner's Guide for This Sojourn on Earth* by heart, especially the meditations on heaven and hell and all the other prayers. Everybody's amazed to hear him pray and meditate right in the middle of the landslide. But he won't go anywhere without his rosary. He tends the animals with it and goes to bed hugging it. The people who've been hit by the landslide say, "What is this? A curse on this land?" "What can we do with this damned earth?" But some of us know the answer. See, my uncle had prophesied, "The time will come soon when boons turn to stones." Some landslides come from water, others from spells. I can tell you about mine. It's enough for me. There's evil people going around doing evil things.

Once there was a landslide at the Daini estate, it reached the houses in Daini and Bruca, half an hour away on foot. I can't tell you how far in miles, I don't have education. I just know from experience. The earth kept moving. I don't know what was at the bottom of it. How can you ever tell why? You try to look and see, that's all. How else can you figure out what causes it or doesn't? Look, this is earth that's made to landslide. They say landslides are caused by underground water, but we'd have to see that first with our own eyes. Once there was a torrent overflowing, now there's nothing but pebbles. We need water for the animals, but it all disappeared with the earth that slipped away. Who knows if it's still underground? The Daini estate was all level terrain. How did the land ever rise like that? It could drive you crazy thinking how flat land all of a sudden is hills. It all breaks down from inside. It cracks and the animals fall in and don't come up again.

I don't think it's the water, it would take too much. Just imagine! How do whole stretches of land disappear? How do rocks as big as houses rise? It can't just be the water; it's got to be the earth getting all shook up. We can't meddle in the mysteries of God, can't figure it out ourselves. You see mountains move and . . . who can get to the bottom of it?

I finally told my uncle, "Look, it's time you rubbed out that signature you made with the blood of your veins to destroy my husband." I pointed to one of my children: "Remember, they'll be grown up tomorrow and want revenge. I'm no Saint Rita, I don't forget. It's best you give them no cause." My uncle's dead now. So many things have passed, and the land keeps on shifting. Once I had a pain in my side for six whole months. It wouldn't go away, not with bicarbonate or lemon soda, or for that matter, bay leaf. It was always that same uncle. Once the calf's chain vanished for good.

Wherever you go, there's landslides. But how can you ever stop them? They're all over. Ficuzza, Bocca di Capra, Giardinello, Mancuso, Chirummu, Suddia, all beyond the Plains of Ivy. The landslide took six acres of my brother-in-law's land. They're all over the place. The roads crack, the earth just goes. It's all we ever talk about. They travel on their own. We can't do a thing about it, not me, not you, nobody. The landslides grind and the earth turns to flour.

13. THE HEALER

We are in the slums of Palma di Montechiaro. She is sixty. She radiates benevolence.

I f you want to charm worms, you better have a feel for cardoons. The cardoons grow in the countryside, like artichokes, and the worms are born under their roots, and you rub these worms come Easter time. Actually, it's best on Good Friday when they put the Lord on the Cross. You rub em in your hands, crush em up, and for three days you better not use your hands. The worms stay on your hands three days just like that, dead. Then you pass your hands over the sick part and say the prayer. You rub three worms cause there's three nails in the Lord.

To cure things up quick you can make a concoction too. Little babies have fits, their eyes get glazed, they foam at the mouth. They'll wheeze and gasp or sleep too much. If the attack comes at night, the little ones die. It happens a lot. The worms get in their throats and choke em. If the worms come when they're forty days old, how can they tell their mothers? It almost happened to one of my son's sons: "Don't die, Pepe, don't die." "Momma, they're eating me up." His eyes were popping like this, but now he's ten. Biagia's son died, it was a mystery. Then the worms crawled out through his nose.

If the worms are in the stool, you pull em out by hand—watch out, they bite. There's short ones and others as long as your arm. You might pull half out but the rest stays inside, they're soft and break easy. You can pull em out through the mouth too.

We're all full of worms. They work hard to eat. All of us have worms, but we're not aware. We eat for ourselves, and for our worms. What we eat goes down to them. The more we eat, the fatter they get. They eat, work, move around. It's just like in life. They go everywhere, up and down, right and left, but they never get to the liver or the lungs. Mostly they travel through the guts, always looking for food. We have two sacks inside and if there's nothing to eat, the worm bites us and causes a disturbance. Just go to a churchyard and look at a dead child. Try to count all the worms, you'd never manage, not even in forty-eight hours. We're crawling with these things, like lice too. They're born inside our bodies. When we die and don't eat no more, they come out and eat our flesh.

There's all kinds, big and small. It all depends if your blood's a bit poisoned or sweet. If your blood's sweet you have lots of worms. There's all different sizes. Animals brood and keep making worms. I've found folk with a seven-year-old tapeworm. It can get up to four yards long. If you get a tapeworm, you're always hungry.

I was seven when Father Giacchino collapsed on the pavement. Nobody went to help him, so I did: "Father, take my hand" (he was old). I helped him up. He took a deep breath, clasped my hands together, and made a sign of the cross all over me: "Be a shepherdess unto the flock." Then he headed for Canicattì.

I wasn't yet thirteen when I started out. A young boy in my neighborhood broke his leg and I heard this voice saying, "Go to him." The house was full of people. I slipped in, nobody saw me. I noticed the bone sticking out, flesh and all. I stopped the doctor cold: "Look, the bone has to be propped up." So I tug at the leg, stretch it out, reset the bone, and bandage it up. Forty days later it's straight. Well, after that everybody lined up to see me: policemen, officers, plain old soldiers, not to speak of peasants. Not a day goes by I don't see ten people. Most days I lose count.

All in all humanity's the same. People here are like they are all over the world. When you come down from heaven, your blood gets all muddy, it swirls around. You get fits of anger. Bad things happen, like a fright: you start to shake all over, in a fit, you get all jumpy, right? This lawyer who always watched out for us, well, he had a short fuse. They made him a judge but the worms got to his brain. He died like a rabid dog, chained up and barking. He'd howl to the moon. The worms drove him nuts. Then there was this lamb ran around like it was loony. They gave it to the butcher and he smashed its head in. The worms had bored in and made a ball. That's what drove the animal crazy. When us humans go insane, it's the worms eating our brain. The turbulation inside your head makes you do anything.

So many things go wrong inside us and all over: nerves and worms, that's it. When the blood gets all embroiled, there's evil brewing. You go into a frenzy and that causes boils. People here get so nervous they faint, crumble down on the ground, and die. You can be sure something's churning inside. Just give a child a fright or a good whipping, he catches worms. We all have worms naturally, but when we get scared the blood embroils and the worms embroil the people. It's like a dog that stops you dead in your tracks. You stare him down, but the minute you panic he gets ferocious. It's the same with worms.

They stay in our food sack, but sometimes they come up on us. Children being born get worms from the milk. But these worms help us out. Who else would keep us going? They make us digest. What else could we do with the food? That's the way it's got to go. The kettle's got to boil to cook our supper. The worms cook our food in the sack. We swallow and the food goes through the tube to the sack. We have two sacks, this one for food and the other one for making water. We gulp things down and then it's the worms' job. Without worms, you can't digest. You die. The Lord made the world this way. Kill all the worms, we can't survive. What the worms can't digest goes down with castor oil. A lot of us here at Palma di Montechiaro know how to pass worms through your body. How many, you ask? Fifty, I'd say.

Trachoma comes from a rush of blood or anger. If it's a real fit, it can split your eye open cause the blood just shoots up and breaks everything open. A fit in pregnant women is disaster. It ruins everything. You heal the eye with water from a trough where scum broods. You put the scum right on the eye and rub it in. The disease goes away, it all gets better. See, the slobber from when the animals drink from the trough is all good for the eye. Mule or cow slobber dissolved in water is best. All diseases come from fits or eating. Of course, if a fit really gets to you, you die.

See this guy here, his brother would always sleep out in the country. Well, one day he woke up all red and swollen. His throat was so tight, his voice all changed. He got back home and banged on the door and his wife said, "Who is it?" By now he couldn't answer, so she wouldn't dare unlock the door. He had this terrible itch, like a big round sore. He looked closer and it was a tick. The fever just about did him in right on the spot. They're poisonous, those spotted ticks. All it takes is one on your body, and you can't just pull em off. You got to use a scissors or else they break and leave the poison inside. Cut em at the roots and they die in one piece.

With animals in the house, there's always ticks. They get born from beast-stench. Worms crawl all over the animals' flesh. Goats have millions, give em a squeeze and the worms ooze out just like spaghetti. Sheep are the same way. Ticks bite and hook into dogs and other animals. Then the animals sleep with us and the ticks try us out too. There's two varieties: the fat white ones, and the coffee-colored kind that cling with little claws. They poison the blood.

Lice are born from frenzy and filth. There's three varieties. The scalp louse that gets in your skull when you think too hard and worry too much about paying the bills and get all worked up trying to figure out how. They ooze out from your brain. Mostly poor folk have this kind, you see, because we have more worries about surviving and feeding our families. They feed off our brains, then go out on their own. Our cares become lice. Wonder about paying the rent, they appear. Why, who knows? They just do.

There's the white louse too. It grows on the body. Sometimes you don't even know it. They dig in and live on your blood, then you scratch and get like a cheese grater. The earth makes em. I've seen how it's done. Then there's the kind chickens hatch. They crawl on humans too.

Urine's a good strong medicine for wounds. You use it with different kinds of snakeskin and the powder from special kinds of bacteria. You spread it on thick for cuts and scratches. The snakes shed their skins whole in briar patches. You save it for any emergency.

You know the cords they use to hang babies' cradles? Well,

you scrape off the fly droppings and mix them with breast milk and administer for colic. Just melt the droppings in a tablespoon of milk. Nowadays they do it less.

You treat dog bites with the hair of the dog that bites you. Motor oil works too, but the hair's better. Pluck out the hair below the haunches, near the loins, apply the hair to the wound, and there won't be any infection.

For a sty, here's the prayer:

Saint Lucy was reading in bed.
The doe's weeping, near dead.
"My eye's sick, I can't see, can't look."
I picked a fennel from the garden,
plucked it with my own two hands,
a sty, I cut it out for you,
a sick eye, toss into the sea . . .

Don't forget to press a clove of garlic to the eye. The spirits draw out the infection, and the eye is healed.

When a mule has a cold, you cook up fifty pigeon turds and when it smells just right stick the mule's snout in the pot. It gets better right away.

When a child's umbilical cord dries up and falls off, you keep it. When he gets a cold, you burn a pinch of the cord and make him breathe in the smoke and the cold goes away. Keep the cord at home. That way the children stay at home and won't run around in the streets or the outside world. Here it's almost a proverb: "Don't throw away the cord or else the child will cut himself loose."

What about miscarriages? Sometimes they come from odors. The baby twists around inside cause he wants the food he smells cooking. You get hungry even in the womb and thrash about till you're in a tangle. Maybe you'll get in an argument with a neighbor and she'll get envious and cook up these nice strong-smelling concoctions and the baby'll smell em and kick up and die. But if you act quick and go get her recipe or concoct something just as good to eat at home, the baby won't get all embroiled and twisted up. That way him and the mother won't die.

14. IGNAZIO

Illiterate, worn at forty by life, he is tall and corpulent and has a nose full of lumps. We converse along his rag-beat in one of Palermo's slums.

ere in Cascino Alley round back of Grotta Alley just off D'Ossuna Street, none of us have ever found a regular paying job. As a rule, we're all ragpickers, I mean the men. The women do laundry. Some of the younger guys get taken on in the building trades or on the docks, but not for long. They're the first to get laid off and they always come back to good old faithful ragpicking.

Seven years ago about ten people here died of typhus. The police quarantined us to the alley. It was catching. Nobody could leave. The cesspools backed up. The alley was one long swamp of filth. You know, some women empty the chamber pots out on the railroad tracks nearby, but others just throw it out the door and it makes these puddles of dead water. The muck builds up so thick, the firemen have to come in winter. But they say there's nothing much they can do, so they drain out some water from the foundations and leave. Well, this goddamn typhus never stops. Two people died recently and lots of kids were bad sick. Mostly it kills the little ones.

The police confined us. See, nobody could go nowhere. They brought us food in big kettles. They'd announce it by blowing their bugles, and hundreds of people would come running out with soup cans or pots and pans and all get in line, just like in the army. They'd feed us cause we couldn't go out and work. When we had to relieve ourselves we'd have to do it in the alley, unless some decent guy on duty would let us go on the tracks. See, they put this medicine in the food to disinfect us. It must have been a laxative because fifteen hundred men, women, and children all had the runs.

The typhus just had to come, with all that filth and overcrowding and no running water. Eight, ten, even twelve people to a room no bigger than a cell. Most houses have dirt floors and some are just caves. A lot of us have nothing but stones and crates for furniture. There's tons of lice. The dead bodies were just crawling with them. You couldn't even count them.

They came with this powder, they called it disinfectant, and sprinkled it all over the houses, in the streets. Then they lined us all up and poured it all down our clothes.

This past winter there was heavy rains and a lot of houses got flooded. The authorities came, inspected, and disappeared. The people heaped all their belongings on carts—mattresses, pillows, the few rags they owned—and went around other neighborhoods looking for a place to stay. We appealed to the authorities. They rounded up everybody who was homeless and transported us to some empty stalls in the market. Hundreds of people herded together, like horses. Men on one side, women on the other. We slept on the ground, sharing a few blankets, for four or five days. We demanded housing. They gave us seventy-five, a hundred dollars per family and sent us back where we came from. They "regretted" there just wasn't any places.

Every morning, who knows since when (I remember my father, rest his soul, did it too), us men get up and go relieve ourselves on the tracks. Every now and then the city health inspectors come and fine us ten, twelve bucks. We pay through the nose to relieve our bodies. The women do it at home in their little room. The kids, around town or on the tracks. Six months ago a five-year-old boy from down the street was run over by a train. Like this guy who went to nap in the tunnel. This is two hundred yards from the Cathedral and the heart of Palermo!

There's the ragpickers and the washerwomen. Others don't do a thing. A few make and sell little pennants with pictures of Saint Rosalia. Then there's the prostitutes, but they do their work in other sections of town. See, we all know everybody's business.

Most of the kids never go to school. They just play in the alley in that stink. When the girls get to be twelve or thirteen, they hurry and try to get married. But it's like intermarriage in this alley. Ragpickers marry off washerwomen to ragpickers, and vice versa.

I was a prisoner of war till October 8, 1944. Then I was released and took a month off to travel. I got home to find my family half-dead of hunger. I still wasn't married. Two friends of mine showed up in Palermo and asked me if I needed a job. I did, so I went with them to cart away some lumber left after all the bombings. While I was working this lady shows up and asks me what I'm doing with her house. Then the cops come and invite me for a ride. The lady reported all her furniture missing, but they didn't find anything on me. The captain interrogated me and asked for my papers. I'd got back the day before and they weren't in order. So he had me locked up. I was charged with attempted robbery and sentenced to twelve months. My family was starving (not to mention me), so I couldn't pay for a lawyer. But I appealed and they cut it down to six months. Still, I had a record. It was like I was blacklisted everywhere.

Luckily I've never been back to jail, but I've suffered for it anyway. I can't find a steady job, and in this trade you can't really support your family. So my wife has to work too. She's a cleaning woman.

I had the Maltese fever for eighteen months. I'm illiterate like most of us around here. Every morning, summer or winter, I get up at seven, take my coat, and go shouting through the streets. I buy scrap metal, used goods, rags. The metal's not worth much, about three cents a pound. So you got to get it for nothing to make it worth your while. The boss advances you the cash to do the buying. He owns the carts too. We rent them out at twenty-five cents a day. There's days you earn a dollar-and-a-half. Whole weeks you don't earn nothing. If you're lucky you make five bucks, maybe more. In this trade come noon there's not a chance, we can't make another sale. There's two hundred of us in all from this alley who are in the same business. This is the center of Palermo for scrap metal and rags.

Then you buy up all the peels of oranges, mandarines, and lemons: two cents a pound. You resell them to the warehouse and they get eight or nine cents at the syrup factories. The kids go around picking butts up off the streets. They strip them and sell the tobacco. What they earn they contribute to the family.

A lot of guys in the building trade and on the docks are so poor they can't afford real cigarettes, so they buy a few cents worth of this tobacco to economize. These kids go downtown near Massimo Theater or Liberty Street where lots of people stroll. But if the cops nab them, it means Malaspina Juvenile Home. Get the kids off the streets! It's prohibited, a disgrace. Yeah, they know who's to blame, so they ease their conscience by putting us away.

When it rains you can't work. Most of the winter you stay inside. Then your job is getting credit where bread and pasta's cheap. You got to go around from store to store because the most they'll trust you for in one place is five, maybe seven bucks.

Afternoons us guys from the alley go down to the warehouse district where work is still going on. See, maybe you can help them load and unload and pick up a little extra. Other guys just hang around, playing cards or going to the local bar, or if they're broke, just sitting in the sun. In the bar you talk about the price of metal, your luck that day, your troubles. "How much did you make?" "Two-fifty, nothing much." And we tell each other our troubles. It's the same old story. We've inherited it. My family's been here a hundred and ten years.

When you come home broke, the fight starts. "What do you mean nobody had work for you? What've you been up to all day?" "What the hell can I do, I'm down on my luck." You're always anxious for tomorrow to come, but if it goes just as bad, husbands and wives are at each others' throats.

It's a blind alley. The only thing we keep up with is this trade. Nobody cares what goes on in the outside world, except when there's a murder in the city.

Religion? Nobody here gives a damn. Sure, I register Christian Democrat, but not so I can vote. See, if I don't, I can't do my business. Sure, come election time the priest comes by with a few outstanding citizens. They give out ice creams, figuring we'll vote for them. Monarchists come too and give out these cards and addresses where we can pick up two pounds of pasta. Most of us are scared so we vote for whoever they tell us to vote for.

Most of us never go to church. For us there's no Sundays or other holidays. Sundays, our only thought is how to put food on the table.

It's a tough neighborhood. Once two people came to take some pictures and this Monarchist neighbor of ours, who was always drunk by ten-thirty in the morning, suddenly jumps them and grabs the camera, and these poor jerks are scared to death that their five-hundred-dollar camera might get busted. We don't want no pictures taken here.

The priests came into the neighborhood a couple of times to teach the kids their catechism. It was two months before the elections. We cleaned up as best we could, scooping up the muck and hiding it someplace else. They came a couple of days to show a movie about the saints and the Madonna, but the alley was just too dirty for them and the kids were all hell to pay. Nobody listened so they packed up and left, and the kids ran after them cussing them out: "Shitheads! Come back next election! Cunt-faces!" The movie disappeared. Like everything else.

15. A STREET CLEANER

A friend of Gino Orlando's, he is over fifty, gentle, almost passive,
but very proud of his small apartment in a new low-cost,
high-rise development on the outskirts of Palermo.

She's a real beauty, isn't she? It's hard to believe we'd let her get
so spoiled. Sure, they keep things clean on the fancy streets,
Maqueda, Rome, and Liberty. But one block away, say Carini
Street, it's all filth—just like most of this city.

Except for the workers, this city's a late riser. You won't see
any traffic before four or five A.M. On the outskirts, yeah, a few
street hawkers start out at six with their brooms or greens. You
might see a few baskets lowered from the balconies and the cowherds go around selling their milk. That's the hour the buses
load up for the city, and come seven the construction workers
leave for work in buses or on bikes and scooters. Most of *us*
begin at six-thirty.

This here's my route, but the dumping's done way out of
town. It takes an hour to just get there, and when I get back the
garbage is as high as when I took it away. Like I sweep up my
turf and by the time I'm through, my trail is all covered with
garbage again. In strategic places where the upper crust hangs
out, like Maqueda Street, I can keep things sort of under control
by doubling back. But around the Capo or Garraffello Square the
filth makes your flesh crawl, so you sweep on ahead and never
look back.

At the end of the day if there's no sign of the truck that picks
our stuff up, we figure we'll get rid of it tomorrow. But we got
to make sure we pile it in a street or a back alley in a poorer
part of town. See, poor folk can take the stench and having
garbage under foot.

There's times the alley between Flag Square and Naples Street
is so cluttered you can't pass through. Those fancy downtown
shops use it to get rid of their boxes, and it's just as thick with
people who come to collect the cardboard and anything else they

can salvage—what we call "all the rejects." Downtown there's lots of poor streets worse than the garbage dumps.

The city gives the contract to Vaselli, but the company tries to economize and make a bigger profit. So they don't buy enough equipment to do a half-decent job. And you have to understand the rules of their game or else you never figure out how to do your job right. We're on the job by six-thirty in the morning, and by seven-fifteen, seven-thirty, the trucks are at their pickup stations and their bins are full already. So then you have to wait for the truck to get back from the dump. By then it'll be eight-fifteen, eight-thirty. If you still don't have a whole load, you have to stay anyway and wait at the pickup station another whole hour or two. That's how long it takes the truck to go unload and come back. So you're stuck just waiting around and piling up garbage in the bins, and it stinks and overflows. But we keep it up for the love of collecting garbage on our route. That's the way us street cleaners are.

There's another problem too. On my day off, from a logical standpoint, another guy should cover my beat. But they don't have anybody to replace me. Instead the super tells another man to do his route *and* cover for me. So Vaselli Enterprises drives us street cleaners extra hard and pockets the money themselves. Meanwhile the streets are always filthy, so a lot of people hate us in spite of our good will. Just look at all these homes and monuments in this city, all this historical and modern-day beauty. Everything looks even uglier by contrast. The whole damn thing is screwed up. We'll do a thorough job at the break of dawn and then people wake up around eight or nine and throw their trash out in the street and all their crap just lies there all damn day long.

Us street cleaners don't see Palermo through the windows of an air-conditioned car. We see it through clouds of dust. With one swish of the broom the dust curls up your pants legs and the public feels it too. Your nose gets full of it, but it becomes a habit. At first, the dust and the stink gets to you. It gets in your eyes, one gust of wind and they burn. You sweep and you taste every particle on your tongue. It clogs your ears, gets all over you. Lots of streets aren't paved, and all it takes is one swish and the dust rises up to the second story. People get really mad. "Hey, down there, beat it. This is no time to spoil my day." Or, "What the hell do you think you're doing? Get lost, will ya?" Or else they cuss you right out. And just let some dust get on a silk suit, then there's hell to pay.

Some people understand the sacrifices we make, but there's others make the blood rush to my head: "So you think I'm a bum, I should get lost, huh? Well, take my broom and do your own sweeping." Now and then somebody'll notice us working like beasts of burden in the dust: "You poor slobs."

Sometimes we'll be sitting there waiting at the pickup points and the truck's delayed and we're itching to get back on the job, and people'll come up to us and say, "It just goes to show you're a bunch of bums." On my route there's this guy so poor I could buy his birthright, and *he* tells *me,* "You bums just don't want to work."

The dust gets in your shoes, down your socks, up your pants. With all that dust and sweat, your clothes get stiff like cardboard. But you keep right on sweeping and all you can think about is dust, dust, dust.

Eight-thirty or nine, the stores open up. Supposedly the bureaucrats punch in, but let me tell you how it happens. Say I'm the office manager. Well, I'll come in to open up, but the janitor's always there, so I'll tell him I'm going out for a coffee and if anybody shows up, just tell him to wait. That way I punch in and go home to do my own business. Then come the end of the month, I collect my paycheck. A few people really do their job, but most government officials in the region, the province, the city, and all the offices for placement, records, and health insurance act like they're smoking cigars in whorehouses. You'll go to offices that are still deserted at eleven, and by one or one-thirty they're all out to lunch. It's like a plague. Sicily was born with it and it just keeps spreading. From birth, we're all dying of the same disease.

Guiliano, you know, the bandit, he put the fear of God into

Sicily. He could of saved us all. He should of been the king of Sicily, but they had him killed the way they do with anybody who wants to help poor people.

Our brooms, the trucks, the wind, it all sets the dust in motion. People pass by and ignore you, they look out for themselves and mind their own business. Nobody trusts anybody else. Sure, maybe somebody'll stop and talk to you, but that's the exception to the rule. You just stay out of everybody's business. Then again, that's why I love Palermo. It's filthy but it's beautiful, and even in a crowd I can have a little privacy. If you're rich, you're in paradise. If you're poor, it's tough luck. Your hard times are all your own problem. Sure, I'd like to be well off. But how could I ever get that far? I'd have to steal for it. Otherwise, it's work and pray.

Let's get down to brass tacks: see, it's all for the family. I'm a plain old working man. In the government the right hand doesn't know what the left is up to. I'm just a street cleaner, but I have to watch out for myself. If a guy wants my job I have to be careful, otherwise he'll snatch the bread right out of my children's mouths. See, he's probably jealous, and if he's like the rest of us, his kids are starving too. Luckily, though, we all stick to our own business. There's Group A, employed by the city, two-hundred-thirty in all. Then there's Group B, twelve or thirteen hundred, we all work for Vaselli. They always get the contract. Between fifty and fifty-three men work to clean up around the Palace of Justice alone. That's not counting the night-and-day watchmen. To tell the truth, they don't do a damn thing. That's what they're paid for—doing nothing. And let's not forget the supervisors—who do less. That's Palermo for you. If you have connections, you get fat by doing nothing. If you don't have any "friends," you eat dust.

After lunch, the bureaucrats are through for the day. They go home to nap and offices are closed till ten the next morning. You could bash your head in against the door and nobody would answer. Afternoons in ritzy sections they stroll up and down the boulevards. Summertime they head for the beach at Mondello.

Come evening poor people sit on the stoops or the balconies, or if they can afford it, they go to the port and eat octopus and squid. Things quiet down on the outskirts, because next day they have to go to work. But downtown, near the Opera and Massimo Square, there's lots of activity in the high-class joints till one or two in the morning.

Us road-maintenance guys knock off at four-thirty, broken bones and all, full of dust and filth, with the stink of all the muck we been dipping our hands in. You know, one of our occupational hazards is lead poisoning, and our eyes are just burning and our skin's crawling, and when we get soaking wet in the cold, rheumatism sets in. I'm sacked out by eight o'clock. We don't have time to stroll around and have a good old time till midnight or two in the morning.

When we go on strike, the city's one big sewer. Two days and you can't hardly walk in the streets, what with all the paper and the flies and the little kids playing in the garbage. Look, we've got to strike sometimes to get our rights, even though we're sorry to see the city in such a mess. If I've got to live in this neighborhood, I want it clean. I want to take pride. Did I tell you I have my own garden at home? I grow jasmine and passion flowers. They say, "Don't do unto others like you wouldn't want done to you." Me, I'd like to see the whole city clean. I was born here. I love it.

There's thousands of applications for our job, thousands of people wanting to push us out and move in themselves. How do you get a job like this? "Every believer finds his saint." What I mean is you have to know somebody who can pull strings for you. It's all a matter of connections. What you have to do in return is get a certain amount of votes for somebody's friend in City Hall. There's not much industry in Palermo, so lots of people's dream in poor neighborhoods is being a street cleaner. That means a steady job all year round, plus benefits.

16. UNCLE ANDREA

He is fifty and virtually illiterate. Having worked near lawyers all his life, he is anxious to make a good impression in spite of his poverty. He lives in one of the more squalid old sections of Palermo. His apartment is adorned with kitsch.

In Palermo the gofer must establish his practice by polling what the public might say behind his back. Then of course there's the ignorance of the authorities, who confuse the letter of the term *goferism* with the spirit of the law that bans *go-betweenism*.

From its conception goferism has been a time-honored profession, but with the onslaught of unemployment it got scandalous notoriety. Some estimate us to number a thousand, but I'd guess there's five hundred of us here gofers in Palermo. Without job security, we're still dedicated to hanging around government buildings. Our goal and our need is to procure and dispatch documents for appropriate parties. With modest recompense we spend whole days waiting in lobbies. If it isn't the civil service or provincial clerk, it's the district attorney or some other kind of court. We apply for the whole works: certificates of marriage, birth, and death, civil bans, notarial acts, records of sentences, and charges pending, and everything else within the public domain.

We serve our clients well. But the gofer is unpopular, even among the people he serves. From his assiduous, exhausting, and clamorous labor, he earns little more than the price of stale bread. Why? Let's take his fee for filing a regular birth certificate: one dollar. But the form costs fifty cents. So figure out the rest. Plus you have to apply, and come back the next day to pick up the certificate and go hand it over to your client. That's just one example.

The law barring go-betweenism, as per the spirit of the legislation, does not outlaw goferism. But the office managers strong-

arm us by issuing peremptory orders, saying we can't loiter in
the lines, and our calvary begins—the fight against human hunger. This is the dilemma: the individual who professes goferism
is constrained to establish connections with certain clerks, and
vis-à-vis a retribution by no means meager, he can acquire the
necessary documents. Goferistic negotiations for clearing of said
proceedings occur beyond the precincts designed for said purposes, being handled in a café or at the gofer's home.

As I was saying, the gofer is unpopular. People think he's
rolling in money because they confuse him with his client. Plus
his fees are considered exorbitant, even mercenary. It's fitting and
proper—no, let's use the technical term, it's *human* if out of absolute necessity and lack of work a man is forced to devote himself to goferism. Look, how else can you bring home bread,
albeit stale, to the woman who's your partner in life and the
creatures she's begotten? What else can you do? They don't treat
you like a normal citizen. You can't even stand in line. You've
got to find an in with a clerk and renumerate him more than
generously.

Let's get back to the matter I mentioned before. Say a regular
birth certificate costs fifty cents and you tip the clerk another
fifty. There's no way you can charge your client a dollar. You've
just got to ask for two. Otherwise how can you make a dollar-
and-a-half?

This kind of life just strains you completely. It's exhausting
because you always need a friend to see matters through to the
verdict. You have to contact your clerk and keep coming back
tomorrow and waiting till after regular hours (when nobody else
is around) so the clerk can slip you the documents. Then you
have to take them to your client's home and that means going
out into the suburbs. Of course, your travel expenses go into the
loss column. And that's the gofer's life for you.

People entrust their business to us gofers because they don't
feel like pushing their way through crowds, or bureaucratic proceedings are just too overbearing, or their schedule's much too
tight (the offices are supposed to open at nine, but it's always

nine-thirty before things get under way, and they make sure to
close a half-hour early, at twelve-thirty), or they're simply illiterate. They hire us out because we're hardened to official abuses
and are sensitive to the needs of the people. Palermo has an
illiteracy rate of twenty percent and they can't really afford their
own gofer, but for two bits or so we'll fill out their applications.
Then there's some forty percent who can't take time off from
work and have to dispatch their business via an individual who
has a day or two to waste. A final ten percent are highfalutin
shysters who won't stoop to bureaucratic transactions that take up
their time. Gofers hang around the courts to apply for and clear
papers and the guards do it too, in the courts and City Hall.

Fascism outlawed go-betweenism. See, the go-between hangs
around lawyers' and doctors' offices and hotels and stores, and he
heads off prospective clients, tells them he knows a cheaper place,
and takes them to all the clip joints. But the gofer is legal, that's
a fact. See, in 1936 or '37, Caciotto, a retired fireman, was charged
with goferism by the authorities, Penal Section Number Five of
the Court of Palermo, Judge Fazio (deceased) presiding. Caciotto's defense attorney was Giovanni Rosano (still living), who in
his summary demonstrated the true spirit of the law and the will
of the legislation. He distinguished between these isms neatly
and Caciotto was acquitted. So goferism doesn't constitute a crime
and they arrest us only when we tip too much.

Until there's comprehensive social action, there can be no
progress for humanity and no mutual aid in all fields that better
human life.

Most of us gofers are practically illiterate, but we've got natural intelligence and reasoning powers and the necessary internal
contacts. If the gofer doesn't have the know-how, then it's his
connection who keeps him on his toes.

My life is my work. I play it by ear. If you're a Monarchist,
it's "Long live the King." If you're a Communist, red's my favorite color. If you're a Fascist, me too. If you're a Christian
Democrat, that suits me just fine. All it takes is rubbing one
client the wrong way and it's three bucks down the drain. I keep

facsimiles of all the party cards to flash at the right moment. I get them all sent to me.

Well, I've summed it all up for you, plain and simple.

Goferism isn't really a profession (see, there's no jobs to be had), it's a calling to go help people with all their affairs.

17. A LAWYER

*Once a hack lawyer, he now has a desk job in the Partinico
City Hall. He is thirty, nondescript. He chats at our Center for
Research and Initiatives.*

Take Big Sweep away from the middle class—I mean the card
game played among acquaintances—and we don't have real
friends around here. Everyone would just crawl back into
his shell.

Mistrust is innate with us. If we organize, it's pure coincidence.

The bar's the place you go for a coffee or a drink, and if you're
short on cash you sit outside the bar with a few of your acquaintances and watch people stroll by. You pass the time of day
criticizing the way people walk and look. Most of your talk is
just gossip. Of course, there's also current political events and
you can sound off.

People get together for weddings and baptisms. The atmosphere isn't like the café, but it isn't intimate either. At least it's
cordial. We're nice to each other for the occasion.

I guess you could say hunters have a certain camaraderie. They
meet to talk about their dogs, which has the best nose and what-
not. They like to brag or talk about how they saw the rabbit
but the dog didn't pick up the trail in time and the rabbit got
away. They always tell the same stories. It's their passion that
unites them. They love to argue. Mostly they're small landowners,
bureaucrats, petty bourgeoisie, so they have their own club.

The Civic Club Umberto lasted sixty years. It was restricted
by its charter to the local elite, the people with titles and money.
They played cards and sat around watching who was taking a
walk. In the postwar period a lot of heterogeneous elements
horned in, but they couldn't afford monthly dues, and even if
they could they were *non grata,* so the club, which was broke
anyway, closed down three years ago. A few other clubs sprang

up. But they didn't catch on so they folded. People always suspected they were fronts for covert political activities.

Now that I think of it, there's billiards . . . There's nowhere else to go, so you find yourself a partner and kill a few hours shooting.

Evenings, Sundays, and holidays, you stroll up and down the boulevard to show off all your wares. All bought on credit, of course. The wives of day laborers and peasants push deluxe carriages. That way they feel important. The students have their own ingroup.

The church is like the boulevard. You go to be on display. Girls go to size up young men. And some do it out of habit, to be seen going to church. A scant minority goes to pray.

Local festivals attract the people, not the middle class. The people want horse races and fireworks. If the bureaucrats, professionals, and petty bourgeoisie have cars, they escape all that hustle-bustle and picnic out in the country with families, relatives, neighbors. But that's the only time they get together.

Among professionals, say doctors or lawyers, there's competition. Professional courtesy's an excuse to scavenge for patients and clients, to enlarge your own turf. Of course, the most successful don't need to step on any toes because they're already rolling in money.

Agriculture is dying. There aren't many people left who work the earth for love.

Political parties don't represent the people. They're out for instant gratification. You become a Christian Democrat because it's expedient. You can exchange favors and make your pile through political connections. Ideology is for the few, the few idealists. Generally speaking, people look out for themselves. So you jump, flippantly, from party to party. The unions are mostly party appendages, pawns.

The electoral canvasser buys his shares of power via his friends upstairs. They use him, in turn, to get votes. The canvasser starts out on his own, pursuing his own ends, but he wins more and more credibility among the people as he makes more connections.

I went into law because I was broke. I wanted to study chemistry, but I couldn't afford room and board in Palermo. So I applied to the school that would cost me the least in the long run and wouldn't require great sacrifices or commitment. I remember I flipped a coin to decide: heads it's literature, tails it's law.

I quit the legal profession because I couldn't stand handling eviction notices and property seizures. I had some principles, you know. Besides, the work wasn't steady and it was hard to make a living.

Unfortunately, we have no sense whatsoever of what democracy means. That's because there's prejudice. We only get together to escape boredom, the anguish of being alone. We don't have compassion for one another. We're all stuck in a situation determined by abuse of power and defensiveness. Just try to say, "Such-and-such has to be done," and your acquaintance retorts, "What's your game? You want to rock the boat? You can't straighten a stray dog's legs. Don't you know you can never change a thing?"

Rest assured, though, the Mafiosi know that there's strength in unity. Unity is the secret of their success. They know they can count on the strength of related elements within a certain radius. So as long as individuals and the people are isolated, which means weak, the Mafiosi will always be extra strong.

The slowly growing gross minority that reads the newspapers and the grossly increasing majority that watches television may be curious about what's happening in the world, but basically they can't do a damn thing. They're resigned. It all seems so remote and they feel impotent to have any say about what determines their lives.

We're trapped in a closed circle. To change things we'd have to take the responsibility to argue out our problems, calmly and objectively. We'd have to learn how to work together. But honestly, we can't stand each other. There's nothing much we can do about it.

We're in a vicious circle, a blind alley.

18. THE WARDEN OF THE UCCIARDONE

*Having returned for a visit to the jail where I spent two months
for participating in our strike-in-reverse, I find him a cordial,
totally decent human being. At forty-five, he is still open, trying
to understand the environment in which his prisoners, his staff,
and he himself are trapped.*

Once they're through with the preliminaries of solitary confinement, they're anxious for the company of other men.
Except for the rare bird who wants to study, they can't stand
being alone. Of course, whether or not they can stand each
other is a moot point.

This isn't a penal institution. They're all just awaiting trial.
So we don't have an effective rehabilitation program. There are
no means or funds at our disposal to teach them to cooperate or
adjust to society. Besides, we're overcrowed. What we really need
is trained experts, but at present we can hardly manage to get
them to be half-civil with each other. It's especially trying when
they represent six or seven different organizations. None of them
can meet on neutral grounds. Plus we can't allow accomplices
to be cellmates. With nine hundred to a thousand persons, it's
complicated. Prisons should be organized in a radically different
fashion. At a minimum, the ratio should be one expert per fifty
inmates. But I don't believe we'll ever reach this goal.

The maximum term here is two years trial pending. Call it
transitory, whatever, it's overwhelming. I daresay it's easier in
maximum-security prisons.

We offer manual training courses, but hardly anyone attends.
Perhaps they figure they'll earn more when they go back to their
former "trades."

Our instruction for illiterates is compulsory, up to the age of forty. They're in the majority here. Most letters sent to the outside have a "topic sentence": "The first letter I ever wrote I'm writing to you, all by myself."

We try to do something for young people. If you're past forty, how can I change your habits? It's just too complicated. But my next-in-command and the chaplain do work with young adults from eighteen to twenty-five. They hold orientation meetings and personalized interviews regarding the family environment. What else can we do? We're just too overcrowded. Nobody really wants to change things here.

Reading matter is available: all the popular magazines plus newspapers like *The Evening Courier, The Daily News, The Messenger*—apolitical, you understand why—but they get bored quickly and it costs too much.

We have two chaplains who try to establish contacts with the families and channel them toward Public Assistance and Catholic Charities. They hold services, but their real job is bearing bad tidings and giving comfort. Let's say a prisoner's mother dies: they're trained to break the news slowly, with extreme tact. Here that's their only appreciable function.

When it's Mafia, there's nothing you can do. It's the mentality, period. In those cases it's "ethics" not to "rat." If a riot is in the offing, the guards will investigate—"Who's the instigator?"— and all they get is the razzmatazz. Nobody talks, so what can I do but punish a whole cell block?

Seeing these people here inside, I can't even begin to understand their nature. The world of free men is another planet. But once they get out, they're back in the rat race, in another world where indifference, alienation, and opportunism reign. Greasing palms and hustling become the rule.

Of course I have to be strict, but they all know I'm fair. I say the latter from certain experiences I've had at the Vucceria Market and in the Capo Ghetto. I'm still a bit puzzled, but take this episode for an example. One day I parked my Fiat 600 at the Vucceria and happened to run across a fellow who'd recently left us. He was selling cigarettes. "What are you doing in this business? Didn't you used to deal in cars?" "Don't you worry about it, sir," and he unfolds a piece of paper with love and care and shows me in writing the number of my license plate . . .

They're weaned on fear, it's in their mothers' milk. If a man's on his deathbed, he talks. But if he recovers, he retracts his statement. And that's what they call being a real man.

What about justice? Around here, we've never seen it work. We've seen nothing but its neglect. It's to each his own: "Justice? That's *my* affair." They say that blood washes out the stain, and naturally that's the vicious circle.

Wake-up time's six-forty-five in here. At seven-thirty, it's coffee in the cells. From eight to eleven we give them fresh air. Thirty to forty men take a stroll in a courtyard twenty by twenty-five yards. I can't allow soccer or bocce. They might do each other injury or get too excited. At eleven it's chow in the cells. Then silence at noon. Rest time on their cots till two. Then the same routine all over again: the cells, the meals, inspection.

The State pays for their manual training, but they refuse to attend the classes. Maybe twenty men will show up the first day, but at most they keep at it for a month. Then little by little they disappear. Attendance drops to zero.

We work on Sundays too, until one.

When you really get involved in this sort of work, you get trapped. It becomes an obsession, a plague. It's the nature of the work that traps you. It makes us prisoners too. Men will explain to me how they've done twenty years, and I'll say, "Yes, I understand, I've been doing my time for thirty." Of course I don't get overtime for Sundays, but I can't just shut these people up and take off. They're human beings, not numbers. In the armed services you can give everybody a pass and take off yourself. Here it's the opposite, and naturally the biggest holidays like Christmas and Easter are absolute torture. We just have to show up and try to give them some encouragement. Legally we can take a vacation, but how can we abandon these poor men on days like that? They almost never see another human face, so the least

I can do is be with them to talk and prevent suicides and riots. As you see, I'm also in prison.

I haven't spent a Christmas or Easter at home now for thirty years. I eat with a lump in my throat, all choked up. People think we're nothing but slave drivers. They don't understand we're all prisoners here inside.

HOME - GROWN
PLAGUES

19. E. A.

We are in the Ucciardone, both prisoners. He is one of the most determined bandits of Partinico. Thirty-five, maybe forty, he is dignified, a man of his word.

I was arrested first time in August of '44, and taken down to the station at P. For interrogating, the Little Box was all ready. Actually, it's two wooden boxes, one on top of the other, about a yard long. At one end there's two iron rings. They make you sit and slip your feet through. That way, they secure you. Then they tie your hands behind your back, and with this leather strap attached to the box they wrap your thighs so tight you can't move. The end of the rope they tie your hands with is put through an iron ring attached to the Box at ground level. Then on goes the gas mask with the hose unscrewed and they stretch you out with this kind of pulley action. One cop'll "initiate the proceedings" with a tug and another'll stand by with a big can of salt water. They've got a whole supply in a tub so they never run out. This guy's specialty is pouring water through the hose.

Captain M. was stationed at the foot of the Box with his rawhide whip about two inches thick, and he'd work over the soles of my feet. Every once in a while another cop'd twist my testicles. He'd grab em and keep twisting to see how much I could take, but I was choking inside the mask. It was so bad I would have been glad to die, so my testicles and my feet didn't hurt me so bad.

They know exactly how much you can take before you croak. Then they give you a break and ask you if you're ready to be reasonable. If you say no, they stretch you out again and do the same thing all over.

I couldn't breathe with all that salt water inside the mask. I'd have to gulp it down. When they saw I was about to bust my gut, they'd untie me and a cop'd push in on my stomach and I'd puke it all out.

Nobody in the vicinity could hear the screams. They were drowned out, so to speak. They did the torturing near S. I'd go through three, four, maybe five rounds. Then seeing I'd just about had it, they'd untie me, pump my stomach dry, prop me up cause my joints were all numb (paralyzed, I should say), and they'd walk me around the room. Meanwhile they'd drape the Box with a blanket so nobody'd detect a thing. See, I put up a fight trying to break loose. I was drowning, scared. It was survival instinct. They'd walk me around till I could stand on my own, then have me get dressed and take me back to my cell.

That's the way it went at P., sixteen days straight. Then I was indicted and sent to prison. Those last days my feet were so swollen I couldn't put on my shoes. After our sessions they had to take me back in one of their wagons. They were mad as hell because I wouldn't confess to a crime I didn't commit. (Fact is, the judge acquitted me later.) So just for kicks Captain M. put lighted matches to my toes.

Come '47 I was arrested again and taken to C. Street in P. It was around eleven at night. When I got there, no questions asked: out came the Box. It was just like the first one, except here they didn't whip me on the soles of my feet. They did twist testicles and had lots of the same old surprises. The third degree began on the Box. I was cross-examined about a whole bunch of crimes. They still didn't have suspects, and they kept up the torture, not giving a damn if I was guilty or not.

Let me tell you I was innocent, but if I could of proved to them I was guilty just to stop the torture, I'd of confessed to killing God or burning Rome or anything else they said.

You know, a hell of a lot of people confess to crimes they never commit, just to stop the torture. After four or five years of trials and retrials, the judge finds them innocent.

Where was I? Yeah, the torture. An hour, hour-and-a-half, and they let me loose, and two cops prop me up and take me for a stroll. Instead of putting me back in my cell (see, they worry that some guys'll bash their heads in against the wall or hunt up a nail or piece of glass to slash their wrists), they tie me down to a cot. I mean right against the springs. They'd take me to the toilet every twenty-four hours. Otherwise they'd untie me at ten P.M., for my appointment with the Box. It went on like this for a little more than three weeks—except for two nights they were tied up with the Massacre of the Peasants by Giuliano and friends at Portella delle Ginestre.*

At Partinico come summer, you can make a little money going around with a cart selling ice cream and ices. Soon as you stop the cart at a corner, all the little kids appear and run home crying to their mothers they want a cone. It's enough to tear your heart out, seeing some mothers fork over the dough. Others say, "No, that stuff is garbage mixed with horse piss. You shouldn't eat it." How could they go and buy ice cream when they couldn't afford bread? But the kids won't believe it cause all they see is other kids licking it up.

Let me tell you about these poor people. Somehow I can't forget it. From '44 on I was engaged. Now that girl's my wife. April of '46 we sort of eloped. That's how you do things at Partinico cause usually you don't have money for a proper wedding. I mean working people don't. So first you "elope," then you have a little service. After we did that, we went to live for a time in the house of a friend of mine in the Madonna Street section. Almost directly across from us there was this family, the husband's name is M. He had a wife and four kids. One was about

---

* May 1, 1947, at the mountain pass of Portella delle Ginestre (literally, Gate of the Broom Flowers) near Montelepre, the legendary bandit, Salvatore Giuliano, and his men ambushed and gunned down a large group of leftist peasant organizers and trade unionists who had gathered to celebrate their Labor Day. There is good evidence (see Michele Pantaleone, *Mafia and Politics* [New York: Coward-McCann, 1966]) that Giuliano was merely a pawn of the forces most interested in crushing the peasant movement, stopping peasants from occupying unused or badly cultivated land (in accordance with the Segni-Gullo Law of 1946), and intimidating anyone who might think of voting for parties of the Left which were making real advances toward building socialism via democratic processes: i.e., the forces of Mafia, Church, State (still manned in part by Fascists in disguise), and the American military and Secret Service. See also the stories about Placido Rizzotto (pp. 189–202) and Accursio Miraglia (pp. 239–49) for other examples of how the peasant movement suffered postwar setbacks.

four months old, still nursing, and the others were about five, seven, and nine. We moved in and right away the oldest girl drops in to help my wife around the house. She even takes our leftovers as pay, but we never guess how bad off the family is. Sure, the kids are going barefoot, in rags, but in Partinico that's the way things are, so you don't pay much attention.

The third day, come evening, my wife's cooking up some pasta for the two of us and this little girl comes in: "Donna Titidda, my mother says soon as you strain the pasta could you leave us the broth, I mean the water?" Well, it didn't hit my wife right away so she says, "Sure, as soon as the pasta's done." Well, I was sitting there and it struck me a little funny, so I asked just out of curiosity what her mother was going to do with that "broth." All innocent-like, the girl says three days now nobody at home'd had pasta or bread to eat and her mother was nursing the baby but the milk stopped so now she wanted to try drinking something to see if it'd get some milk flowing.

Well, hearing that pitiful story I cursed God for letting us be born, I cursed the government that ran our lives, and that child's father (he was unnatural). Me in his place, I'd have robbed anybody and anything to feed my children. Only a coward could see such poverty and torture and take it lying down. Just put the most honest minister in that family's straits, I'd like to see him. I'll bet he'd become a bandit too, one of the most vicious, but he wouldn't be a coward to his children like that little girl's father.

Instead of that pasta broth, I told my wife to give her the two-pound package we had on hand plus some oil and a loaf of bread, and I told her to have her mother eat that. Soon as the child left, my wife and I burst into tears. I set the table. There was some pasta left, but the bread was all gone. When we started to eat my wife decided she just couldn't. She kept making up excuses about not being hungry: "Listen, I don't feel like eating. Would you mind if I gave it to those children?" So I figured out she was testing me. I told her I wasn't hungry either, so she could give them my portion too. That third night as newlyweds we spent with empty stomachs, but it was worth remembering how we at least got one chance to feed those poor kids.

A few days later, the landlord gave that family notice—I guess they couldn't pay the rent—and he called the police and they threw the few things they had out in the street. There was an old bed and a few chairs. They threw it all out in the street.

20. CIOLINO

He is one of the two alcoholics from the fishing village of Trappeto. Still the local clown at forty-five, he is steadily wasting away. Yet there are traces of a good nature left in him.

Well, to start with, I was born in America and they took me back to Italy. Some fifty years ago, my mother and father, they took me to Terrasini.

My father was doing just fine but he had a brother. They went into business together with two fishing boats. That was in Terrasini. They had all the equipment and two warehouses to store the nets. At Tabachi, Tunisia, Cicere, we had ten fishing boats with all the gear to dive for coral and we'd go to sell it in Genoa and Naples. We rented the boat to haul all this here gear, and after we got some skill we had a three-master built and went sailing without a motor.

Several years after that they sold it and had one made like it but bigger. It had three masts too. Come wartime the government confiscated it. That was in the war of '17, and then they didn't go fishing no more anyhow.

One day my uncle says, "Look here, brother, how's about us making a contract? The first of us to die leaves everything to the other brother." My father says "OK," cause he was younger. My uncle was getting old. "He dies before me and I get all the inheritance. Then I die and it's all my wife's and my son's."

Well, it was just the opposite. My uncle lived and my father died. My uncle took it all over himself, all the wealth, and my mother was in poverty. I was just a kid, about seven. She went to work sewing all the rags in Terrasini and I had to go work to help her make ends meet. I hauled baskets of salt on my back from the boats to the dock where they sold fish. We had to walk across planks laid between the boats and dry land. In those days they paid you ten cents a day. After that my mother opened a store that sold bread, pasta, soap, kerosene, and we managed to live hand-to-mouth.

Some months later my mother got married again to this guy from Trappeto, a widower, with two kids and some vineyards. He liked me a whole lot and he sent me to school to learn the woodworking trade. But the master cabinetmaker didn't teach me a thing, except how to drink and cuss.

Well, then I grew up and started off making hay with this little lady. It was all hush-hush so her family wouldn't know. As thing progressed I bought her this whole outfit. The guy let me take it home for a few bucks, but then he came to collect the balance. Well, I was busy at work, at my apprenticeship, so he called on my mother and she says, "How come my son's buying this stuff, he's not even engaged. Show me his account, I mean who's the interested party. I'll pay you the rest." So the guy tells her my fiancée's address, she pays him, and he leaves.

Two days later my mother pays that young lady a visit: "Maria, if you show me what he gave you, I mean bought, I mean my son, if I like it you can keep it, if not I'll buy you something better." So the poor girl went and got it. My mother kept saying, "If it's not good enough I'll buy you much better stuff." But then she scooped it all up in her apron and carted it off. Before she leaves she says, "If you mess around with my son I'll blow your brains out." She talked that way so the girl would ditch me.

A few days later that young lady's godfather invited her real father over and killed him. He did it because she was through with her time of service in his house, which meant he had to give her linen and money for her dowry. But he wanted to break the contract that goes with custom. He told the father, "Tonight you can stay over. See, I've got to go to Giardinello and get the money from one of my relatives. He has to loan it to me being as I'm broke." The poor guy said OK and the godfather left and went to talk to two Mafiosi about a contract on the girl's father, name of Duilio.

That's how it happened he died in that gentleman's house. The girl slammed her door but a pistol shot nicked her too. It was nighttime. Next day the authorities got wind and saw the body and right away sent a telegram to the Partinico headquarters and this doctor was ordered to do an autopsy.

When the commissioner called in the girl, she was still alive: "Did you have any pending lawsuits? Were you in bad with somebody?" "Nobody. Except Ciolino's mother, she told me I better get out of their life." The commissioner had me arrested right away and an hour later they nabbed my mother and stepfather. He interrogated us and we told him we wasn't in town that whole day. We had several witnesses who were with us. Well, he rounded all of them up, even arrested the relatives who brought us stuff to eat. We hadn't had a bite all day. Next day they tied us up and two armed guards took us to the Partinico jail. We were handcuffed too and they gave us the once-over and said, "Too bad you poor suckers are innocent."

They released my mother after a month. Me and my stepfather stayed. Well, my mother dropped by a few days later to bring some food and they nabbed her again and put her in jail. They held my father and mother and let me go.

I went home, except my father's brothers kicked me out. I had to go to the house of a cousin of mine in Terrasini. She had ten kids but she took me in anyway: "Yeah, there's room. I'll do your cooking and cleaning, but to eat you've got to work."

Woodworking didn't pay for food or the shirt on your back. It wasn't even beans. I had to take odd jobs at sea and scrounge for food. If I made a buck, I ate. If not, I went hungry.

Three years and my father got out of jail. My mother too. I went home again, skinny as a rail, but they fattened me up bit by bit. I still had to work, fishing all the time.

Then I went off to Mazara del Vallo, Selinunte, Marsala, Marinella. I stayed away a year. I wouldn't go back cause I earned such piddlings my father'd be ashamed of me. But my paisans told him, "He won't come back. He's afraid you'll scold him. He sleeps right on the boat deck." So my father came for me and I went home.

I got sick from all that misery, but with the help of God and my mother and father I got better and went out hoeing. I gave up fishing. Then I joined the navy. They sent me to Messina on mess duty. My mates went to sea, and I applied to do it too but they kept rejecting me. I kept it up so they transferred me to Trapani.

Finally, I shipped out on a tanker. It was like a tugboat. We stopped at Palermo, Cagliari, Trapani, Messina. Then I shipped out on Destroyer Twenty-Four (from Brindisi), where I did officer training with Admiral Dopoto, and from there it was the gunboat *Basile,* where I did signal flags (we had to signal when leaving port) and flares when it was dark.

I was so good they didn't want to give me any leave. They wouldn't till three months before I was discharged. Well, I got home and hung around and decided to change the dates on my pass, to sort of extend it three months. Then I took off and traveled around dressed as a civilian. Headquarters wondered why I didn't report back so they contacted the local MPs. They show up at my house: "Your son, where's he at?" "He's gone."

They contacted Headquarters: "He left for Trappeto." Headquarters answered: "No sign of him here . . . order issued for detention at parents' home." The cops knock on my door, they want me handed over. My mother and father go hunting. Me, I'm on the move. I run across this guy from Trappeto: "Hey, your family's on the lookout, if they don't get you first, the cops'll get them." So I head for home, that's Trappeto, to spring my family loose. Overland so's not to run across the law. I dropped by the lunatic asylum to check out the truth of this story and this guy says, "It's true. Look, give us a hand, we'll give you food and a horse." "OK," and so I stayed. Later that night I decided, "You got to get me some booze. They're sure to arrest me but I'll fool them, make them think I'm nuts. That way I'll know what they're up to."

So we did that and later, in town, people start to say, "Ciolino showed up. He's gone crazy." My stepfather's son took me home, they called the family and had me locked up down at Headquarters. One hour and I was out: "Get on home," they said just to see which way I'd turn, figuring if I headed the other way I was crazy. I had it all thought out in my head, what they was up to and all that, so I headed the other way. But they escorted me to my uncle's place, and to figure their next move I made believe I was stark raving mad. One of them laid a cloth on a bench and put down some roasted chickpeas and fava beans with a bottle of wine. They started eating: "Come on, Ciolino, eat and drink up." I made believe I was plain dumb. Then they handcuffed me and took me back to the cell.

Next morning they called in the doctor from Balestrate to examine me and see if I was really crazy. I knew him. It was Dr. Cicalone from Public Health. He asked if I knew him. I said, "Sure, you're His Excellency, Benito Mussolini." And I gave him that Fascist-type salute. So Dr. Cicalone says, "Take him to the hospital and put him in a straitjacket. He'll stop fooling around. We'll see if he's crazy or not."

They took me to the hospital and locked me up with a whole bunch of people and I said, "What are you all doing here?" They told me all their troubles. I wouldn't eat for two days so they left me all alone in a room without a roof. There was an iron grating so they could hand me food and water and I just stayed there in my straitjacket on a straw mattress rolled out on the ground. The attendant would look through the bars to see if I felt cold when it rained or if I'd call him or try to eat or drink or go to the toilet. If I did, they'd say I wasn't crazy. "If you're crazy you can't do that sort of thing." I'd hear them talking and wouldn't do nothing.

As far as the toilet, I did it in my pants. The officer on duty saw me all filthed and stinking and next day the doctor came for a visit. "Has he asked to go to the bathroom or have something to eat?" "No, he hasn't asked for anything." So they left and pretty soon ten soldiers showed up to take me for a bath. But then they left me alone to see if I'd try to escape. I saw my chance but didn't take it. I just kept running up and down the halls, past all the patients' beds.

Finally the corporal on duty grabs me. He's hopping mad and punches and kicks all hell out of me. They all grab me and throw me in the bath. Bath my foot, it was a beating to make me talk or say "What in hell are you beating me for?" But I wouldn't say a word or else they'd say, "He's not crazy," and go report it to the commanding officers.

So I put up with my troubles. They took me back to my room with that iron grating and no roof and waited for me to ask for a blanket. See, it was cold. Well, I could grin and bear it, but I couldn't take being called a deserter. I was doing it all for me and my family. Then a chaplain came in with another official and a doctor. This army doctor looked me in the eyes: "He's out of his mind; we'll have to send him to the Psychiatric Hospital." Back comes the straitjacket and into a van I go with half a battalion destinated for the nuthouse.

They put me in a room, took off the straitjacket, gave it back to the soldiers, and brought out one of their own. I put up a little fight, wriggled loose, and ran off and banged my head against a wall, making sure not to do any damage. But I got tired and found this ironback bench, sprawled out feet and all, and started twisting and turning like I was fit to be tied.

So a guard up and gets me in a strangle hold, squeezing so tight I can't move, and the rest of em put me in the straitjacket and strap me to a bed. I'm spread-eagle like I was Jesus or something, and they leave me locked up all alone in this room and won't feed me just waiting to see if I scream for help. In the hall they keep saying, "If he asks for bread and water that means he's not really crazy."

Next day they brought in some bread and milk and tried to feed me. I spit it in their face. "Eat up. Have a drink. Can we get you something else?" I made believe I didn't even notice. Around five, they came back with some food. I wouldn't eat. "Come on, eat. If you don't, you'll die." I wouldn't say a word.

The day after the doctor came in and looked me square in the eye. Then he turned up my lids and checked my "progress" out with the guards. "He won't eat or drink, just urinates in his pants, messes in the bed. We have to clean him twice a day and he keeps talking to himself about discipline." "What does he say?" " 'Hup two, ten-shun' just like drill." "Remove his strait-jacket, and put him in the general ward with the men from the First Division." He left and the guard took off the straitjacket. "Buck up, they've declared you a case of nervous breakdown."

So I joined the other nuts. They gave me a new bed: "Be a good boy, help us around the ward. We'll write a report about how you get mad sometimes, but basically you got sense in your head." And I started to wise up, help serve meals, do laundry, sweep, make the beds. They'd warn me when the doctor was coming and I'd jump into bed and start talking to myself. He'd check up on me and they'd say, "Sometimes he's fine, then he flies off the handle." "But does he get aggressive or violent?" "No, he just goes through his drills."

One month later they signed my papers and escorted me to the military hospital. But they fouled up and put me back on active duty and I wound up in the stockade. The health officer had to take me to the Harbor Office Barracks. There was no straitjackets or guards for us lunatics, so they shipped me back to the psychiatric hospital and delivered me to the doctor on call and gave him my whole crazy story. They took my case history and read up on it. It's on record I'm a nervous breakdown, suspicious for any group activity. See, I'm sick. That's the way they printed it, and off I went back to the military hospital. They received me and took my whole history and put me in my mother's custody. She came and took me home.

Twenty days after that I found a job.

The year after, I started up with my woman again, she was still alive, and we kept it all hid from our parents. Five, maybe eight months and I made a marriage proposal. That way I was welcome in her house.

Well, a year went by and a cousin of hers decided he'd steal her on me. I mean elope. I got wind: "So you want your cousin, huh? Just tell me yes or no." "You were my first love so I have to marry you. If there's talk or competition you and me'll go off and elope so's we can live in peace." But I couldn't sleep nights, I was always afraid her cousin would give me the horns. Every second I was on her back: "OK, so when do we elope?"

Finally she said, "Tonight's the night. Get a place and some food, I'll go with you." Well, I got everything together, bread, pasta, meat, eggs, everything we needed, and I go to the place. No sign of her. I had to share the stuff with my friends. I can't tell you how mad I was. I'd had it but I kept on coming back for more.

It just so happened one evening her parents went out. They went to the dock to buy some fish to sell in town and she was at a neighbor's place, just sitting around. And I went and hid in her room between two mattresses so she wouldn't see me, and when she came to bed I jumped up and shut the door and I had her where I wanted her. But she excused herself to attend to certain necessities and made her getaway downstairs. Before I could shut the door again I heard her crying to her parents. Her mother said, "What are you crying about?" "Ciolino's up in my room. I spotted him and escaped. He's still there."

Well, her mother ran around looking for a stick to beat out my brains or at least make me a cripple. I couldn't get away clean cause the stairs was too narrow. "I'll run down and knock her over and take off." So I did. She got me twice in the head with her cane, but I pushed her over and got away.

Next day I go to work and announce, "I'm as good as married," so nobody else will go near her. After that it was all over town, everybody, the family too, was saying, "They better hitch those two up quick. What'll happen if somebody else tries to court her?"

That's what they were thinking. So one evening her mother and oldest sister drop by: "You marry my daughter or else . . ." And the sister says, "If you don't marry my sister we'll tear out your guts."

Then my mother snaps at them: "It's right what you say. I want my son to get married, but right now I don't have the proper dress, besides we're broke. I can't do much but I'll do my best. Sure you're worried about your daughter, so soon as you say the word they get married. Just remember my son can't afford no fancy suit." And the sister says, "We'll make the suit ourselves, the whole outfit, shirt, hat, shoes, tie, socks, we just want it all done right away." "OK," I tell em, "can I come visit?" "Yeah, starting tomorrow." So they bring the bride-to-be to kiss my mother's hand, and my stepfather's too.

Two weeks later I got married, and come noon we head for my mother's house in Terrasini. Then she decided not to live with my mother. So we rented another house, but she didn't like it there either. I was set on staying in Terrasini, but she sent word from Trappeto after a month-and-a-half asking me to come live with her. I didn't want to but people kept saying, "Go be with your wife. You're all alone. How can you manage to cook and clean?" So I got talked into it and went back to Trappeto. Well, I scrounged up work, fishing, hoeing, town crier for the council and private groups, cleaning water wells and cesspools, all for the love of feeding my family.

In 1933, I found work down at police headquarters, washing dishes and floors and doing odd jobs. They paid me three cents per officer with a nickel from the sergeant. After I finished at headquarters I'd go clean for the sergeant's wife. They let me have some of their rations, but there'd be plenty left over and I'd bring it home.

Then I quit, because they wanted me to report whatever I heard around town and I couldn't stand making enemies, especially with all the crooks. See, I could of got shot. So I backed out and took up fishing and other things.

Well, 1935 finally came around and I went to Mazara with a motor fishing boat. In one year I earned maybe fifty bucks. The second year I went to Porticello. In five, maybe six months I made fifty bucks. Some other years I didn't make a thing. The years went by and I went to fish at Lampedusa. My debts were piled up high and I was starving. But I wouldn't go home because I was ashamed of being broke. Besides, I didn't have enough to pay my way. I kept saying, maybe next year, who knows, I'll strike it rich, pay my debts, send money home for food and for all my wife's debts. Instead the catch got even worse. So I snuck off one night on a trawler headed for Palermo. "Hey, pal, would you take me to Sicily?" "Sure, just hide so nobody sees you."

We got to Palermo with God's help. Soon as I got ashore I started walking. I got as far as Terrasini and stayed at my ma's cause I heard in Palermo that my wife wouldn't have me and her family was ready to beat the hell out of me. I wouldn't be a laughingstock, not me, so I went off fishing on a sailing ship around Mazara del Vallo.

Then at Cefalù I saw this brother. I mean a monk. I asked him for some bread and a bit of cheese, and he gave me money for cigarettes and wine. "Go with God, my son, but come back right away and I'll set you straight."

I was back in a flash: "Here, my son, help me with my luggage." I carried his suitcases and he led me to this hotel and ordered up a meal. They brought us these gigantic dishes of pasta with tomato sauce and cheese, a steak for both of us, a bottle of wine, and even some fruit. Well, that made us sleepy but before we took a nap, one man to a bed, I told him my life story.

"Take heart, my son, man proposes but God disposes." Next morning we got up and he took me to mass and back to that hotel for a delicious meal of fried fish. Then he paid for the whole thing and we took all his stuff to the station and he bought two tickets for Palermo and escorted me to his convent and introduced me to the father superior and told him all about my "trials and tribulations" and how I'd survived the winter. "Both of you go and sup. Then you, brother, get a room ready for our son to rest, and tomorrow we'll give him a ticket and a letter of introduction and he can go to our Carini convent and be the cook."

So I did that. In plain-clothes, not dressed as a monk. I stayed there a year and a half, but then I ran across this guy from Trappeto. Seeing me he calls the father to one side and tells him I'm married with kids. They called me in: "You may keep all your things and accept five dollars from us and go where you will.

You're married, which means you cannot reside with us. If your wife knows you're here, you understand, she can prosecute because we are housing you. And if the monsignor discovers us he could have me defrocked. So you see, it's not my fault. It's your fellow citizen's."

So I went back to being a fisherman, a peasant, and a watchman in the vineyards. Then I guarded the sand piles along the shore, worked as a cowherd at Borgetto, and finally as a tile worker.

At the tile works I got a buck-fifty a day with board. I stayed on about a year. The year after, I heard it was a good fishing season at Trappeto, so I said to my nephew, "Take me out fishing, will you?" He agreed and I made about twenty-five bucks. I sent half to see if my wife'd accept something. She did and bought the kids pants. I slept on the boat and cooked in a shack.

Ten days later my wife sent word to me: "Well, you're back, let's set up a household." So I went to see her and we got back together after those five years. The whole town was talking but we managed some peace and quiet and I went to work to support my family.

21. GASPARE

He is thirty, a jack-of-all-trades from Trappeto.
We are at his home.

I found out I was sick in 1949. It hit me when I was hoeing. I felt sick all over. It'd come on at night, I'd feel tired, strange. At night when I'd come home I'd tell my wife I'd never make it up tomorrow morning. It kept up like this for three months, maybe more. One day I get this sharp pain in my right side. Some people said it had to be muscle spasms. Others said rheumatism. So they gave me a few massages and I kept driving myself into the ground.

Four or five days, I was going from bad to worse, so I called the doctor and he says to me, "It's a touch of pleurisy." Couple more days I'm in bed, then I'm up and back to work.

I worked some two, three months more. Then one night it hits me like a landslide. I get up and turn on the light: there's a big gob of blood.

Next day I tell my family I got to go and have an X-ray. A little spot shows up on the picture. But they keep telling me it'll clear right up. I can have it taken care of under the Health Plan.

A few months later they call me in for a checkup. After the checkup they say I'm fit for work. That was at the Health Insurance Office in Partinico.

They say I'm fit for work, but my condition keeps getting worse. Three days and I'm headed for Balestrate (cause if there's doctors in Trappeto they're in hiding). Being it's the Easter holiday, the doctor in Balestrate does a quick checkup and finds fluid in my lungs. But seeing it's clear he says, "Go home. Come Tuesday Dr. C. will pay you a visit."

So Dr. C., he lives in Trappeto, drops by, to draw off the liquid. He's got a bag of instruments, but he's missing a few. Fact is, all he's got is a worn-out syringe and needle. And he starts to poke around inside me. With the first hole he hits my ribs. Second shot he finds an opening, but can't get right in where the liquid is, so he drains till he breaks the needle there inside. Well, the needle's broke and he's all tensed up and it never occurs to him to cut it out. See, the needle was still in sight, even *you* could of taken it out.

All in a panic he rushes me to the station and sends me to this emergency ward in Palermo. For two hours, maybe more, they're taking X-rays, putting me in this or that position, never turning up the needle. When they finally located it they said they had to operate cause it was in a bad place and without an operation I wouldn't last the night. So I stay put in this room and midnight comes and goes and nobody appears. And the needle stays put. Five years, maybe more now, it's right in here. See, now the doctors've told me it's not doing much and the operation's dangerous.

I stayed in there twenty-eight days, to be treated for this "inflammation of the lungs." I still wasn't cured but I had to check out so's to be with my wife when she was going through labor.

At home I got cured by myself—not completely, but at least I was sick without feeling it too much. Seeing how the family needed it, I scraped up a little work. I started to repair shoes, anybody and everybody's. It didn't pay, but the family had something to eat. Still I couldn't get rid of it. Fact is, now and then I'd spit up a little blood. But only when I'd move around too much. Five months or so it was like that. I was always out of breath and about ready to cave in. When they explained how it could lead to TB, I started feeling lousy all the time. The more I thought about it, the worse it got.

Nineteen-fifty, around the month of May, I had to check myself into the hospital, the Military Hospital of San Lorenzo Colli. I didn't have other choices. They treated me and found "seepage" so they tried a "pneumothorax." It didn't work cause the "pleura" had been "attacked"—or "attached," I forget. They proscribed me an operation, that "phrenic cut." It was supposed to be done before four months was up, but I had to wait a half-year because I always had a fever.

First thing I wanted to do there was puke, and not because of the "gravity" of my illness. I'd see these old people with their bones sticking out and kids not even seven. But I was always careful not to get too close to my fellow inmates. Otherwise you get too neighborly, see, and eat together and . . . The beds are so tight it's easy to get close, touch. I was afraid of touching up against the other beds. Everything got to me. It was hard to breathe in peace.

You'd see people die. They'd do it everyday. That's what hit me the hardest. There was twenty per division, forty in a ward, all packed, with partitions that hemmed you in. And us inmates always got into arguments because there was a draft coming through the door. People near it wanted it closed, but the others wanted some fresh air. It was stifling. Many a night we had to complain to the orderly or the doctor on duty. All the doctors were lieutenants or captains.

One time, Scirocco season, there was forty of us in this room. It was deadly hot. We were the most serious cases, hand-picked for this new medicine called "hydrazite." They had us in confinement. There we were in this deadly heat, just stifling, especially these two guys: one old man from Montelepre and a young fellow from Bagheria (he was twenty, a nice-looking youngster, tall and handsome). Well, they were having a specially hard time and that particular night they wouldn't leave anybody in peace. Every five minutes they'd ask for water. Around eleven, the guy from Bagheria got real sick, he starts ringing for the male nurse and won't stop. See, he wasn't himself any more. He was death warmed over. The male nurse, he was a paisan, a friend of the family, gets real pissed off and decides he'll play the hero. So he takes the boy for a nut and ties him up in a sheet.

The kid couldn't hardly breathe. I was six beds away and could see him squirming. I got under the covers to block the view. Then an inmate near him calls out to the nurse, "Let him loose! Can't you see? He's dead, take a look."

Meantime, the old guy from Montelepre was going crazy for

water. The nurse, the orderlies, none of them on duty could find him a drop so they just let him croak, moaning and groaning "water."

This other old guy nobody ever came to visit. The wife had died and left him all alone with his disease. When our families brought us stuff, we'd all share it with him. Then there was kids. Mothers forget about kids too. Sure, not all of them, but a lot. And many a time—you know how kids love chocolate and stuff like that—we'd share it with them or give them some spare change.

Some men the wives didn't visit at all. The disease is catching and it'd be hell at home if they have to be confined. Still, the way I see it, if it wasn't for your family and their concern and their visits even if it's dangerous for them, it's better to be buried alive. All the friends I had when I was healthy, now when they see me they turn their heads the other way. They don't even say hello any more.

Come the sixth month I had to have this here "phrenic cut," but it didn't work. I wasn't any better. Fact is, I was worse. I stayed on in that clinic three years and two months. I passed the time reading newspapers, magazines, anything I could get my hands on, being I had no money to buy them.

As a boy I went to school till I was eleven—up to the second grade. Then I dropped schooling till I went into the service, because I was always doing farm work, day and night. I happened to get hired by this landowner. In winter we got up at five, some of us at four, and got home two hours after dark. In summer it was two A.M., maybe two-thirty, and we'd get home by eight in the evening. All them hours, for the same lousy pay. You could hardly afford the bread and pasta.

Just turned twenty, I had to go into the service. When I had a mind to write home, I begged this other guy to write my uncles a postcard or a letter to my ma. See, I'm fatherless ever since I was born. My father died. From Spanish flu, they say.

A few days later I got an answer. The postman came with two letters, and I start to open them and burst into tears, partly because I realized I was far away from home and partly because you get to know the ins and outs of the family only when you're far apart. I didn't want to offend my buddy, so I had him open the letters and read em out loud. Then he says, "You want to answer your mother's letter?" But thinking you should keep your own skeletons in the closet, I told him, "Look, Giuseppe, I went to school. I can write too. I'll do it, but when I need a word, you fill it in." So we did it that way, practicing for seven months, and I worked on that skill the seven years I was in the service, the air force, prisoner of war, all in all from '39 to '46, from the Aegean to Syracuse, from Udine to Naples, from where I was deported to Prussia.

See, at the hospital they let us read as best we could. When you have nothing to do, you start to learn things. You start to open up your eyes. I know that from experience. Hoeing, I never got involved in politics or stayed tuned to the news or what the State was up to. I'd hoe cause I knew I had to eat. If I didn't work from before dawn till after dark, I'd never bring home enough to keep my family from starving. But nowadays, down on my luck and just stuck here, I've tried to read the papers and think about these things, all these past and current events, and I've learned how lots of things work.

Then there's my own experience. Now I know it, my disease started to develop in Germany. It was there I started to complain of not feeling very well. Then I came home and being young and cocky I made believe I wasn't sick.

When they told me I was really sick, I applied for a pension. Don't you think I'm entitled after seven years in the service? Who deserves it? The guy who goes and plays with a bomb and breaks his arm? A cowherd who gets crushed under a cow and loses his eye? Or the jerk who falls off a jackass and breaks his back? I don't say this just for me. There's a whole bunch of us in my shoes. They tell us we have no right and reject our application. These seven years I'm sick, nobody took it in hand to say, "You have the right to a pension." If it wasn't for my family, my mother and my mother-in-law, who fed me when they had it, I don't know what I'd of done. Some days I just go hungry cause I sacrifice to be able to watch my two kids eat. You know kids don't understand things like that, and if there's misfortune at home, you should try to hide it from them.

Being there in the hospital for that little bit of treatment, I came out worse than I went in. Fact is, I was called in one day to consult with Surgeon A. from Naples. He was in charge of the serious cases. He proposes to cut out half my lung. Of course, he couldn't give me guarantees. The operation was dangerous, the odds against me. Sizing up the situation, I talked it over with my family. They didn't want me to go through with it. So because I decide not to be operated on, the director of the hospital asks me if I want to stay or go. Since I'm getting worse in there, I decide to check out and go home.

22. POTATO

I meet this healer in her straw-hut village way out in the country (at the eastern limits of Palermo Province). She is about fifty, small, dark, earthy. Michele Pantaleone (author of Mafia and Politics) and his brother Angelino have accompanied me—both carrying pistols. After this meeting word gets back to me that if I return, I will be eliminated. It seems that the Mafia doesn't want us to study its exploitation of the straw-hut people any more.

You can buy leeches from this guy who comes from Canicattì. He catches them there in the fountains, but we go buy them in Palermo. Fact is, we just sent for a hundred or so, since not all of them work. Three or four'll die off every day, even before you use em. Keep em in a bottle of water. Change it every day, specially like now in summer. There's the Sciroccos and the heat kills leeches. When they all die off (that takes two months), you send for more. Buck apiece, and those of us who use em in our trade rent em out at a buck-and-a-quarter.

It all depends on the disease. For bronchitis you put them on the shoulders or the breast. If it's whooping cough in children you apply them, then throw them away cause that's catching. You can use em two times, maybe three. If the blood's poisoned the leech can die right there on the spot. For meningitis in the brain you apply them behind the ears just like when an arm or leg's injured. For sunstroke too, it's behind the ears. Let me tell you, leeches are better than injections, the best. You use them for pneumonia and bronchitis in babies, newborn or a week old. Around here, Valledolmo, Alia, all these towns, everybody comes to me. Rich or poor, they all come to me with their diseases. Around here in small towns there's two or three of us in this work. Other places there's plenty more.

The leech sucks our blood and things work out fine. They're beautiful little things. When they're all blowed up with blood, you milk them gently and all the blood squirts out. Leeches get drunk too, on wine. They spit blood. Just put out a bowl of wine, they'll jump right in and puke all the blood right into the wine. Then we wash them, all milked, and put them back in fresh water.

For typhus, it's behind the ears too. But after that we cut them in half and throw them away to get them out of circulation. They prick the skin and start sucking. When they're full they drop off all by themselves and right away you milk em. Cause if you don't the blood curdles in their guts and they die. The only way to make a profit is using them lots of times. They die if they're not milked. The blood's bad and they get indigestion and that does em in. They get fat like little fat jugs. They'll bulge so much you're afraid to milk em. Some folk get all flustered trying to handle that blood.

There's times you use six, seven bloodsuckers all at once. We used more than twenty on this guy getting meningitis from the heat. He went a touch deaf but at least he didn't get meningitis.

It all depends on the disease. When there's paralysis you apply a whole bunch to get out all the rich blood. Come threshing time you use a whole bunch of leeches for a stiff kick from a mule. For heart trouble too. When we don't have any leeches we call on the barber to puncture the wrist. He finds the right vein and when it bleeds it's for real. The blood gushes out like crazy. People don't go to doctors cause it costs a lot more. Instead you give the barber a little something, a buck or maybe a gift. Doctors charge five, even ten bucks a visit.

When a woman gives birth and she's got a fever, you put the leeches on her womb. When her milk stops coming they go on her breasts or on other private parts in case her veins are popping or she's got piles. We apply them for toothaches too. This science is handed down from grandmother to daughter. You just watch and learn. The other day there was this woman with her navel cord dropping and I cured her by winding my finger around the cord three times and spinning her around, so the cord'd turn three times.

I'm good at driving worms out too. You rub em and say this prayer:

Monnay holy
holy holee
Tuesdee holee
holy holee
Wensdee holy
holy holee
Tersdee holy
holy holee
Fridee holy
holy holee
Sattadee holy
holy holee
Easter Sunday the worm
falls and he'll squirm
Cut off the head
cut off the tail
may this poor soul be
set free.

And the worms work their way out in a split second.

Then there's curdled milk. When a woman washes up with ice-cold water her milk'll curdle. The baby can't stomach it. It's just too cold. Then you say:

Almighty Saint Martin
I met a man and woman
bound in a ball of yarn
water flow thaw pain
depart—I cast you out
in the name of the Father
Son and Holy Ghost.

Then you say a Credo to the Sacred Heart of Jesus so He'll cast out this evil, and a Salve Regina to the Madonna of Altomare so she'll cast out this evil. Do it all three times, and before you know it they stop crying.

There's times the worms'll come at night and the baby'll scream. You got to rub em saying the prayers, and it all goes away quick.

Doctors, they don't know nothing about these things. They don't believe a word of it. Come harvest time the men's wrists swell so bad cause they always hold the scythe too tight. So you give em massages with fox-fat. You can even get rid of the evil eye. Just sprinkle salt on their heads and say the prayers . . .

Families spend whole nights out here in the countryside, in these straw and mud huts. Some live here the whole year round —on these estates at Turrumè, Túdia, Vicarietto, La Niculiddia, Berboncando, Susafa, Mattarieddu, Belice, Polizzella, in all these shanty settlements, all around Palermo Province.

Of course, then you find these huts where families get a few acres of land but can't scrape the money together to put up a house, so up goes a hut. The men work with the boss, and the women and children harvest the grain. Last year R. and his wife were way out there harvesting and their two kids were near the hut. There was a bottle inside. The sun was scorching and the glass got so hot it set fire to the hut. The mother spotted the blaze and ran to save the baby. When she went to get the baby out safe, she got burned all over the face and hair and arms. Everything they had was inside and it got all burned up and they were left with nothing. The baby got trapped inside, all eaten by the flame, and the mother couldn't do a thing but keep shouting and crying and all the overseers came running, the husband too. Sure we cried, just like them. They left their son with us for the harvest and went and settled the case with the authorities, accident report and all.

The huts here burn up a lot. People die. Like M., a few days ago. They were working out in the countryside and they saw bad weather coming and ran for cover: the two mules, a mare, and two brothers, Calogero and Rosalino. A young man passing by saw what was brewing and wanted to get out from under it. They said they couldn't make any room. So he went off and took cover in a house nearby. It started to rain, lightning and thunder, and the hut went up in a flash and burned down with the two brothers and the animals and he saw he'd saved his own neck. But he came running anyway, he wanted to help out, and when he got there he couldn't do a thing. It was all ashes. So he went to town to report it.

23. VINCENZO

*We meet in jail. He is twenty-two or twenty-three. His words
come out like pieces of rock hewn from caverns. Built close to the
earth, he is from another age: perhaps the period just after Cain
and Abel. At the same time, there is a warmth to him.*

Three nights ago I dreamt of pigs. Cows too, and stretches of
grass. I always dream, every night, about cows, mountains,
goats, sheep, lambs. All my life I've tended these animals. I
think about them all the time. Last night I dreamt about how
I was home and somebody came in looking like my father. He
was carrying a sheep with two lambs on his back. The cow was
nursing one lamb and the sheep was nursing the other one. And
an old man came and killed my lamb and there was this chicken
squatting, laying eggs, and he crushed the eggs and sucked them
dry and threw them to the ground.

He escaped, he did. I ran after him with a club to kill him. I
stopped. My mother came in: "Who did it? Who broke these
eggs? The lamb, who killed it?" But it was the old man. He was
mean. And my father said, "It'll make a good omelet." I said to
throw it away under an olive tree cause there wasn't enough.
And he did and it just stayed there.

I dreamt of finding a stake in the ground, with a pig tied to
it and the chain stretched back inside. It came out and grunted
out loud; you couldn't tell what it wanted. There was water but
the pig just snorted. Somebody popped out of the door: "Well,
did you find the broccoli?" "Yeah, I did." So then I up and went
in this dream, and he was there and kept saying, "So you're off?"
"No, I'm not, you haven't paid me lately, I'm staying." So he gave
in and forked over a couple of bucks. "This isn't enough." Sure
enough, he thought fifty cents a day could do, but he was
tempted to give me a quarter. "Take it or leave it," he said and I
left.

One time—what month is this, February?—yeah, last February I dreamt about two bulls. They were goring each other and I was galloping along the shore. I had a Tommy gun and the sheriff came a day later and handed me the summons. That wasn't a dream—the bulls were. See, they'd sentenced me. I was in a cell. The sergeant says to me, "You degenerate." So I said it back. I don't know what it means, but it must be a bad word. Then he showed in the priest—this wasn't a dream—and he said if they called me those things I should be humble. "How?" "Trust in God. If they slap your face, swallow." "Son-of-a-bitch, you got no balls, just like the cops, *and they call me degenerate.*"

I dreamed of women too. I recognized some of them, they were lying by my side. I dream of animals on the loose all the time. See, I've tended em since I'm five. Hell, I was born with em.

When I was born I was all alone. Then brothers and sisters started to come along. Then I tended to animals—I mean other people's. My father got hired out by the year—a year, how many months is that?—or by the half-year. Maybe they'd give us five, six bucks a month. Don't know how many months make a year. I'm not sure if I'm seventeen or nineteen. Maybe we could get a letter wrote to check out my certificate. I can count up to fifty, but I don't understand how money works cause I was always out there in the country, never saw civilized, Christian folk, just my father now and then. My ma, she doesn't know about money or counting neither. I knew how to cook wild grasses and turnips and cabbages, so I ate. I can figure out what a half-a-dollar means, but after that I'm lost.

If there's no work you eat grass. You do anything if you're starving. You can't see any more through your eyes. You kill, do any damn thing. Find work, everything comes your way. Get paid fair, you do good work, stop to chat with people, don't get into trouble. Let's talk plain and simple: everywhere you go, we're killing each other. Sure, if you get on with the big boss, he takes you in, trusts you now and then. But people like me, who trusts us? My head's not screwed on right. I never know what I'm about. Let's say you and me grab this guy who's loaded and snatch his purse, what do we do so he don't talk? Kill him, what else?

Once I fell from a horse and broke my arm. I was watering him for my boss, but my arm got broke and nobody paid.

There was six of us kids at home sometimes. None of us knew how to figure money. Mostly I was alone. And all those rich fairies stomp up Main Street in fine leather boots.

In here, there's one way to go: six feet under. We have words, kill each other, wind up in jail or the graveyard. When you get out, it's no better. You're still hopping mad and show it: "You son-of-a-bitch, you screwed me, now I'm going to get even." And you do. If there wasn't spies, nobody'd catch us. Take us three here, say there's this guy who's crossed one of us and we kill him. If nobody squeals, you get away with it. But there's always spies, they always get you. If not, the authorities would sweat blood and choke on it.

I was gone six months, maybe a year, and coming back, the kids threw sticks and stones. It was like I was an animal. Nobody knew me, I'd run away. Once somebody threw a handful of confetti at me and I bit off his finger.

I have a brother thirteen and one twelve. They can't count money, or numbers neither. Then there's a brother five and a sister six. There's two others dead and a sister a few years younger. How old? Twelve, maybe sixteen, I don't know. She's got married since I'm in jail.

When I was little, the cops took us all to jail. All of us was crying. They took my mother and us kids. My father they got later. The first time he jumped the wagon and ducked the cops. But they locked my mother up with the kid she was nursing and sent the rest of us home. Kept her six months, but then they found my father and let her go.

After that it was countryside and animals. I slept in the straw in my clothes, no covers or nothing, no shoes neither and mostly hungry. The lice was as thick as dung-flies. The boss said no drinking from the cows, he'd beat me with a stick. I'd eat bread and ricotta for breakfast, and at night bread with onions or olives when we could find em. Then it'd rain. The boss'd come by every once in a while. Or I'd look for shelter down in the valley. The dogs'd bark but I'd go begging for love or money or a piece of bread. I was starving. Sometimes people'd feed me, and if they gave me more than I needed I'd bring it back and maybe they'd take it.

Once I was walking back to town, arm in arm with my father, and he saw the cops and took off. I was all alone. They started shooting and he dove into the river. They were on horseback, on foot, with Tommy guns. They fired lots of rounds and got him in the back. Higher or lower he'd of died. There was this stoolie, kept saying, "There, that's him, there in the bushes." They kept combing them but didn't see him. Then the stoolie said, "Look," and they spotted him, nabbed him, dragged him out like he was a sheep or a lamb. "Is he dead or alive?" "Dead." And my father perked up: "You're the ones've croaked, not me, you fairies." And he spat in their eye.

Three years, one month, fifteen days. My father counted every one. Then they sent him on home, on parole. He was confined, couldn't even work. Three years, all the time being watched. I worked but I was little, couldn't do much. We always went hungry. I worked the cows somebody gave me: halves on one of them, a share on four others.

I took baths summertime when I led the herd down to the shore to give the sheep and cows a bath. Wintertime, not a chance. There I was by the sea not knowing how to swim. Then I herded the cows into the grasslands of this guy who squealed on my father. He wanted to beat me and I escaped. My uncles found me. They wanted to know where I left the animals. The son-of-a-bitch was taking them into town and my uncles got them back. Another time they all got in a fist fight.

I never went to school. There never was no cause for it. Nobody in my family ever learned to read or write.

Last night I dreamt my uncles were skinning a sheep—it was white. Cows were munching grass.

What are the stars in the sky? I know that. There's the moon —it's like the sun. I understand them stars at night. They lean out, a whole lot of em. There must be a fire with all that smoke. It all rises into the sky. All that smoke, it all rises into the sky at night. Sometimes you see it, sometimes you don't. The moon is made of sky. The sky is made of smoke, it's made on earth and rising. Sometimes at sunrise, the moon's still there and the stars that travel at night keep on traveling. At daybreak, they disappear. Like cows they go into their barn. Us men and animals are just like the stars.

I've dreamt of fire, too. What's that mean? And a river with scummy water, running quick. What does that mean? Fire, I got scared and ran. In my sleep. How else would fire scare me? Then I was dreaming of drowning and calling for help, drowning and they were clubbing me.

The earth's an island, the sea's all around. I know because I been there at the Colombaia Jail in Trapani and got to know the earth is earth and we're plunked down here in the middle of an island. So I said in my brain, "Damn, if there's sea here too all around like toward Castellammare, then the earth's got to be an island." So when they brought me handcuffed to Colombaia I understood what "island" means.

Italy, what's that? Yeah, there's Italy too. Being here I realized everything's "Italy," like the Ucciardone Prison. Here there's jail and Italy too and it's all in Sicily. What's the difference between Sicily and Italy? When you say *The Journal of Sicily* it means the paper for everybody.

In the world there's countries. They put up houses. It's all like half your ass. Since I been in jail I had new things. This bed, it's got sheets, blankets, mattresses, pillows. When did I ever have things like that before? I know I was born in the sticks. They told me so. My father did too. Houses I saw from the outside, far off, but what business did I have going in? Was I the boss or something? When the cops came to get me they found me with the cows, I saw them and started to run.

Shoot? Yeah, I know how. I can pick off a human if I want

to. I learned how. See, I saw this thing: "Gimme that tube, will you?" The guy said, "It's a shotgun." "Show me how it works, will you?" I watched him make it go bang! Then he handed it to me and I shot at two prickly pear stalks and hit em dead-on. He taught me everything, holding the gun and having me pull the trigger.

But rabbits I know how to catch by hand, in the summer, when they hide between the rocks. I'd break their necks, clean out the guts, skin em, and cook em over the fire. Just like that, no salt or oil. Who'd of given me oil anyhow? I'd take two stones, rub em together, make sparks, and light the fire. Flint- stone, it's called. I'd set the rabbit over the fire, and when I saw it was burned a little on one side, I'd burn it on the other and eat it just like that. Other times I'd eat em raw. Raw snails, too, with the shell. And wild asparagus and turnips. The borage I'd eat roots and all when I could ever find it. That I really like. And frogs where I found water. I'd skin em and cook em over the fire. Then there was fox. I'd set traps outside their caves. There was little ones and big ones too. Once I caught one so big she bit me on the shoulder. I grabbed a rock and smashed her head in.

I'd eat wild dogs when I could catch em. I'd throw em off the mountain and they'd die or else I'd throw em down till they did. Then the crows'd come and try to have em all to themselves and I'd scare em off throwing rocks. I'd suck the baby eggs of finches and robins. I'd put straw in front of caves to make porcupines slip and roll over. Then I'd kill em with a stick, cause they're good to eat. Rabbit meat's good too. I'd skin em by hand. What I could tear I teared and threw it in the fire. At night I'd eat it, the whole thing in one night. I didn't have bread. I'd just tear at it with my teeth.

In jail I got some education, at the Colombaia. They brought me an orange and I learned me the "o." Then an "o" with a tail, that's called an "a." Then the "u" like the cow's mooooo. Then the "e" and the "i." That's all.

How would I like my life to be? Tending to animals. Know- ing how to add and subtract. Understanding about money. Working hard, buying things and selling them for a profit. Like buying shoes for half-a-buck and selling em for a dollar. How much does a pair of shoes cost? I've had four pair of shoes in my life. When my father got out of jail he bought me my first pair, but they got all busted so he got me some others. Now a cousin of mine brought me these here rubber ones during the trial. I had one other pair, but they had nails. I kept slipping and falling on the cement or down the stairs, so I sent them back and went barefoot.

Is there a way to live a good life? I bet my ass there is. Know how? Blow up all the police stations, we'd be better off. They say we'd all go around killing each other. Yeah, we'd kill each other, but it'd be the ones who deserve it that got it.

Sure, somebody's in charge of Italy. Who? Mussolini. I think. All these lawyers suck our blood dry. All these judges meddle in our business. The ones who screw you we should kill. Burn em up and throw out the ashes.

What's the difference between my mountain and life here in the city? I'm savaged, and if I go down into the city nobody gives me the time of day. We're different. People in cities learn to read and write, to work hard. They know how to act with other people. City folk keep in touch with humans. In the mountains you're all alone. Being with God-fearing folk is nice, but only if you talk proper. If you don't talk right, don't know how to act, they kick you the hell out, kill you, crucify you, arrest you, jail you, send you packing. They won't even look at poor people cross-eyed. No, it's the rich they look up to, the big shots. Them they should kill, not us poor folk.

If I could do what I want, I'd study and learn to write, but I'd want to stay with the animals too. They can't talk but they need to hear things like words. They don't talk, they go "uuuh." Animals, soon as I tell em, stop making mischief. The boss, if they don't mind him right off, he beats em with a stick or a stone and they get skitterish and won't come when he calls. Me, I understand when they're thirsty. Like now in the month of May, the whole season, they're always thirsty cause the grass starts to get tough. They don't say a word, but if you're tending them and don't notice, they keep getting weaker. I understand cows and sheep and goats better than humans. The cow, if I take good care of her, pays me back. She gives me milk. I respect her, she respects me. But humans don't pay me back. They keep on robbing me blind. These animals—the cows, sheep, goats—I know how to deal with them, but with humans there's no hope. I don't know how to get across. Animals have always treated me better than humans. Certain animals always stay close to me. There was a kid and a lamb that'd follow me wherever I had to go. I'd share my own bread with them when I had some. They'd come up to me and share my spaghetti, so we'd get to know each other. I loved them and they'd stay close to me. Wherever I'd go, they'd follow. If I went inside, they would too. If I went to the sea they would too. I'd call em and they'd answer in their talk and come running and jump all around me. I like company, but not when it means hate all over the place. There's some of that hate even between animals. Once a bull hated me, a few cows too. One always kicked me and stole figs and never listened. Another greedy bitch with a fat-assed calf always strayed off to eat.

Even if animals hate now and then, they're much better than humans. Cows get tamed much better. If they don't, you sell em or you kill em and don't have to pay for it. You can't trust an ornery beast, so you sell her and lose money. With humans it's much more dangerous. Let's say I kill you or you kill me and they find out: you got to pay the price. Cows don't know how to scheme or do me dirt, but God-fearing folk are good at that. They starve me out, don't let me be.

I never had no friends like that kid and that lamb. My father was always in the army or jail or on parole. I hardly ever saw him. Anyhow, I know who he is. My mother and brothers and sisters love me too. But not even God loves me like that kid and lamb did. I saw that kid and that lamb get born. I raised em. They stuck in my mind. I think about em all the time. I'd suckle them under the cow and they'd follow me. Just like little puppies.

I don't understand it. This love I had for that kid and that lamb is god-awful. The kid'd jump around me and my brother'd be playing. I never had any kind of company like that kid.

I had to sell her to buy some food. I thought it over a whole month. I needed the money and I wanted the kid. I kept thinking, do I sell her or don't I? I wanted both. She was white with red spots all over her head, all down her neck. She had eyes like a human, like you. A little tail with tufts of hair. She started to grow up and her horns started to curve. I really loved her. It was real love. If I sell her I don't have her. But I talked myself into it and sold her. And I went out and bought two pounds of bread, two pounds of fish, and I started to eat. I was eating, thinking about the kid. After that I couldn't eat for two days, just thinking about her and crying. Even when I was working for eight months I couldn't forget her. I still think about her.

My mother loved me too. When I was set to leave for the mountains she told me to watch out and not fall, to do an honest day's work, to stay clear of people who wanted to hurt me, stay clear of everybody. She'd kiss me when I was going off for six months. If she had bread in the house she'd give me some. If not, she wouldn't.

Christmas and Easter I spent twice in jail. Sometimes I was in the mountains, other times at home. In prison I saw my first movie ever. I never seen anything like it before, couldn't understand a thing. Horses galloping, guys swinging swords, all over the place. Then I saw a circus with this girl who walked on a balloon and a horse that went across this plank. The first time I went on a train I was eleven. I went to see my father in jail, at the Colombaia, but the sea was too rough and we waited at the dock and had to go back home. The second time was when I fell off a horse and broke my arm. The third time, I came here.

What about political parties? There's three, maybe four. Socialism, the Priests' Democracy, the Monarchists, and the Communists. The Democracy, they should slit their throats and play soccer with their heads. The Monarchy is the rich guys with all the power. They get on the people's backs and milk em dry. I hate all the parties. I'm not in any of em because I have a record.

I'd just like to line em all up against the wall. They're all sons-of-bitches. Lawyers, fink-judges, none of em's honest. Those other guys, come election time, give us clothes, the motherfuckers. I know so cause I heard all them God-fearers talking and I picked up a few words.

In America and Russia there's the same government as here. Russia, what's it like? I bet it's a little island. China? What's that, a kind of grape? Never heard of it.

I'm in jail over two bunches of herbs. I went to pick herbs in a field. A boy was watching. Soon as he whistled, a stone flew at somebody coming. I got away with a cow that was running ahead of me. The cops came a first time. I was in the barn shoveling manure and I heard the noise of horse hoofs. They wanted to take me to the station and pin it on me. I decided not to go.

A second time they came when I was milking. They herded me between the horses and took me to the station. They stuck knives in my face, beat me over the head, kicked me, all the time writing with this machine, clickety-clack, who knows what the fuck it was. They made me make an X and I left.

After four months they came to get me and take me to jail. They shipped me to the Colombaia. Then they tried me and gave me a sentence of four years and twenty days. Actually they pushed for six years. Anyway they asked me if I was "appealing." I was crying so hard I couldn't see. Now here I am at the Ucciardone, waiting for this appeal. But the "injured party" never shows up.

24. GRANDMA NEDDA

*She is our neighbor in the Spinte Sante district of Partinico.
(We've bought the "haunted house" next door.) Seventy-five,
always dressed in the same black, she loves and cares for our
children as if she were their grandmother.*

O f course a husband can beat his wife. At least when he's in
the right. That's fair, no? Like if she gabs or talks back.
Husbands won't put up with it and don't spare the rod. You
bet. But what about a woman raising a hand to her husband?
Born to walk the streets, they say. See, your *man* can club *you*
if he's got a good reason. He's acting just like a man. If it's the
husband does the beating people say, "Now why'd he do it? He
must of had a reason. She's always provocating him. She should
be ashamed." When it's a woman who's been around, everybody
says, "She defies her husband and we know why. It's in the blood
from birth." We got a name for that kind of woman, a well-
traveled mare. So her husband tries to knock some sense into
her, but she'll talk back: "So I'm only good when you're on top?"
Things like that and we say you can tell she's been straddled
plenty. She's just that kind of mare.

We need it every now and then. Sure, there's some that report
him. But those are the mares. Is it right to blab about your husband when he beats you? No, you just take your medicine. See,
one time my granddaughter Saridda's husband just about beat
her to death. I said to her, "What did you do to your eyes? Who
was it?" "Grandma, I fell down the stairs." She was laid low, all
tensed up. "How'd you fall? Be more careful, you're expecting."
Her eyes were all black and blue. "But my belly's OK, it didn't
do nothing. I landed on my face." A good woman never says it's
her husband. Not even to her mother. It'll get around town. Once
my man busted my rib and I shut up, said I had a headache and
went on making the bed, down there on my knees. I could
hardly move.

When there's nothing to do you set down and chat with a neighbor, maybe four or five all together. "That one there's dirt. She don't do a blessed thing. Her house is a pigsty. The laundry stinks. Don't she wash? Trouble is she got no time for housework, always gossiping and criticizing good folk like us. Her husband breaks her back. That's the way it should be. The kids scream all day long and she goes right on gossiping. She never shuts her trap." It's nice to chat, it keeps your mind busy. The sun comes out and so do we. "Hey there, the sun's out. Time for a chat." The sun is nice coming out. You breathe better in the sun. You can sit there and hear how folks think. It means the same thing: the sun coming out and folks sitting in the street talking.

How should a woman make her husband happy? Stay indoors, cook and clean house, always have clothes ready and mended, and mostly be all his. The husband's the boss of the house and the wife. The wife can't ask for nothing except the linen from her dowry. He's got to strong-arm her. If not, you never know where she'll wind up. He's got to keep her in check. That's the way we're accustomed around here. Is it different in other parts? How do them Americans do it? What about Russians? Aren't they the ones with red faces?

When they beat us we crouch in a corner and let come what may. There's one God, but the husband's another one. That makes two, they say. We have the right to caresses—and beatings. You don't go outdoors unless he says so. Ask for permission and wait for the command. See, he's the boss.

How did my mother die? My sisters told me. I was still being nursed. My mother had a real bad headache so she stretched out on the hope chest with a pillow. Her head was killing her. She'd just put the bread in the oven. My father, rest his soul, comes in and says, "Rosalia, get up." "I can't just yet. Call your daughter, she'll roll out the mattress and make your bed." Now he was a little drunk, and the kid snaps back, "The old man's gone to the tavern and drunk up all our money." She was mad cause she was hungry and there was nothing to eat (of course, husbands usually provide), so she wouldn't make that bed.

He don't back down and rushes up to my mother: "The brat won't do it so you got to." "I can't, I just can't, my head's splitting." So he grabs her and slams her one in the face. Her whole upper jaw just dropped. Her teeth locked. Her mouth wouldn't open nohow. My father was a blacksmith. They rushed in my godfather—he was a barber, like a doctor—and he applied the spoon, but her mouth just stayed clamped. Her teeth were locked. She was dead.

If your husband's sick, you make special promises to the Blessed Mother if only she'll cure him. If your man's sick you say, "Save me my husband. Take one of my children." Come a holy day, to make good your promise, you lick the center aisle from door to altar. Everybody says, "Make way. Here they come. That good soul's licking her way to the Madonna to thank her for the gift of grace." And there's weeping high and low. My daughter-in-law done it too.

When he's real sick, you pray, "Madonna, I lick your floor." The whole way you go barefoot and inside the door you start licking on your hands and knees, just like sheep. You lick all the spit. That's real faith. And the dust, the mud, all the filth. The church is packed and they spit and leave mud on the floor and the little ones' pee. When your tongue's all numb you raise your head—"Thank you, Blessed Mother"—then go on licking. At the altar you get up and stretch out your hands and thank the Blessed Mother from the bottom of your heart and you weep and praise her for the gift of grace and make sure everybody hears you. It makes a good impression if you weep. Everybody's there, everybody's weeping. The men are barefoot too, but some don't tear their flesh to do penance. There's young and old, but mostly the young, the old folks've got discouraged. Everybody says, "Make way, step aside." That's the way it's done at Romitello and Tagliavia. Then you wipe off your tongue with a damp hanky—it'll be bleeding, skinned, torn to shreds—and you dry your tears. We didn't always do penance this way. It's a new thing come these five years.

Now and then there's disasters, and plenty of them. The Lord's taken five of my little ones. One was three, I was still nursing him. He got the whooping cough. One day his friend comes to see if he can come out and play. The kid had whooping cough and he and my baby took this same rope between their teeth, to play horsey. So my son caught it too. He was slender, blond, delicate. Beautiful like my grandson Fifiddu. His name was Carmeluzzu. See, my father-in-law was blond.

Well, I went to the druggist: "Please, I need some medicine. He's got to cough this thing out." He was slender. I was scared he was dying. So I got the syrup, but my baby wouldn't take it. "Momma make cough go bye-bye." I'd hold him in my arms and put the spoon in his mouth. I had to do it every half-hour, but I only got one dose in the whole day. I tried to make him take more: "Momma take some too." I tasted it: "Look, honey, Momma like it." My baby, he finally took it. But then he started getting belly-aches. I didn't understand it was making him sicker. "Shoo, shoo, wicked old witch!" he'd curse. The pains were burning him all up there in his belly. "Shoo, shoo!" (little ones say that). The medicine was eating him up inside. He was that way all day and all night.

My little girl snuck a drink too, figuring it was candy. At first she licked the spoon, then she started to get belly-aches. She was five. You know how kids are with sweets.

Nighttime he's all worn out so I nurse him. He cries and quick I give him the nipple to calm him down. The second day he's worse. I try to nurse him. He stares at the ceiling. He doesn't want milk no more. I fall asleep. The third day, it's like my breasts was dry. I forced a spoon of water into him to cool out his mouth. I poured it in and it stayed in his throat. I tipped his head forward so the water'd run out, but how could my baby swallow? He was dead. And still warm.

Nobody was around, I was alone: "My child . . . my child

. . . my child . . ." I was crying there all alone, and my daughter Ciccina came. I was all in tears: "Look . . . here . . . my baby . . . dead." We dressed him up. My godmother tied a lovely sky-blue ribbon on him and Ciccina went and bought him white stockings.

They filled out the papers right away real quick. It just beats on my brain when I think about it. I had him there with me hardly an hour. But the druggist was a friend of the funeral carriage driver and he called him right in and they took my baby away. They took him off quick so nobody'd know nothing.

My little girl was dying too and she told me how she tried that candy. My oldest son grabbed the bottle and threw it out. I grabbed my baby and took her to another druggist, near the fishmarket. He shows me into the back room and has me hold my child. I felt like I was dying too. He feels her ribs and her belly and gives her this medicine. "You're the one whose little boy was poisoned?" What did I know? It turns out that other drugstore had a new guy and he wasn't much good at the business yet, he didn't know the trade, so he took down this jar and didn't notice the skull and crossbones. Well, this druggist gave my daughter a purgative. "I'll be a good girl and take my medicine." She understood. For a while I gave her nothing but my milk.

A week later a man came and said to my husband, "Peppino, my friend, I'll put it to you straight. It's just your tough luck. There's nothing you can do. You're poor, they're rich. You've got to swallow it. What else can you do? If they dig up his body, you'll have to pay for it, pay for everything. They always win out. They're rich."

25. XX

He is one of my fellow prisoners in the Ucciardone. He is
thirty-five, with a long wild beard. In spite of a mind partially
destroyed by his diseases and a rankling hatred for women and
life, he is relentless in his search for what this world really means.

In the country the old folk rang a bell blessed for protection against thunder and lightning. Many wouldn't sulphur the grapevines because the Lord might get offended and hail punishments down upon them. Whoever was gluttonous paid a tax to the Church (they called it an "indulgence") so they could eat meat and eggs during the Lenten season.

Two months each year I'd be called on to play. At private homes, Ziganet, with Sicilian cards. I'd clean them all out and split it up later with the guys who were my contacts. My share I'd bring home to my mother. See, I started young, at about twelve. I hit nearby towns and all the hotspots in the city: slaughterhouse row, the red-light district, all the dives and the ragpickers' hangouts. They'd go bats seeing me win and never figure out my game. My hands were just too quick, so I'd sweep up every pot, even without marked cards. They'd cut, but I'd have the cards back in the same order so quick they could hardly blink. Shuffling the cards I'd stack the deck, four cards on top, the one I wanted on the bottom, and so on and so forth. When the cards weren't marked I'd do it my style, bending them ever so slightly with a flick of my finger. Just by shuffling I'd get em all going my way.

We played in groups of fifteen, maybe eighteen. They'd lay bets on all the cards and try to guess what'd come up. The poor suckers would lose their shirts. With every bet on a card the money'd leak through their fingers, and as is fitting and proper, the less they had the more I'd raise the ante.

Ziganet is played mostly by the lower classes at Mussomeli, Villalba, San Giuseppe Jato, Palermo. But they're hooked on it all over the place: Rome, Reggio Calabria, Naples, Milan, Turin, Trieste, Venice, Florence, Pescara, Chieti, Aquila. I've played almost everywhere in Italy: Bari, Lecce, Brindisi, you name it. I'm so well known nobody'll play with me any more.

In new towns I'd have an escort. He'd introduce me around as his nephew or a close relative and take me to all the private card games. See, Ziganet is strictly forbidden. It's considered illegal gambling so you have to play in secret. Of course, many a time I'd find myself dealing to officers of the law—and they wouldn't have a sneaking suspicion of my maneuvers either.

What with losing all the time, people become lunatics. Word about me got around and they'd try to get my number. One guy'd say I slipped a card on the top. Another, no, it was on the bottom. Everybody was sure I was a cardsharp and crooked to boot, but then they'd start fighting among themselves, punching the table in desperation and accusing everybody left and right. Somebody'd shout, "But this is our own deck. The cards aren't even marked. How the hell is he taking us when he isn't even shuffling?" They racked their brains trying to figure out how I won all the time whether I shuffled or not. Next day there'd be no hope for a repeat performance, so I'd get my show on the road.

Cards is a nocturnal activity, and before the war I could earn a good ten or fifteen dollars a night. Of course, I'd go halves on my winnings. That is, half for my contacts and half for me: I'd set my own terms. After all, I was the expert. I was also good at Sweep. I could deal my opponent almost all the low cards and get the high ones myself. When I dealt, I'd get all four points.

But I really hit the jackpot when I played Baccarat at high-class joints frequented by the nobility. Let's discuss that some other time. What I meant to talk about was the human drama of the game. My eye was so sharp I'd often see certain "associates" using marked cards to rob each other blind.

Once I saw they were up to their tricks even before I sat down to play. They were sure they could beat me too, these sharks, but they lost their teeth and their skin. Well, they cussed out me, God, and the Saints—they were so desperate they spit all over the cards: "You're hell's operator himself." They couldn't believe they could lose with their own marked deck. Then they invited me to dinner so I would tell them the secret of my success. Let me remind you that I'd learned to tell fortunes by studying *The Book of the Five Hundred* by Rudilio Benincasa, F.S., so I told them it was all my merit for possessing a talisman of virgin parchment that was designed in harmony with the movements of the planets and the phases of the moon. It was this pentacle that brought me good fortune at the tables. Well, they all asked for one as a little gift. I said I'd love to, but they cost seventy-nine dollars each since they were made with magical essences: the dust of Saint Rita and coral and amber powder, all three united together with a pinch of incense and myrrh by singeing them at twelve o'clock midnight and invoking the spirits of Gabriel, Michael, and Samuel. Thus this talisman is composed in harmony with the movements of the planets and the phases of the moon and brings good fortune to all who bear it on their person, not only at the tables but in business, love, and all things that come to pass. And with this talisman we are free from every spell, even the evil eye of some envious person or the danger of accidents.

Well, they were enthralled, so they accepted one per person for the sum of seventy-nine dollars each. This happened after the war.

I played only two months a year. That's how it's done around Italy. The season lasts from November through January. Christmas and New Year's are the big nights. Wherever I went I made a big name for myself. The rest of the year things cool down, so I'd go back home to work as a stonecutter.

I got as far as second grade, but being too sharp for them, they didn't want me around any more.

At fifteen, I came to know womankind. The minute I touched one, my peace ended forevermore. My mother had a stand where she sold milk, ice cream, and deep-fried foods, and I'd sneak money out of her cigar box to go and mount those strumpets.

Well, around my way there was this red-light district with this special little hideaway I frequented. The fifth time I went to my regular woman, I felt something portentous happening inside. It was all hush-hush, behind closed doors. After all, I was only fifteen, see. Three days later, when I'd take a leak I'd feel this tremendous burning like a match was lit in my tube. Well, I checked it out with this older guy and he told me it was the clap. I went to the emergency ward for treatment and the doctor proposed I check into the hospital. I was a good case for instructional purposes. He said he'd pay me on a day-to-day basis. Not wanting to give my mother grief, I refused. So he gave me this medicine. Dissolving this tablet in a quart of water, it got like wine that's so red it's almost black. I hid it so my mother wouldn't find it, but one day she did and thought she'd try it. Right away she threw up. I saw her and got scared it was poison, so we rushed her to the hospital. The doctor said, "Don't worry, she only had a sip." But I couldn't bluff my mother any more.

I was still getting a little pus here and there, but a friend of mine advised me to forget it: it would clear up all by itself. So I forgot about the treatment, but this chancre materialized and I had to check back into emergency. They had to operate. That did the trick.

When I was on the road I met this guy who blew his wad every night, and I was curious to find out how he could afford it. He told me he got rich with a simple con: you stop people in the street and show them a free sample, Benson and Hedges or Lucky Strike, hint you have other imported brands. Then you have them pay and say, "Wait, I have to get them" and go around the corner and make a run for it up the alley. I decided to go in with him, but the cops got wise through their stool pigeons and this plainclothesman set me up. They were out to get me from the start and they did. I was arrested for attempted fraud. They gave me four months, but it was suspended. I was released on bail. It was my first offense.

By now I was eighteen. At home we were in dire need. I wanted to set myself up good and get married. My mother made an offer: "The schoolteacher's daughter, she'd be just fine. She's been through a lot with her parents and all." I knew her since we were kids, but I hadn't seen her for a while. First time I saw her again I fell in love. At first, I wasn't too enamored with the idea of actually marrying her. I was thinking of having a fling. But my mother guessed what I was up to and put her foot down: "You marry the girl or else." She said yes right away because ever since she was little she was just like a member of the family.

I presented my case to the grandmother. At first she was opposed because word got around I was a gambler, but getting to the bottom of it she discovered I played only two months a year and was always ensured of a good take. Deriving I was a normal sort of gambler, they agreed to it. Fact is, they were tickled pink. They saw I could do an honest day's work and provide. During my engagement, I dropped stonecutting because I'd never support a family on my daily wages. I took a job as a traveling salesman in fabrics. That meant going all over Sicily with my commuter rail-pass.

I was delighted about having a girl with a real artistic build. It drove me wild. She looked just like a queen. I kept thinking about this new, imposing responsibility. Meanwhile she was content. She had a man who brought home the bread and everybody in my family loved her. We had a wedding feast with lots of cakes and cookies and all the relatives, and the celebration lasted till one in the morning.

Well, I felt I'd settled down to a simpler, hard-working life. My days as a drifter were behind me. I could tell because two days after the wedding, I was busy selling cloth again. That way I managed for two years, living a happy life—till '37. She was a bit sloppy with the housework, but she had the right spirit, and when we'd fight she'd never let me walk out before kissing me and making up first.

We'd go out a lot to the movies, and when those unbreakable-glass high-heels hit the fashion world I bought her the first pair out because I took so much stock in that artistic build of hers. Two months of marriage and she got pregnant, and in '36 I had a baby girl. Come '37 I was working a certain town and I knocked on this door to try to sell some dresses. The lady of the house answered: "Please, leave us alone. I've had a misfortune in my home. My son, they put a spell on him. He's cursed." "Madam, have no fear, let me see him." I figured he was touched by evil spirits. Well, his head was blown up twice its size. I examined him and promised to cure him in thirty-three days, but it would come to twenty-five dollars for the purchase of ingredients. It was Saturday so she says, "Give me time to find the money. Come back Monday." And I did. Two cops were there to greet me. She pressed charges. They sentenced me to thirteen months for attempted fraud.

My mother made terrible sacrifices to feed my wife and the baby. My brother was a volunteer in East Africa and he'd send me a dollar a month. Out of this I'd keep enough for three airmail letters and send the rest to my wife. I felt good about this sacrifice I was making. But my wife failed to show due respect to my mother. She forgot who was feeding her. It got so bad she had to move out and rent a room from one of the neighbors. She met two women from the alley across the way. One worked in a medical laboratory. The other, let's say, was of easy virtue. Anyway they were a comfort, and gave her some advice: "What do you expect from a husband? Being free's much better. Come on, we can work in a good house and make a pile. That way we'll be on Easy Street." Well, some of the neighbors got wind of it and my mother got an anonymous letter: "Watch out, with the kind of company she keeps, this girl might go astray."

End of '38, I got out of jail. My brother came to pick me up. I asked if my wife had behaved properly. "She's been a complete mess, but as far as your honor, there's nothing to say." If it wasn't a question of honor, I had nothing to worry about, so I went to greet my mother. Later I went to see my wife and she really made a bad impression. The room was so tight a bed and chair could hardly fit, and the ceiling was so low it just pressed down on my brain. I went right off to look for a place closer to my mother's and found one without a floor, I mean it had a dirt floor, but it was bigger.

My wife was unbearable. I felt a tremendous resentment against her too, because she actually went as far as abusing my mother, and that's the most sacred, inviolable thing in my whole life. My mother, she raised me all alone without a father from when I was four. Well, my wife and I had some real brawls. She talked back to me. She didn't fear and respect me any more.

I'm back thirteen days and they summon me to headquarters and read me this charge for draft dodging. Well, I had an alibi, being in jail. So they sent me to Rivoli to do my military time. I was there two months with other recruits and about two thousand veterans from the War of '17–'18. They put all the Southerners in one barrack and the Northerners in another, but sure as shooting I'm the one Southerner they stick with those Piedmontese. Every night the whole damn bunch of them would come home loaded, and this one time the guy who sleeps in the bunk above me hits the sack and the wine he's been guzzling comes up on him and then comes spraying all over me. So I reported it to the lieutenant and asked to be transferred in with my people because I was fed up with those goddamn polenta-eaters who got stewed every night and made me want to puke. I never would have guessed it, but the lieutenant turns out to be from Piedmont. "You lousy no-good son-of-a bitching dirt-eater! Just remember, when Garibaldi landed in Sicily he gave your kind soap and you thought it was cheese." That upset me a bit, so I took my belt, secured it to the bunk, and wrapped it around my neck to strangulate myself. I did that little maneuver with the aim of getting transferred. But two soldiers were playing cards near my bunk and they cut me loose and took me to the infirmary and kept me under guard.

I decided to write home for a care package. I asked for a pound of that globby soap, the kind we use in Palermo Province that looks just like apricot jam. I also wanted three pounds of extra-fine powdered sugar, the kind you sprinkle on pastries. The package arrived. I mixed the sugar into the soap and put it back together like it wasn't opened. Pretty soon after that I was sent back among the Piedmontese. About ten o'clock in the morning it was, I carry the package in like it was worth its weight in gold. My buddies notice: "Goddamn your horse's ass, a package from Sicily. Come on, open it, let's have some goodies." I did and they jumped for joy. "I'll be a pig in holy shit! Jam! Let's have a party." I told them I had to refrain because I had a toothache in my wisdoms. They got some bread, spread the jam on thick, and belted down just about the whole package without suspecting a thing. I'd added just the right amount of sugar. An hour later one of them has a little belly-ache and checks into the infirmary and that starts a chain reaction. Finally the lieutenant of the infirmary summons me: "What in hell did you do, poison em?" "It's soap, sir. See, the company lieutenant said Garibaldi gave us dirt-eaters soap for cheese."

After that episode the lieutenant and this sergeant kept on giving me extra shit-detail until I couldn't put up with it any more. So I had a friend I really trusted tail that sergeant to see where he got his kicks. It turns out it's every night with this blondie in a little hideaway. So one evening at seven he's waiting for his girl and I take him by surprise: "You son-of-a-bitch, what's all this shit every day! I'm up to here! When's it going to stop?" Then I took out my bayonet and smashed him a good few times with the hilt. He crumbled up and made believe he was dead. I scrammed.

I was in bed faking a snore when an MP interrupted and took me to prison. They cussed me out so bad I had a fit of despair. They left me alone, but I asked for pen and ink to write home to my mother and drank the whole bottle. They decided to keep me under guard in the loony bin. Two months later I was released and sent to the stockade. After that it was court-martial. The chief prosecutor of the Ministry of War wanted to give me eight years, but I was acquitted on circumstantial evidence. My next assignment was Verona, where I did two stints of six months each to get cured of piles.

Back in Sicily. I was hoping with all my *savoir-faire* and good hard work to restore my wife to obedience and have some peace and quiet. But she never listened to my word. She wouldn't give in to my authority. I'd go around town hawking cloth, but when I'd come home to roost, it was nothing but grief.

Just to show her, one night I went to the movies alone to hunt for the first thing I could get. All to punish my wife. I sit down by these two dames and start talking about the movie. We get friendly. One of them gives me her address and a date for tomorrow. I show up, and she's got four kids and tells me her husband's in Africa and she hasn't heard from him, so this guy is keeping her. She has to feed her kids. I didn't have it in me to go with her. The poor dame, she was doing it out of need.

But she was pushy, so we coupled and she gave me something. At first I didn't know it, so my wife got it from me. Finally, we suspected it and went to see a doctor. He announced the verdict: the syph. I started crying, thinking I'd defiled my wife's blood. We both took a little cure.

I kept on working the towns. At home, little squabbles and lots of grief. You just can't make it by selling cloth, so I did some fortune-telling and two months a year I'd play. Ziganet was out at the time, so I got specialized at Baccarat and was invited all over to play. This game is in vogue in business circles, the nobility, big industry, and Christian Democrat headquarters at Syracuse, Caltanissetta, Agrigento, Castelvetrano, Santa Teresa, Sant'Agata di Militello, and other vicinities. Of course, I'd always need a contact, but more about this later.

Now remember, my wife was comely, and this ugly little prick starts passing the word around he was intimate with her when I was in jail in '37. My family gets wind and my mother starts weeping, lamenting just like the Madonna: "My son! My son! He's lost to me. He'll commit murder!" She went begging to my older brother: "Save my son from perdition, he'll kill them both." So my brother came to see me one morning around eight. My wife was doing some housework. The radio was on full blast. My brother whispered, "Go get *The Book of the Five Hundred* and the cards and come with me."

Outside my brother says, "Look, do me a favor and go tell the fortune of the wife of this certain somebody who's spreading the word he was intimate with my wife while I was in East Africa. That way we can plot our revenge." When I heard it, you can bet I shuddered, it was a matter of life or death for our family: "But who is this ball-buster? Do you really believe your wife's capable of such a thing?"

He points out the house and I go. When I get into the courtyard, I see this woman doing laundry. She looks up, gets pale as death, and rushes inside and slams the door. I'm wondering if maybe she recognized me, so I knock at the door across the way. This woman's in the middle of brewing coffee and I ask her if she knows a certain lady. I invented the name. "She called me to see her sick child." "You a doctor?" "No, a fortune-teller." "How about reading my stars for me?" She invites me in. "How about calling that other woman too? She ran inside but from her wrinkles I could tell somebody's given her the evil eye." "No, no, we're on the outs. To the death. She's my sister-in-law." "Which side of the family?" "Her husband's my husband's brother." It was too bad for her, but I was set on revenge. I was defending my brother's honor.

I read her palm and warned her a spell was cast on her too. I saw it in the cards. It was written: "By the power instilled in me by the mystical brotherhood of the Cobalistic Circle of Saint Paul's Church in Rome, if a spell is cast upon you, in the name of Michael and Samuel, a certain card you are holding will vanish." I named the card. She couldn't find it and got all flustered thinking she was hexed.

"Madam, you have quicksilver in your pubic regions and if it isn't drained off within thirteen days you will be paralyzed and bedridden for three years." She was scared to death: "Drain me, I beg you." Through certain massages in the genital area, my fingertips incited her lust. I got her to the point where she didn't know what was what. Our magnetic waves were in the same field, there was contact and a mixing of tongues. She was saying, "I've never done this before, not even with my husband." She was ecstatic and contented. Then I snipped off some of her pubic hairs, doing the exorcism to drain off that quicksilver that came from the evil eye. Plus I had her give me a photo.

I wouldn't have given a damn if her husband walked in on us. I could have taken on a whole army and fought to the death to wipe out the stain on our family honor. I could have slaughtered him in his own bed.

We were sitting there talking and she caught sight of my ring. It was made of bone with a picture of me and my wife. "How come you got all worked up over me when you have a real looker like that? I hear she really knows her way around in bed." When I heard that, that my wife had screwed around, I tried to poker-face it: "What do I care? We're not married. I was off in Africa. That was her business." "No, you were in jail." Thinking maybe she could be mistaken, because my sister-in-law's about the same height as my wife, I took out a passport photo of my wife. "That's her." "I'll bring her where you can look at her in person, that way you can be sure it's her."

I went right home and invited my wife to come with me to borrow some money from my big brother. I took her past that woman's house. She was stationed where she could see my wife and nod to me if she was the one.

When she nodded, I stopped short and told my wife I forgot something. Then I left her at home and went to see my brother. "I owe it to you, Sherlock Holmes, I'm the one holding the bull-shit by the horns. But now *you* got to tell me who it is said he did monkey business with my wife." "Let me talk to you as a brother: be rational, go get proof. If it's true, then just leave her." And my mother rushes in and throws herself around my neck: "Son, I bore you in my womb, don't lose your head. If she's tainted, it's her that must bear the cross." I tried to reassure them. See, I had to clear it all up before I decided on murder. She was seven months pregnant. Besides, maybe this guy was being paid off by somebody else who wanted revenge because he couldn't seduce her.

They brought the guy over to meet me. On the spot he begs

my pardon, my mercy. "I didn't know. Your wife seduced *me*. If I'd of known you, I wouldn't of gave her the time of day." He confessed the whole thing—see, our go-betweens assured him I was a man of reason. I'd understand if the door was opened from the inside, not forced. There wouldn't be any reason to lay a finger on him. You know it's the woman who's always guilty. I swore I wouldn't do a thing if he gave me proof. Then the woman would pay for her crime. Otherwise I'd kill him and his whole family. He said, "Look, it all happened two years ago. Who knows if she'd get familiar again." I gave him the game plan: "I'll tell my wife I'm off on a sales trip for three days. You go to my house and set up a date with her at such-and-such a place to talk about pressing matters. If she says yes, you tell me and get your ass home and hers I'll kick the shit out of and ship back to her mother." We agreed he'd go the next day.

I couldn't let on anything was afoot. My wife was always sharp, quick on the draw if I let my guard down. "I'm leaving tomorrow, for three days." I got all packed and went and hid in my uncle's house. I was just itching to hear from that punk. I figured he'd send word out of fear, if nothing else. Instead, he told his mother everything and she blubbered like he was in the grave already. "Are you crazy or something? Those two are brothers in crime. They know the ropes since they're six, they know how to hang you and go scot-free." I heard all about it later through some neighbors who reported to my family.

She's desperate to save her son's life, so she sends a trustworthy friend to my wife to tell her the whole story. Well, my wife knows what sort of man I am, prizing my honor above all things in life. She's sure I'll kill her, so she grabs the baby and runs out in the courtyard and calls the landlady. "Madame, it's finished. My husband's going to kill me. I'm innocent, I swear." But my brother's always on the lookout—he hears her screaming for help. "Now you know what's up," he says to my wife, "so take what you need and get out. Go to your mother's or else my brother'll kill you." So she hustles up all the stuff for the baby she's expecting, grabs the baby girl by the hand, and takes refuge in her mother's house.

I had a pistol and a knife, and was all set to slash her womb open and throw the fetus in her face and then go to the cemetery and shoot myself, right over my father's grave.

Today I have the courage to tell the whole story. At my age with my vast experience, twenty years as a fortune-teller, and with all my research into the nature of womankind, I've come to a profound understanding of what the female sex is and isn't. If I had all this experience and knowledge in the first place, I wouldn't of beaten my brains out and let despair push me into committing crimes. I've acquired this knowledge at my own expense, all by myself. If the same thing happened now, I'd say, "That's just like a woman for you."

My brother rushed to tell me what had happened. Before he finished I was on my way to strangulate her, right in front of her mother. I storm in and grab her mother by the throat: "Where is she?" Suddenly her relatives are all over me and kick me out.

Several days later my wife finds out who it was smeared her honor. So she gets up next morning at seven, dresses like a man in her father's clothes, takes a knife she's rubbed with garlic to poison it, and goes to the neighborhood tobacco store where she's found out he buys his cigarettes. She whips off her cap: "You there, do you know who I am?" "I never saw you in my life. It's all my sister-in-law's gossip." She grabs him by the hair and stabs away in the genital regions. The proprietor is shouting, "What the hell are you doing? Look at the mess you're making! Get him out of here!" See, he doesn't want to get implicated. So she drags him out on the sidewalk and dumps him in his own blood. He's passed out already and she starts shouting, "Police! Police! Arrest me! I'm innocent! I've restored my husband's honor!" They took her down to the station and then on to jail.

Two months later she gave birth to a nice little baby boy and named him after my father. I heard from this woman who got out that she played crazy. She wouldn't stop screaming and imploring in my name, "I'm innocent. I've restored my husband's honor."

There was this baroness who did charity work for the needy and the animals. She had certain pull with the police and the examining magistrate. She tried to make peace between me and my wife. I said OK, let her stay out of trouble at home with her mother for two or three years, then maybe we could get back together. See, I wasn't sure how guilty she really was. Meanwhile I supported her. After all, she was the mother of my children. After six months they let her out on probation.

I kept on working and found a card game in Foggia. I was commuting from Pescara where I'd shacked up with this married woman. I was convinced my family life was shot for good, so I concentrated on seducing wives to wreck their marriages. I was taking revenge on the human race. Once I made contact, the woman naturally got syphilis, and that way the husband would find her out. I didn't get cured on purpose.

When I was heading back from Foggia one day, my wife ambushed me from an alley. She wasn't a good shot, but she nicked me in the leg. The cops broke it up and arrested the both of us. Right in front of them she says, "It's hopeless, kill me or I'll kill you. She'll never be yours. I wasn't born to be everybody's whore." They let me go and shipped her back to Sicily.

Pursuing my sales and cards career, I moved on to Milan. But I returned once to Sicily on a sales trip and was held up by the landing of the Americans. They arrested me for transporting stolen goods and confiscated everything because I didn't have the bill of lading. My brother went to a lady who knew certain judges to get me released on bail. She asked for the sum of five hundred dollars. My brother forked it over and she went to work. She found this cutie who sold herself to anybody and everybody and promised her fifty bucks. Then she had her dress up as this shy little housewife and go to the judge to beg for her husband's freedom (that was me). Meanwhile, the lady handling my case had gone to see her judge friend and urged him to give an audience to my poor dear "wife." The girl came crawling to him and he tried to comfort her: "We'll see, my dear, but it's a serious crime, you know. Three to seven years at the least." He was stroking her by now, his hands straying all over. Next time she came back, he deliberated and held forth all the way to the bed: "It's a shame a pretty girl like you is in the clutches of a black marketeer, a bum who's so stupid he gets caught." Out of the kindness of his heart he gave her five bucks, but he took so many prerogatives she wanted fifty more from the lady. He let me go on probation.

For a few years now, I've had some lucky breaks, and a little peace of mind. I've found my ideal and I'm living with her. I'm awfully happy about our union. I never knew before what love or real connubial affection meant. It's a real comfort to have a nice old-fashioned girl, a homebody, obedient, neat, clean, and thrifty. She got sick from me and had a miscarriage, but we took the cure together and got healed. The germs aren't active any more.

I've been devoted these past few years to my work telling fortunes. I got licensed, for the cards too, and I got renewed every year so I could exercise my profession in every city in Italy but the capital. The pope has his own dominion. The priests don't want competition.

I've treated people with fixations on the brain and a woman with a fallen bladder. She'd been to lots of doctors and they were stumped. I proscribed an elastic girdle and she was cured for good. I'd visit a family in desperate straits and tell them the evil eye was cast on their house. To convince them, I'd ask for a wad of cotton and on the sly put a pinch of metallic sodium in the cotton and lay it on the floor. Then I'd have a bottle of water fetched and I'd pray, "By my power in the name of Samuel, Michael, etc.," sprinkling the water on the cotton. It'd burst into flames and they'd be terrified thinking the house was really cursed and beg me to save them from the evil eye and offer to pay me anything. Naturally, that's fair.

To rout out fixations, I'd call for half a bottle of vinegar. So I wouldn't tip my hand, I'd bring my own bicarbonate in different earth-colors—yellow, red, and green—saying it was coral and amber powder and the dust of Saint Rita. I'd mix them in with vinegar, chanting, "Draw out the quicksilver incarnate in this house, etc." and corking the bottle tight. It'd start to glow inside and the cork would explode and foam would come shooting out. "Ladies and gentlemen, behold, the quicksilver is passing forth." What was left in the bottle they'd have to divide into thirty-three doses and every day put a few drops in the four corners of the room reciting three Credos, three Paternosters, and three Ave Marias. When the doses were used up, the house would be purged. Sometimes I wore my robes with the rosary. That makes a better impression. But you have to do that in secret. As I was saying before, the priests'll have their competition arrested.

You have to remember it's not just women who believe. Men do too, illiterates and doctors of philosophy alike, in the country and in the city.

Once this guy walked in blubbering, asking to be set free. He couldn't muster any conjugal contact with his wife. It'd got so bad she'd showed him the door. He wanted to kill the suspect, a neighbor of his, with a spell. I put him in a trance and he went home and worked magic. He came back to thank me personally, with some gifts and twenty bucks.

On my way into a town I'd have my apprentice pass out handbills. Under my photo it said, "The Wizard of All Science."

I've told many people's fortunes and discovered all their family tragedies: fathers with their own daughters, brothers with sisters, sons with mothers, girls seduced by fiancés, married women with secret lovers, selfishness, envy, revenge through evil concoctions, magnetic attractions to procure love or infection, attempted poisonings for the treachery of fiancés, people cured only to embrace the same disease again.

At N. a girl came to have her fortune told. She looked like a goddess, Venus in person. The prefect had seduced her. She wanted him bewitched so he'd marry her. At V. this woman who was quite a looker got involved with this dandy and wanted me to kill off her husband with a thirty-three-day spell so she could be free to enjoy her lover with a clear conscience.

The long and the short of it is, these things come to pass because the priests get mixed up in politics and play filthy dirty tricks to their advantage and forget to preach goodness and justice to us sinners all over the world.

Looking beneath the veil of reality I've learned that women and men are nothing but scarecrows or feathers blowing in the wind. Women are movable objects, and man is so weak, generically speaking, that he exposes himself like a peacock. Savage beast that he is, man in the presence of woman is like a new-born lamb.

If human beings had the slightest inkling of the secret, that we're only on this earth a fleeting moment, we'd cherish every day month and year a lot more. We'd see time flow past and our life with it, which is all the more reason to cherish it and help each other out, physically, and be at one in peace of mind. Instead we only see the rich man hunt down the poor, trampling and enslaving them, while he sits with his legs crossed and fancy ladies at his feet, and they all, his wife too, they've got limousines and chauffeurs and harems with slaves waiting on them hand and foot. They're decked out in gold and studded with diamonds and the wife's like a Madonna on the high altar. The world is in the palm of these selfish, vengeful people's hands and they don't give a hoot about the real needs of their fellow creatures. Look at me: when I was a child of four, I lost my father and my whole life's been one long battle. And now I have no other choice but to put my son in reform school.

With all this experience reading the stars all over Italy, I've plumbed the depths of the universe. All of humanity under Christendom, the poor, the rich, princes, barons, counts, have revealed to me their hidden desires and secret practices. That's the reason I'm saying all this, I've been everywhere, on trains, in cafés, bars, all sorts of dives, talking to anyone and everyone, and I've learned it all in one way or another. If I'd known I had to spend my life like this, I would've refused to see the light on the face of this earth. But all of us are condemned to life.

Who'll give an ex-convict a job? Who'll give us ways and means to work? Wherever you go they slam the door. It's always the same faces back in jail. Aren't we members of the human race too?

At my age I can't work with my hands. If only I could have a little hole of a grocery store with a counter and scales, I'd give credit to people in need, but still earn a living for me and my wife. I'd forget about all this wandering. I'm tired, depressed . . . Maybe I could be a foreman . . . When people buy me a coffee, they always want a favor in return. They want me to solve all their problems without paying . . .

Man is so ignorant he finds more beauty in things forbidden and private, not in what's open to us all. Like when you're in jail and the guard leaves the door open, you don't feel like going out into the cell block. But as soon as it's shut, you suffer. It's always been that way for our race.

Being here in jail this time, I've let my beard grow wild. When they send me out there again, what else can I do? I don't have any cash to pay the charges overdue on my license, but I still have to go back to telling fortunes, sending handbills around, a dollar per consultation . . . or even fifty cents. A half-a-dollar, how far does that go? . . . Look, we all need stage presence to put on a good show. I wear spectacles, it makes a better impression on the client.

Wandering around I'd hear of another fortune-teller, the best in the business everybody'd say, so I'd be eager to go see him, disguised as a regular customer. I'd want to see his act, hear his pitch, see if he knew his stuff and had the right aura, charisma. Maybe he'd say, "I see evil spirits working in your life, especially along business lines. You need a good-luck charm, one hundred dollars apiece." But I'd surprise him: "Let's see if it's in my magnetic field. Look, I'm invested under the protection of a benevolent spirit. Here's my talisman." Still, I'd be afraid his talisman might be unique, and more powerful. He'd have the same fear.

Our hypnotic power is so strong that many young girls, married or not, will do anything we command. You know engagements never last long, or she gets hexed and the baby's born sick, or people go broke and marriages collapse. Whatever the case, women pay with love, sell themselves, let us touch them all over. The line of the ones easy to seduce is endless. So is the one of those who want to put the curse of death on their husbands. That costs fifteen hundred dollars . . . When I start up a séance I bat my eyes in a frightful way, shut them, and go into a trance. Then I turn on one of my other voices to make them think it's spirits talking. I was so good once in Gela, I brought them to their knees: husbands, wives, males, females. They gave me free room and board.

If you make a name for yourself, people flock to your door. You mention in your brochure that reservations must be made a day in advance, limit of ten consultations per day. I have special cards with a phone number and my initials for people who don't want to leave their names.

I don't feel like part of the human race any more. I have a record, so I can't find a regular job. I don't have capital to set something up on my own. This is my only way out, the only thing left. At least there's no capital investments, no overhead, no nothing. When I can't afford handbills, I go around drumming up business myself. Sometimes people come and pick me up.

WASTE

26. XY

We are at the Center for Research and Initiatives of Corleone.
A fifty-five-year-old illiterate peasant is speaking. During our
conversation, his closest friends help him remember all the details.
Thus the whole group expresses itself.

The first contract they put out right after the war was on a guy
named Cianciana. They got him in the square, maybe for
political motives.

Then there was the guy whose father worked at Belvedere.
They wiped him out because he had an inside job and they were
afraid he'd talk.

Michele Randisio and Zu Matteo Capra's son, the one with
the bad hand, they disappeared. The bones were found when
everybody was looking for Placido Rizzotto's body. It was in the
same pit where they threw Donna Calorina Saporita's son. We
could've loaded up a whole cart with all the bones from that
hole. Angelo Gulotta's and Ciccio Navarra's brother's. This pit
is on Monte Casale.

Grisi had three brothers living here, at Corleone. One was
found on the railroad tracks. A second came home on leave and
that evening they settled accounts with him near the gunsmith's.
The third left town and nobody's heard of him since. The brother
who was a soldier said that the Mafia here was only good for
picking your teeth. They heard that and got him in broad daylight, right out there in the street, point-blank in the head.

Pietro Montesanto, from Palermo, he lived in Corleone since
he was a kid: disappeared. He always had his hair slicked down.
This other guy, too, he used to wear a velvet suit with kid-leather
patches. It must of been worth one hundred–fifty, two hundred
dollars. They told him, "Lower the flame or the gas tube'll burst."
His mother used to cast spells and cook up poisons. You know,
this whole town is full of people crippled by these spells.

Pino Orecchione, his brother's the street cleaner, he was found in the township of Frattina with an army rifle slung over his shoulder and his head bashed in. He could never find a job so he robbed the peasants' straw huts to support his family.

Here in town there was Vito Capra. He figured out who was sending all those extortion letters. They shot him at night. Another guy, name of Selvaggio, was coming home with a load of grain and they shot him. People say he was just a bit too cocky.

Then there was Mariano Governale, killed at the second crossroad out Sant'Elena way. They used the sawed-off shotgun and split his head open with the butt. People said it was a question of honor.

We found another out-of-towner shot in front of the Madonna del Mal Passo. He worked at Madonna di Scala.

They shot Mariano Scalisi in Bingo Township. They cut off his hands too.

Somebody was killed in Pozzillo Township, but he wasn't from Corleone. Nobody said much about it. Here in Corleone it's a free-for-all. You can't find a cobblestone that's not stained with blood.

Salvatore Amenda, we called him the Sheriff because he was a retired cop, they got him with the sawed-off model. There's more security that way. With a pistol there's just one shot. Allegedly he was an informer. "Good for slaughter," we say when a mule collapses. That means, dead meat.

You know Vallone Street at the edge of town? They killed Michele Scuzzulato right there, nobody knows why.

In front of Saint Christopher Chapel they shot Bagarella at close range. It was after a brawl over a matter of engagement.

Here the criminals are protected by the government. Even when they catch your killer, ten days later he's out of jail. See, it's the government that's crazy. It's awful how many murders there've been since the war. Here it never stops. Get in an argument and for one angry word like, "Dammit, this goat's mine," they'll bump you off. It's the way their brains are. It's habit. It comes natural, like killing a goat. They're like animals. Worse. They kill us all because they want all the power. They want to be superior.

If you foul up and get killed, people say, "He deserved it." If you're OK and still get it, it's "Poor guy, why'd they do it?" Let's say you kill me today. Tomorrow my son'll try to wipe out the stain on our honor by wiping you out. But maybe my son is a decent sort and doesn't have it in him. Or let's say I have some animals and you steal em on me. Naturally I'll come and kill you—if I have it in me. If I don't, I'm like a grapevine in bad earth. I shrivel up and die.

Then there's woman's honor. This is a town that doesn't stand for scandal. Say I have a daughter and you take advantage of her. You stain her honor, then you won't marry her. What happens? I come and kill you, understand. I won't stand for such dishonor and people'll say I'm right. Sometimes the women do the killing themselves. The whole town'll be in an uproar, but we'll agree, "He deserved it." It's just natural.

If a man steps out of line they steal his mules or burn his house down. They usually leave you alone if you don't give em any trouble.

There's been Mafia heads at Corleone since the old days. They steal and devour everything, and we just sit and watch. First there was Mariano Cuddetta. That was when I was a kid. He was a real cutthroat, stealing animals, killing people. That's their line of business. Then came Piddu Ucceduzzu. He was an orphan, they found him on the convent doorstep. Then came Cicci Figatellu, and he was something. His word was law. "Go kill So-and-So, confiscate their animals"—and boy, you had to go do it. They killed two of his brothers. He was my height, stocky, nobody crossed him. Pino Ucceduzzu and Mariano Cuddetta were young but big and tough, with beards. Then there was Vincenzo Crisciune, he was a straw boss, like the rest of them. They killed his son, then they got him. After that it was Doctor Navarra, he had his claws in every pie. A doctor, sure, but what a cutthroat.

He ran the whole show in town and all around it. He was chief of staff of the hospital, head of the Health Plan and Accident Insurance, chairman of the board and health inspector in the Farm Owners' Association. He made everybody vote for the priests' party. The more votes he got the more superior he was. He even made plans to have the president killed up there in Rome. See, these guys aren't afraid of anything. Anyhow, nobody knows nothing and the priests always protect them. Everybody knows this story: Placido Rizzotto was a good man for the people. He always made demands for us, so they killed him and threw him in that pit, and a little boy was tending the sheep and noticed. Well, he got so scared he was sick. They took him to the hospital, and right there Doctor Navarra gave him this needle and the kid died on the spot. They were afraid he'd talk so they poisoned him. It was an open-and-shut case. But at the trial they fiddled with the evidence. What could we say? What about the kid's parents? If they talked they'd have been killed too. Everybody knew, but he had the power.

Honey wouldn't melt in their mouths. You see these Mafiosi around town and talk to them. They're buddy-buddy, all smiles. They're all one crop. They play the father to us, but it's just to know everybody's business. The people try to keep in their good graces. We give em fruit, cheese, goats.

If she's married to a Mafioso, a woman runs the whole neighborhood. Let's say you become a Mafioso. I have to show your wife respect or else you'll be my enemy. People have to watch out what they say. There's only one way to live in peace: have ears but make believe you're deaf, have eyes but say you're blind, have mouths but just shut up. Say they steal some animals, it's see, hear, and speak no evil.

Mostly they kill each other. Everybody wants the power. The Mafia's like the army. They have lieutenants, colonels, majors, major generals, they go from rank to rank, demanding obedience from their inferiors. The Mafia head is the general. If he orders me to kill or steal and I don't, it's me they kill. But if I want a good position, like straw boss on an estate, I have to give in to the chief. If I'm not in their party, I don't get the job. If I'm not with them, I'm off the list. Nowhere.

Us tenant farmers are good hard-working men. We know our trade, but our hearts aren't in it. See, every year they relocate us. There's no security working the land. If there was, we'd plant orchards, clear away the rocks, dig drainage ditches, make terraces to stop the landslides. They give you a piece of land, you work it one year, next year they kick you off, and in comes another guy. Listen to what happened to me two years ago. We rented out this land, spread manure, did the sowing. Naturally I paid for the seed myself. After twelve months the boss took the land back for himself and wouldn't even pay me for improvements. I didn't want to budge so the boss came and threatened me with a rifle. He wanted to make his own law, but I went to the police. The commissioner takes down my complaint and sends two cops. They couldn't find him at home, but they confiscated his rifle and pistol. He didn't have a license. I went back and forth to see the commissioner and press charges. Maybe fifteen times. No results. "Forget it, don't make enemies for yourself, there's always plenty of land." They gave him back the guns because they'd been "declared" and because of "invasion of privacy." I lost everything.

When they allot you land, it's almost always full of rocks, so you've got to rent it out as pasture to the overseers of their estates —at the price they fix. There's no competition over this pasture land. Besides they've grabbed up all the good estates already. That was right after the war. We got some good land, we were all ready to harvest the beans and the clover. They came and said, "This is our land from now on." We just had to leave. Show of force, that does it. They go around with gunbelts and shotguns always cocked. Their word is law. It's all-powerful, even with the big landowners.

They killed Tana Cascietta's son down by that fountain below the police station. Business interests, people guessed. His father was shot at Malvello.

On the Plains of Women, Schillaci got it. He was hired to tend the livestock. Maybe it was a dispute over stolen goods. Why, they only know.

They killed Police Captain Anzalone by the brook in Nascè Square. First they gunned him down, then fired point-blank when he was on the ground.

Here just below the prison-castle, we found a young boy dead. He was a shepherd and they killed him. He was twelve, maybe thirteen.

I don't recall any women being killed. Di Palermo was killed in this woman's house, though. He was getting ready to leave for America.

In Bichinello Township, Vincenzo Guarino was mowed down right in the street. He was a Mafia big shot.

This all happens because they're greedy for power. One guy says, "I'm running the show," and another guy says, "Oh no you're not."

Recently, Biagio Figatello was coming out of the barber shop and they got him point-blank. They gave him Easter greetings with both barrels. Then they killed his brother Giovanni. He was coming home from the fields with his kids, and they tried to finish the kids off too, but they ran away. It was figured he talked too much.

Then the executioner of Roccamena got his, with his child, the mule, the dog, and the goat.

They finally got Navarra while he was driving his limousine. They used a Tommy gun from a passing car. Got him and another doctor who just happened to be with him.

Collura got hit at night. The papers are full of the most recent incidents. The Marino brothers: the first on Misericordia Street, at night, with a pistol; the second on a cow path. The father found him after searching half the day.

They shot two sheriff's deputies, but just one died, in the hospital. The other one escaped to America.

Carmelo Lo Bue was the last to go—gunned down by you-know-who.

They were all birds of a feather, but then they started to squabble. I forgot, there was Cammarata, he never worked but he did all right. They killed him in broad daylight, right on his doorstep.

The women scream, the kids bawl: "Blood of my blood, my son . . . A curse on your murderer!" You may know who did it, but you check around to be sure. Then you plot your revenge. "My husband! Me and my children are abandoned!" "Traitors, how will we ever survive?" "Men of no conscience! I have a family! Why couldn't you talk it over?" "Daddy! Daddy! Daddy!" Everybody argues about it and some just let it pass. But hate sinks in and some folk wait for their chance. If you don't get satisfaction, you just wait for your chance.

Right in this house they killed Nicolosi with a rifle. He was chief of staff of the hospital and the Health Plan. Maybe Doctor Navarra was getting itchy . . .

Cacascio's son was killed below the graveyard. Nobody knows why. You can't get to the bottom of it sometimes.

They killed Turiddu Bono in the square, in front of the public toilet, around the time we say the Hail Mary.

They shot Leoluca Mondello at night. Who knows why?

I'm just talking about the ones after the war. Nobody could ever remember them all.

Three of my children died. Three are still living. One daughter died from typhus during an epidemic. Who knows how it came? Maybe it was in the air. The doctors said so anyhow. Or maybe they threw germs in certain places to kill us, to get rid of the opposition. See, they can't stand the people. We guessed it was poison they were spreading because in three, four days, you were dead. It wasn't all over, just in certain neighborhoods. If it was the air, it would've killed them too. How many died? About sixty, I think.

My other daughter died of jaundice, three days sick and she was gone. Maybe it was from fear. The last one was just a baby, two or three months old. I was in the army, so I don't know what kind of death she died of. We can't read or write so there wasn't any mail. I did manage to get a buddy to write a few lines for me, but not much.

If I want to raise livestock, I need connections. You can't raise livestock and be an honest man. I don't have animals, so there's no milk. To have cheese I've got to go out and buy it. That's the way my whole life goes.

The ones who left Corleone went and set up two groups in America. They say Iriteddu became king of the New York underworld. When the heat's on here, they leave and let things cool off. When the case is closed, they come back.

People don't talk. Keeping things secret is a way of life here.

It's the guys in power who kill each other—for the time being, at least. First they had it in for the trade unionists because they gave poor people some direction. They kill to get power or out of self-defense. With all these doings the people get demoralized, paralyzed, I'd say.

They reason things out like this: "I'll get him before he gets me." It's like a race, they're all competing to be the first one to think of it. The people stay out of it and shut up. We just live in fear. We're terrorized so we don't get involved. There's always been a Mafia head. He has a host of friends, under the table, across the board. All over people make believe they're his friends, but deep down we just want to be left alone. Maybe one of them will greet me in the square, but if I give him a cross-eyed look, they might kill me. If you ask me, there's no way to get rid of this way of thinking.

Good kids grow up in fear. The rest want to follow in their footsteps. They want to be one of the rough bunch. The kids play cops and robbers. They hide in cellars or around street corners, ambush each other and shoot away with sticks. "Got you!" "Now I'll finish the job." One'll jump the other and make believe he's blowing his head off. I've seen little kids, lots of times, beating all hell out of each other, and the people just sit there, laughing and egging em on. A few of us'll break it up and tell the kids off a bit, maybe send em home with a boot in the can. But then they get big and turn on you if you give em a hard time.

Among the young people there's those who start to murder to be big shots. The more they murder, the more they can boss the younger kids around. They get real skilled at their trade. Take Pietrino Maiuri, he was twenty when he took part in the killing of Navarra, Russo, and one other guy. The same year he got his too.

During Fascism people were freer to speak. Now, since Fascism fell, the Mafia has free rein. It's even worse than before Fascism. Nobody's free to act, or talk. We were free only during Fascism.

When there's a big dispute, the boss settles everything. "Just stay put," he says to the injured parties, and they do. When families fight over land or money matters, they try to make the peace. Sometimes they try to do as much good as they do harm.

It's hard to raise livestock here, they always get stolen. For us to breed stock, first there's got to be respect for law and order. We need to feel some security, then we'll start to be civil. We need law and order, good country roads and dwellings.

For the time being, Mafia and Church are the same thing. The Church needs them in politics. They get protection from the law through the Church. And the people go crawling to both of em. The Mafia heads here have always supported the Church and its party. The Church uses them to get votes and they use the Church as a front.

There's no sense of humanity here. Everybody's out for himself. "Get out of my way, I was first." Just about everybody thinks that way.

Here's how they think: "Better to run the show than have it run for you. It's always best to be the boss, even if it's only leading the jackass hauling sacks of potatoes." That means it's good to have anybody and everybody under your command, so you can push and shove em where you want. You can even hang em from a tree. They say it's better being boss and having us little guys as their doormat: "What else were these nobodies born for? They don't know their ass from a hole in the ground."

If you show you got balls, the Mafia takes you on, uses you to their ends, and bumps you off. At first the young toughs work with them. But the stronger they get the more they want to go out on their own and have their own show. Then it comes to a collision. A lot of kids choose this career cause they're poor. That makes for a lot of family quarrels. The hell of it is when you look for an honest day's work and can't find it and come home to hungry kids and you go from friend to friend and they're as broke as you are. Then it's total desperation. You're at the end of your rope.

The people say "He deserved it" in three cases: honor, blood, and tragedy. We talked about honor and blood already. Tragedy? That means, say, I have a dispute with X and Y takes advantage of the situation and kills me. X is suspected and winds up in jail. Y, taking advantage of this dispute, is the "author" of the tragedy. In all these cases the people look the other way, it's like it never happened.

If somebody gives the author's name to other people or to the police, most people say, "Finally, the guilty are being brought to justice." But others just wait for the chance to kill the informer. If they arrest a suspect who's really innocent, people send anonymous letters saying who really did it so the wrong guy won't have to pay.

The man matters most in the family. He's the provider, he supports the family and deserves the most respect and love. When a man handles himself well, he's respected among friends. That's if they're good people. They'll even loan him fifty dollars or two acres worth of wheat. As far as other classes of people, the ones who don't mind their business, if you don't take advantage of them when you need something, you're a fool. You're considered a nobody. Then there's the real Mafiosi, or people with such leanings, or their followers—there must be about a hundred in Corleone. Most of us wash our hands of their business, because for them a man's life doesn't mean a damn thing. Fact is, nothing matters. When they kill somebody people say, "Well, at least we didn't have to pay for the midwife." They're used to it. It doesn't make em bat an eye. It's like the first time you go out hunting and bag a rabbit, you're all excited. Then the more you do it, it's no big deal. For them they're the only ones that count. The rest of the world could drop dead. Men go wrong here without a second thought. Money matters a lot here, but a man's worth something only to his family and friends, not to other people.

All this damage done to the people, these endless abuses, are tolerated by the government. If the Ministry of the Interior wasn't in cahoots with them, all this violence could be eliminated. The guys with all the privileges stick together and protect each other. The guys in power stick with the haves. I'm trying to tell you what goes on behind closed doors.

After the war the barons and big landowners wanted to crush the peasant movement, so they set the Mafia up on their estates. But the peasants were unified. They occupied some estates. Then the barons and landowners got together with the priests and sent out the police to arrest the peasant movement. Now squads of police, deputies, rangers, a hundred at least, all occupy the land. It's them who support crime. They protect the Mafiosi and step on the poor. Sure, we make mistakes sometimes, but it's all these forces that keep us from having land and making a living by good hard work.

I just remembered some more.

Baron Mangiameli was picked off his balcony. They wanted his land.

Giovanni Pitarro was shot in '49, but he survived.

Giacomo Moscata was a real gentleman. They killed him in front of the Bentivegna Bar at five o'clock in the morning.

Because of a grudge, they shot Biagio Paternostro and smashed his head in.

Pietro Splendido was a watchman for the contractors building the tunnel. They killed him and bashed his head in, to add insult to injury.

Leoluca Canzoniere was a watchman in Figazzano Township. His co-worker Vincenzo Steva disappeared.

Sometimes before loading they wax the barrels of sawed-off

shotguns, so when they shoot it also sets fire to their target. They get a lot of people that way.

They shot Morello and Giovanni Marino . . . How the hell can I remember them all?

27. A FRIEND OF PLACIDO'S

Placido Rizzotto, Accursio Miraglia (whose story is also included in this book), Salvatore Carnevale (who is written about by Carlo Levi in Words Are Stones) : *these men, among the most extraordinary and courageous of peasant organizers and trade unionists, were assassinated by the Mafia shortly after World War II.*

The friend, with whom I'm speaking at our Corleone center, is a Socialist with some formal education. Forty, he is now a town clerk. Speaking from behind dark-tinted glasses, he is cautious and insinuating. There's something vaguely disturbing about him.

He learned how the Mafia operated through his father, how it was in the service of the rich. When Mussolini came into power, the rich didn't need the Mafia any more so they put his father in jail. He started to develop his own ideas, especially when he saw how his father and some of the relatives still had dealings with the old-time Mafia of Angelo Spatafora while they were supposedly working with Bernardino Verro's cooperative. When he was younger he went to jail too, for six months. I don't know why. Then he joined up with the unions, because he understood that was a way to improve the lot of the impoverished peasants. He was against the system of renting out and taxing land, because the overseer was more of a slave driver than the feudal lord. He insisted that this system had to go and explained why. He learned this from his own experience. His father had been an overseer and never had to do a single day's work. So he saw how the peasants were treated. I'd ask him questions: "How come you're not following in your family's footsteps? You're crossing them, you know." And he'd tell me what the Mafia was up to: murder, abuse of power, the never-ending tale. "I'll croak from hunger before I beg the Mafia for land."

He attacked the people who ran the olive-oil presses because their prices for the pressing were too high and in the over-all production they robbed the peasants blind. Right in the square in front of City Hall he held a heated debate with all these middlemen, and you know in that crowd there's always Mafia. Many a time he'd accompany trade-union representatives into the countryside to look over all the uncultivated land the Mafiosi were hanging on to. Then he had a real confrontation with them in person. It was in the days of rationing and the Mafia ran the warehouses, making all sorts of shady deals on sugar, flour, and pasta. They'd managed to jack up the price of these staples through an arrangement with a town councilor who later was denounced. Well, he took action to have this warehouse taken out of their hands and run by a public agency or by people who understood the needs of the population.

That's why they killed him. He got involved, kept trying to discover the truth, refused to mind his own business. People said he got involved in matters that didn't concern him. The sad irony is, I'd tell him the same thing: "Look, Placido, the sheepskin won't change the wolf." And I'll tell you what he'd say: "In bed, it's always a tug-of-war for the quilt." By that he meant he was against private property. "It's time to end this rat race to earn an easy buck." This is the way he saw it: "If private property as a way of life is eliminated, there won't be any more tug-of-wars." He never went to school. Instead, he studied life. I'd warn him: "Aren't you afraid that they'll kill you?" They'd been killing a lot of trade-union people. It came out to a goodly sum. But the guy was just a dreamer. "They can kill me. It won't solve a thing. People will take my place. Killing me won't stop the trade union." We talked about it a lot because they'd just killed a comrade at Sciacca—name of Miraglia, if I recall.

Let me tell you his dream: "If they kill me, all us hicks'll bring the wrath of God down on them." He believed the peasants would rebel because he always fought for them. But to tell the truth, it didn't turn out that way. He was one hundred percent mistaken. They killed him and nothing happened. He and I were like brothers. We'd have each other over for dinner. We were always together. For about two years after his murder, nobody would even say hello to me in the street. People were afraid to greet me. I had to make sure to be home before sunset. It was like a curfew. I'd peek around the corner before walking up the street . . . But I was telling you what the peasants did. They disappeared, out of fear. It's said, "Whoever serves the people, feeds pigs," and it's true. For Godsake, the alley cats knew who killed him. The motives were blatant. Everybody knew the murderer. A name was on the tip of everybody's tongue and it was the right name.

Frankly, everybody was afraid. I mean everybody. People were saying, "A jug and a stone can never meet on equal terms." The people are the jug. Do I make myself clear? The Mafia's got ways and means. They're organized. Some people think the only way to eliminate them is rising up and resorting to their tactics: the sawed-off shotgun, the rifle. But who carries guns like it was second nature? Not decent people. They don't do this sort of thing. So the other guys always win.

The attendance at trade-union meetings dropped to eight or ten. Then bit by bit it picked up again, partly because they saw the Left was looking out for them, and then again Comrade Siracusa took his place immediately and wouldn't scare off. "They can kill me. People will take my place." Siracusa restored their confidence. He gave them courage to face the danger. Of course, they started coming back because they also needed job lists and any help the trade union could offer.

But there was no public protest. Placido Rizzotto believed we were organized, the people could see right from wrong. The people didn't see a damn thing. You want to know the truth? He could have made a career for himself. He was a sure bet to be elected a regional representative. If it was me I would have gone ahead and set myself up, continuing to be active in politics far from Corleone. But he refused. His head worked different. "Let them kill me. I'll have lived a lot longer than a pig." He never was satisfied with what he did. He felt it was his duty to the trade union and the peasants to give of himself one hundred percent. And still, for him, that wasn't enough.

His father wanted him to pull out for two reasons. First, he understood how real the danger was. "Listen, son, if somebody invites you to come and talk, put it off half-an-hour and come tell me the details." His father understood the whole business, he'd been around. In fact, that March afternoon about four Placido wasn't back yet, so he came to me: "Where did you and Placido go last night?" I just thought he'd still be debating some hot issue, that's natural in politics, so I said casually that he left the trade union with Pasquale Criscione. "Pasquale Criscione, you left Placido alone with him? Christ, they're sure to have him killed." And he burst into tears. "They had some plans to go to Ficuzza or Palermo." "Ficuzza, Palermo, nonsense, they've killed my son." He knew Criscione and all his connections.

Second, his father wanted him to pull out because he spent all his time working for other people and not for himself. He thought his son was too much of a zealot, always involved in business away from home. He couldn't understand his son's way of thinking. He did when it was too late for Placido. Then he saw his son had been for real, so he stepped out into the front line. Even though he was too old by then, he tried to push his son's work ahead. Sure, in part it was a reaction. He wanted revenge for his son, but he wanted to do it legally, through popular support from the Left. After all, his son died fighting for the Left, so out of necessity he sought their support. Then again he'd moved toward the Left before his son died. As soon as they killed him, he joined the Party. He was proud of his son, but he wouldn't say so in public. Just to me. He'd brag about how nobody could ever say he led his son wrong. His only interest was his son's life. There wasn't a day he wouldn't tell him to look around every corner before going up a street, to watch everybody and keep a lookout for shady characters, especially if they were friendly. But Placido'd say, "Everybody respects me, even Doctor Navarra." I heard his father tell him, "Be careful, when the devil courts you,

that means he wants your soul." Placido thought about that and
we talked it over, but I'm not sure if it made much of an impression on him. Of course, his father was obsessed with fear for his
son's life, while Placido went on thinking nobody had any reason
to kill him and that most people loved him as much as he loved
them, even if there were political differences.

Let me give you one example, exactly the way it happened. In
those days there was a shortage of kerosene. Through the trade
union he managed to get a supply of it to distribute to the people.
Of course the people out in the countryside needed it most so they
could tend to their land and herds and light their homes. One
evening this Mafioso—I was telling you yesterday about how he
got killed just around the corner—well, he comes looking for him.
I was with Placido, but the Mafioso called him to one side. When
Placido rejoined me I asked what that guy, a well-known cutthroat, wanted. "He needs some kerosene for his estate." "What
did you say?" "Sure, why not?" "I'd give him arsenic." "All right,
you and me know who they are, but they're out there all in the
dark." He knew how much work it took to keep stables. "They
must be having a hell of a time working by candlelight, and
this way they'll see we're not a bunch of bastards." You know
they went around saying Socialists and Communists were just
out to devour the little guy like wild beasts. "And even if he's a
cutthroat, he needs kerosene." He was so noble, it's like he was a
fool. In the end, to thank him, they threw him in a pit, sixty
yards deep. That's my point of view. He could separate a man's
thoughts and actions, however evil, from his essential human
needs. Maybe people reading this won't believe it, but I've got to
withhold judgment and tell you the simple truth.

He was fair to everybody, even the cutthroats. But if they ever
wanted him to do something that meant selling out on the
workers or the trade union, he'd turn on them like a wolf.

He'd seen lots of things with his own eyes, but his life in the
Resistance really made him aware. He came to Rome as a Parti-
san when I was there in the army. Back here, when we were
trying to organize, he'd refer to the way the Partisans did it and

tell stories all night about Fascism, the German Occupation, the Resistance, the War of Liberation, our victory. When he got back from the war, the Mafia played up to him. He told me he was offered a position as straw boss. But he knew what he wanted to do. I noticed a change in him. Every chance he got, he talked about the evils of Fascism. He wasn't educated, he just knew from experience. He had initiative. He was determined, sure of himself. Decisive and aware of the consequences of his actions. Maybe he was just a happy-go-lucky peasant before, but he was never a fool, he was always sharp. And when he came back, he was a man, he had charisma. At trade-union meetings of a hundred people or more, he'd have them on the edge of their seats, and they'd understand and like what they were hearing.

Fascism stifled Bernardino Verro's dreams of utopian socialism in peasant trade unions. Maybe some of us had an idea of what organized unions could do, but growing up under Fascism, you just weren't allowed to talk about it. If you discussed Bernardino Verro, you risked political internment. So nobody breathed a word. You know how jackasses are. Lead them by the bridle wherever you want them to go. That's the way we were. Older people remembered Verro, talked about him at home, said he did a lot of good. It was hard to make believe he didn't exist. At first he'd been a tailor, then he worked for the town, headed the peasant movement, organized a cooperative, became city manager. At that point they killed him, just like that. He did succeed in dividing up the Zuccarrone estate. That's where he collided with the Mafia. He made real advances and they got scared, so they blasted him with shotguns. (They'd already tried to get him once before when he was sitting in a drugstore on Rome Street.) Everybody knew the house where they killed him, but the cops never asked any questions.

Placido would write letters, agendas, reports. He'd do the drafts, then have me correct the grammar. But he wouldn't let me alter the meaning. The main idea had to be left intact. He'd work out all these plans with facts and figures. Sometimes we had to laugh at him. He envisioned that getting rid of overseers would

mean an increase in production and a reinvestment of capital
that could create more jobs for people. He maintained that you
could reduce the twelve-to-fourteen-hour working day and still
increase the workers' income. He never got tired of debating
these issues.

Did he ever read Karl Marx? He borrowed a book once, but
he put it down after a few pages. He said he didn't have the education to understand it. But still he racked his brains and wore
himself out to make it all real in his own way. Funny though, I
started to suspect that he was doing all this so he wouldn't have
to really work. At any rate, he put it like this: the rich suck the
blood of the poor and put the money in the bank, investing it
just for their own profit instead of creating jobs and producing
for others. He'd argue half the night about how wages would
never improve if things stayed the same. In every discussion he
made the same point. Getting to the core of this matter was his
passion. He was demanding and critical of himself and others:
"It's fine to talk, now let's do something about it." He never
studied books. He had a mind of his own.

So Placido came back from the war, and I'd have to say he was
possessed with the idea of organization, of fighting to unite the
people. It looked like the trade union was functioning, it had a
lot of members, but people were complaining that they were
being robbed. They didn't trust the guy in charge. Naturally
Placido tried to find out if this guy was selling the peasants short.
Well, he was, so they denounced him. He was found guilty and
went to prison, and Placido was nominated right away to take
his place. Of course, now the guy's a syndicalist with the Christian Democracy.

Why exactly did they want to get rid of him? In my opinion,
the local Mafiosi got jumpy because Placido was getting to the
heart of our problems. He had a hand in city government, and
the people looked to him as a spokesman. They saw the people
were with him, that he was loved. Everybody knew that the
Socialists wanted him to run for regional representative. But he
declined. Lawmaking wasn't his field: "Who needs me to warm

another seat?" The Mafia saw the writing on the wall. They knew that he was sharp and knew their ins and outs. Besides, he was up-front, and as his father's son, he was in a position to hang their dirty laundry outside. They saw he was a real threat.

If they didn't have enough proof already, they saw he was dead serious when the Partisans came to town. It was something to see those young guys and hear them all singing. They came in a truck and stopped in the square. One of them went to look for Rizzotto. It was late afternoon and the square was packed. The Mafiosi were there too, checking up on anybody who might be passing through, or who had a new suit on, or who wasn't there that day. There isn't a stone they want to leave unturned. Well, these Partisans are mostly students and they mill around asking embarrassing questions. You can guess what happened. This group of Mafiosi was standing around, not more than twenty-five yards away, and they put the local students up to harassing the Partisans: "Hey look, we got some Russian spies in town." (That's the same thing they were saying about Rizzotto, and he couldn't even find Russia on the map.) Naturally the Partisans got their backs up. They weren't one bit frightened by our local punks. In fact, they slapped them around. Things got a little rough—let's say it was a free-for-all. That's when Rizzotto showed up. He throws himself smack into the middle of the brawl and tries to act the peacemaker: "What kind of hospitality is this? These people fought our war. They deserve respect," and so on. He urged them all to calm down. The punks backed off and he stayed there with the Partisans, but he understood the ground rules and knew nothing had been settled yet. After a while he escorted them to the edge of town and said good-bye, but the hecklers were laying in ambush around a bend a hundred and fifty yards up ahead. They shout out insults. The truck stops. More words. Then things really got out of hand. Slapping, punching, kicking, you couldn't tell who was who. Finally Placido arrives to break it up, and he has no other choice but to tear up a stake from a vineyard nearby and start swinging it to scare off the locals. To tell the truth, he did more than a little damage because the stake still had some

barbed wire on it. There happened to be this little Mafioso with
the contingent. I should add he was thirty-four or thirty-five, and
he got a few good licks from Placido too. Well, in town the
word spread quick: "You see, Rizzotto's a Russian spy, or else
why would he fight with them against us?" For a number of
weeks after the confrontation, the young guys in the trade union
would escort him home, but finally it was Placido who told them
to forget it, nobody would dare do a thing. That's what he said.
I guess they would have killed Placido anyway, but that whole in-
cident was the straw that broke the camel's back. He really never
indulged in personal attacks. Instead he tried to root out the
Mafia by dividing up the land fairly.

He was a true friend. I loved him. He had absolutely no super-
stitions. He saw the Church as useful insofar as it checked man's
perverse instincts and taught him how to behave in a civilized
way. But his criticism of priests cut deep: "If the poor acted like
the priests, we'd all be damned to hell." To him they were a
bunch of spongers, they had no shame. He opposed the Church's
political and economic policies. He thought their job was
awakening personal conscience and social consciousness. But he
worked with the priests as chairman of the committee for the
Feast of the Madonna della Rocca. He tried to open the feast to
the public, without any charge for admission: music, films, activities for all the citizens out in the street.

"I have a mind of my own," this is how he saw and expressed
it. "It doesn't matter if I believe or not. I'm not hurting anybody. I'm committed to trying to do some good. I don't need the
fear of God's judgment to do it. Some people do and they thrive
on guilt, but that's OK, that keeps them honest." He didn't accept
the dogma. He didn't believe, period. He respected everybody's
right to be free to believe the way they wanted to, but he never
went to mass. Maybe you shouldn't write that down or else people
will think he was an animal. He wouldn't go into church except
for those committee meetings. He'd get impatient with the church
bureaucracy: "Damn, let's give all this money to the kids at the
Salvatore"—that's the orphanage. "Let's stop wasting it."

Let's take an overview. Most people go to church so as not to be criticized. If you go against tradition, it's a sin. Me, I don't go to church. The priest tells my kids, "Bring your father along." "Hey, Dad, how come you don't come with us to church?" "I do, I sit in the back. It's just that he doesn't notice." That way I try to educate my children right. Look at it this way. The environment we live in is what it is. Nowadays nobody'll bring your children up for you, not the community or any other institution. You're free to choose not to baptize your children. But are you really free? I live in this environment. I have to conform, especially if I want a job. It's that way for everybody, especially the peasants, if they want land or work. If you don't like it, you got to go. "Eat your soup or go for a loop." Lots of people go to church without believing in beans. Today they murder and tomorrow in the procession they carry the Madonna. "Jesus, Mary, and Joseph, what a host of good Catholics!" It's a hoax. They're all thieves, murderers, desperados. It's all camouflage, they put on charades for the Madonna and when their bellies are full they forget about the poor girl.

Almost none of us have any faith left in our representatives, but we go right on voting. If somebody's down on the ground, you trample them and stir up the old mud puddles. It's always the same old dirty water.

The rich people and the Church are afraid they'll lose their power if things change. The poor trust in nothing. There's absolutely no hope. I try to keep in touch with the people. That way I've come to understand that the rich want to keep the world the way it is. They'll do anything to maintain the status quo. It's all at their disposal, the political parties and the Mafia. Then again they have their private clubs, where they can play cards and bad-mouth each other. They resort to violence over a Scotch-and-soda. And the local government, even though it's leftist now, just lets them run wild. "The shotgun is the law. Why should I get my head blown off?"

The Church is perfection itself, at least that's what *they* say. The Church zooms in mostly on kids. They'll stop at nothing.

They hold on to power with a design, not to maintain the status quo, but actually to regress. Look, I'm not making this up. They say so themselves, in public: "The Lord's creation must not be tampered with. By sending things to the moon, the Russians are in mortal sin. Divine creation must be left as it is." To want change, something new, is a sin. Development is perdition. Of course, they can use TV to promote their ideas, no matter how antiquated and stagnant they might be.

Just talk to day laborers and peasants, they'll tell you, they used to believe things could change. But nowadays most of them have stopped believing in anything. There was hope just after the war: lots of promises, not much action. Now they're apathetic, mistrustful. They see how weak they are. A lot of poor people say, "I've got to survive, so whose elbows do I rub? To scrape something up, I've got to stick with the rich guy."

It was different with Placido. He wanted them to organize themselves, on their own initiative, but they needed proof first that things would change if they pushed themselves. Then maybe they would have believed him. Instead their heads got all twisted inside. See, the establishment's propaganda is just too effective. Tell somebody what's really good for him, and he still won't believe you if he doesn't have his own proof.

Placido believed men could work together and produce better things. So he urged everybody to unite through cooperatives. In a town like this we've got shotguns on the brain. You're always watching out to see who's armed. So the saying "There's strength in unity" has a very special meaning. If you talk to a guy you don't trust one hundred percent, you never say exactly what you're thinking. It's a complex mechanism, this business of conversation. For example, X will ask me something about Y. But I'll never state my real opinion because you never know. One bad word and X will be cooking up the tragedy already, planning to go see Y tomorrow and tell him I called him a bastard or something. Of course, with me he'll be all smiles, nodding his head, sure, sure, making believe it's nothing, or agreeing with me wholeheartedly. The whole conversation becomes a performance.

All of life here is a play. We know each other well. You know how the other guy thinks, but you've got to act dumb. You've got to be on your guard all the time and weigh every word. *You* tell *me,* is this kind of life worth living?

Because of this phenomenon, the few people who want to do something for the community are blocked, stifled, wiped out. We lose all our focus. It's all clouds of vicious words, gossip in the squares, hot air in the assembly, blather in the courts. We're all scared. Some show it, others don't. A few of us flex our muscles, but inside we're all jelly. We've been burned and not just once or twice. Just try to find here in Sicily one single conviction for a crime committed against a union organizer. When Judge Marcataio came to investigate the disappearance of Rizzotto, I was afraid certain interested parties would find out everything I said right away. As you write all this down, do you know what's going through my mind? You took my name down, OK? And let's say they call you to the telephone and ambush you. Then the cops come to investigate and find my name on this document. You can guess the rest.

Placido realized that everything in this sink was going putrid. It's all stagnant like a swamp, rotten. Only insects breed, and epidemics. Everything gets polluted. "We don't have to be beasts forever. The time will come when people will open their eyes." That's what Placido said. His commitment was to make things move forward and develop. How can I judge him? He's dead. But that means he was wrong. At least that's my gut reaction. Still, from another angle, you had to admire Placido for his ideals. He worked heart and soul to better humankind. But I keep hearing this echo: "It comes down to the fact that they killed him. He's dead and buried." To avoid any repercussions, they'd planned to kill him outside of town and dispose of him in the Roccabusambra Pit. Even the crows wouldn't smell anything and flock there. That way the whole thing would still be in the dark.

I guess we all learned a lesson. The trade union suffered a real shock, but then it bounced back as strong as before Placido came. To be honest though, it's achieved absolutely nothing and the people just crumbled. They stopped following us . . . Why did that poor guy have to die? Maybe I'm just selfish . . . See, we were friends . . . I don't know anything any more . . . All that the peasants who followed Placido had to do was pick up one quarter-pound rock per man and they could have annihilated that whole pack of Mafiosi. But they didn't do it. When the Mafia killed him, they vanished. Of course, they loved him when they needed his help: job lists and a fair share of produce. Then they flocked to Placido, and he never acted without listening and trying to educate them politically. He'd have everybody speak their mind, and he'd try to get even the most resigned to participate. He never rode his own bandwagon. He tried to share his ideas with others and have others do the same.

This is the way I see it. Still, it's all confused in my mind. I know there'll never be any development without more people like him. But who knows? . . . One thing I'm sure of, I loved him. Children die every day, and they kill anybody who takes steps to change the situation. What can we do? If one part of the body is diseased, the whole organism has to be cured. The only real remedy is good blood, circulating everywhere. The infected parts don't heal by themselves. That's the way I feel, but who knows?

If you could live without lying all the time, that would be paradise on earth. Am I too pessimistic? Let me tell you how it happened. Placido had worked all afternoon. Then he went out for a walk. Around nine, that certain individual dropped by. For five minutes we hardly noticed him, we were so busy, but he kept trying to make jokes and strike up a conversation. We had to do some shopping, so we excused ourselves. He follows us. We head for home. He says he'll help us with the bundles. We can't refuse. We get to my house first and I say good-bye, unawares. The town is full of people. Placido and this individual descend toward the square. Two men come out of a bar and tail them. They get closer and stick guns in his back. He stops and asks them what they want. This all happens in the middle of the square, at market time. It's March. By now the days are long.

It's nice weather, everybody's outside. Suddenly nobody's in the square. It's deserted. All the shutters slam. He has no choice. He accepts their invitation to come and have a chat. Dozens of people see them pass by. Where are the cops? "Nobody sees nothing." They lead him up the winding steps from Bentivegna Boulevard to Saint Rocco Street. Two more men are waiting in ambush. Then he gets the message and tries to escape, running up the right-hand stairway. He gets to the top and two more guys trap him, throw a blanket over his head, crush him like he was grapes, carry him twenty yards or so, and throw him in a waiting car. They take off. He shouts for help. Nobody'll even dare to say they heard it.

Is it right for a man to die for people who play deaf, dumb, and blind when they kill him?

I can't bear my agony, do you know why? The people could have saved him. Why didn't they run to help? Why did they let them kill him?

28. SALVATORE

We are talking for two hours in some fields near Camporeale.
Sixty, bent by work like the ancient Sicilian hoe, this illiterate
peasant struggles and finds a means to express profound values
of his culture.

A re things "basted" around here? What do you mean? Oh, you said "wasted." OK, now I understand. You don't mean "basted" cause around here the women do that to patch things up.

Waste, huh . . . You mean like letting things go to seed? Yeah, we do that plenty. The broccoli shrivels all up, a nice blood-orange falls and rots. It's all wasted because we can't sell them. Flat out on the ground they start dying. They can't be sold when they're rotten.

I go out and milk the cow, and then the calf comes up to her mother and wants to suckle and gets so hepped up she kicks the pail over and it's all spilled milk.

Peaches come into season and at first they hang just right. But when they droop, an animal can nibble at them, or the bugs get to them and they fall on the ground. So they're a waste.

Also, if an animal gets sick and dies on you, you can't use the meat, so you burn him.

Tomatoes get sick too, with black-blight, ash-blight, oil-blight. And then there's ants. The fruit falls and goes rotten. Plants go bad and rot—like animals. And humans too.

I can't think of any other kinds of waste in the country.

What about water? Well, yeah, water carries disease. People and animals get sick from it, because it's full of sand and the sand carries the disease to the kidney and makes stones in the liver. Through diseases you get waste—of money too.

Then there's fruit the worms bore into. You can't sell it so you throw it out.

That's about it for ways things are wasted . . .

Wait a minute, you know I never thought about it much before. Say you work hard on something for a whole year and it turns out bad. That's a waste worse than death.

And we work out in the fields and our clothes get all worn out. Then we throw them away . . .

Do we talk things over at home? Like earning and saving money? We don't have to. It's obvious. Instead of working in the fields like an ignorant peasant, if you can buy and sell for profit, it's much better. You sell whatever you can come by, fruit, greens, snails, so at least you can have a roof over your head.

Say you buy some fruit, but can't manage to sell it, four or five days and no luck. So you've got to throw it out. That's real waste. That's the way it goes with a lot of stuff, if you can't sell it.

Well, that's the story about farming and bartering. Those are the two arts I know. You got it all in black and white.

29. ANTONIO

*Born in Trappeto of a long line of great fishermen (many of
whom emigrated to San Pedro, California, and fished from
three-masted salmon trawlers in the seas of Alaska), this
thirty-year-old virtual illiterate embodies the best of the local
culture. Given the occasion to express himself, he wants to
respond with epic generosity by giving me the fruits of his
expertise in classical archaeology. We are sitting on the beach
near Marinella's port.*

When you flash the light, the fish just about jump straight
out of the water. Then they hang there just below the
surface in the spotlight. They're beautiful, peaceful, gentle
as lambs. You can tell they're fat and their flesh is solid.
See, the light warms the water up for them—it's like wintertime
with a touch of good weather or sitting around a fire. There's
always a big rush for the light. They dart and splash and leap
to get there. Then they all bunch up in one school and puff out
their gills.

But here's the problem. At Sciacca, just to mention one place,
there's about a hundred motor fishing boats, and every boat
carries sixteen, eighteen men, and they all go out at night to
comb the sea with two or three dinghies and the spotlight. And
then there's the bombs. The fishermen bring crates, kerosene,
gauze, carbide, and eight to ten pounds of clay and stones to use
as weights.

This is how you make a bomb. You take two dynamite sticks
from a thirty-stick keg (every boat has one), and put your explosives in a can, pack em in nice and tight with the fuse and
the cap. Then you cover the can with a piece of wax paper and
seal it all with the clay, so water don't seep in and ruin the
powder. Then you pack stones and more clay all around it again.
Every fishing boat going out at night carries a cargo of about

a hundred bombs. They want to be ready for anything. Of course, the poorer fishermen don't carry that many. Dynamite costs twenty-five dollars a keg.

Depending on your fishing rights, you station yourself out there at sea. When the fish start to crowd together and you can see there's maybe a ton and a half packed so tight you'd think it was a net, you throw the bomb . . . When things die down again you can see the whole school. Some are just floating, some are staggering like they're drunk, others are thrashing all around —see, their backs get broken—but all of em go limp and flabby. You won't find any left with nice solid flesh. The ones closest to the explosion just die and drift away with the current. All the little ones are dead too.

You destroy many more than you catch. Besides, the little ones never get the chance to grow up. Look at it this way, you drop a bomb in this port and maybe us older guys'll survive, but those kids out there diving from the rocks'll all die. Don't kid yourself. There's a hundred boats and each one destroys four to six tons. Add that up and see what it comes to. There's times one boat alone kills off tens of tons. I'm sorry to say I know it from experience. When we throw these explosives into the sea even the water gets destroyed. The water gets all troubled, mud churns up, you can see where the fuse burns all the way to the bottom. Then it goes whoosh! It doesn't exactly blow up. Sure, people far away hear a nice big boom, but if you're up close you hear this hiss-and-whoosh. Then the water divides because the force of the explosion shoots the water out every which way. It all goes flying into the air—water, mud, and fish—and comes plunging down again. When the water finally clears up, you see the whole wreck.

Fish aren't born to travel alone, so when it's dark they all crowd together in schools. Maybe they're a little bit afraid in the dark. Even if their backs are broken they stay near the light cause they like it. I'll bang on the side of the boat to scare em off, but they'll keep coming back just like humans when they're in shock from a broken back. Finally, you cast the net and haul them in.

But you miss a lot of them. You just leave fish dead all over the place. For as far as fifty yards you'll see dead fish. They disappear with the current and we can't get them because we're anchored six yards deep.

All during the night you see fishing boats on the move, some along the shore, others out to sea. From the shore you'll hear that ba-ba-boom! If you're out there you hear the rumbling under the prow and whoosh! You think the boat's gonna split right in two, like a shark or some sea monster's attacking the boat. You know how they attack. They see a shape, it might be a dead fish or a dog or a human, and they shoot for it with jaws wide open. Off the coast near Selinunte a shark attacked Francesco Russo's boat and pulled him under with it. When they salvaged the boat they found a whole set of teeth imbedded in the wood. Sure, most of em were broken, but one was still whole. The shark must've weighed more than a ton.

Sometimes dolphins'll attack the nets and tear em apart and devour everything, fish, nets, and all. So you throw bombs at them, making sure they go off in the air. There's a deafening explosion that echoes all over the bay and the dolphins take off. The flesh of the dolphin's like human flesh. It's not good to eat, just too oily. Like us, we're made up of a little blood, a little meat, and mostly grease. You cut the dolphin open with one good rip and it shoots blood, three gallons' worth. It's like us, all blood and oil. Not much meat. But the way fish are, they don't squirt blood.

When there's no full moon, it's a hundred motor fishing boats and three hundred dinghies. Every dinghy has about half-a-dozen bombs to use with the spotlight. Just figure it out, you get the average, but a lot of boats use so many bombs, you'd think it was a war. I hear at Terrasini a man blew himself to smithereens with all his sons. This guy from Mazara had the cap blow up in his hand. His hand got blasted away just like that. The new-born fish all die off, there's no chance they'll survive, and the spawn on the bottom, every single egg, all the little ones die off.

If you go out fishing in a regular boat, it's hopeless. The

motorboats bomb the sea and the fish all scare and stay at the bottom close to an hour. You keep shining the light and they start to surface. Then another bomb explodes and they disappear again. The port authorities forbid bombs on board, consequences are they'll confiscate your boat. Sometimes they come on board to search you. But they leave the big shots with fleets of motorboats alone. Certain agreements are made.

When the sea's calm you can haul in some of the dead fish, but just test em out to see if they're still good. They're like rubber or mud, so you throw them back into the sea.

I've also done fishing at Terrasini, Trappeto, Castellammare. There they don't use too many bombs. At least they don't destroy the sea like we do here. Sure, if they spot a school of sardines or fish like that, the kind common folk eat all over Italy, they'll cut loose their bombs. Otherwise they just fish. But the big motorboats come from Palermo for the spawn. They use these special kind of nets as tight as cheesecloth. The nets are so tight water hardly passes through, and they haul in the eggs and the minnows that are smaller than a needle-head. They don't even have scales yet. They haul them all in so the fish go to waste because they never get a chance to grow up. That way you have a real shortage. Then there's a special kind of trawling net that catches or kills all the eggs and babies too. So there's not many fish left. They just go to waste. Same with baby shrimp, what's left of them. See, fish like to eat them, but when they're finished with their nets it's like a forest fire's passed through. There's nowhere else to go for food so the fish give up and disappear. They don't lay their eggs there any more. There's nothing left to eat, so they migrate somewhere else.

Here at Marinella there's about sixty of us with rowboats. I know the coast up as far as Mazara, Marsala, Trapani. Here, especially at Mazara, they destroy tons and tons of fish with potassium. They get it ready-made. You throw out your nets, row around sprinkling the potassium in a circle and when it's spread a bit, start to haul in the fish. They can't escape because there's a ring of poison. For months after that it stinks so bad, no fish'll come near the place. It's so strong we get sick, but it's worse for the fish, just like poison gas. Take my tobacco here, you and me hardly notice the smell, but that stuff's like spot remover. It gets rid of stains on cloth, but for fish it's deadly acid. They won't come back for months. It takes tidal waves to get rid of that stink. The stuff comes from China, or maybe hell. It comes in little chunks a bit bigger than liver pills. It dissolves right away and the sea gets all white. It looks like lime, and the fishes' eyes get red and they can't see where they're going. After you bomb, the fish stay away for two or three days, but use this poison and it's months the fish are gone unless there's a real bad storm. All it takes is one time where people go to fish, and whole villages go hungry. What they do then is try it in different parts of the sea, but that way they've destroyed all the eggs.

From Partinico to Castelvetrano it's about eighty miles by land. By sea it's more than one-twenty, all a complete swamp. If you watch from the shore at night, everything's lit up so nice you'd think it was a regatta, and instead it's us who are butchering and skinning each other. You throw a bomb and I'm out of work. It's all a waste, all those treasures destroyed at sea. Hundreds of boats used to head for Selinunte and fish in Marinella Bay. Nowadays even our own fishermen are just landlubbers, because the sea is worse than a sewer. It's nothing but a floating graveyard, and we have to find other ways to support our families.

There's no cemetery at Marinella or Selinunte, so when somebody dies we take him to the station and send him to Castelvetrano. Then us fishermen stick together. We pay our respects to the strickened family. "He was a good man. It's a real loss, he had lots of good years ahead of him." Then we go off to tend to our business in the port, but we never stop talking about the deceased and for three whole days we don't go out to fish. And close relatives or friends feed the mourners' families for at least a week.

See, somehow you've got to survive. What do people do where they can't earn enough to feed their families? You get by as best as you can. All around Selinunte, Gela, Segesta, Solunto, Agrigento, if you don't have work, you go tomb hunting at night. Sure, it can rattle you, down in there looking for valuables, groping around in the dark. Dead bodies don't mind a thing, but then again why should I disturb them? See, I rush to steal whatever they got and get a move on. I'm so terrorized I snatch an arm or a leg, and what right do I have to intrude on his peace and quiet? He's sealed in so tight there between all those slabs, not even the air can get to him. Many a time you'll find the skeleton in one piece, though sometimes it's all broken up. In the old days they put little bottles in there with the corpse, amphoras they called them, and little painted dolls, oil lamps, cups, jewel boxes, clay pots, statues, silver rings.

Even then there was rich and poor. They left that stuff with you so you wouldn't have to start from scratch in case you came back to life. I've found fruit bowls and bracelets, always made of bronze, and rings made of terracotta. You climb down with a flashlight, the whole six feet under. It's spooky, let me tell you, especially when you're all alone and you run across a skeleton. It takes guts to touch it. Some places they dig with tractors and unearth tombs. There's thousands of abandoned tombs in those places they call necropolises. You start to learn if a tomb is nicely made or if it's just slapped together. Some tombs are gold mines. In others you won't find fifty dollars' worth of stuff. But you do find really wonderful things, even knights still decked out in their armor. Hundreds of us folk live off these tombs.

Sure, we all have dreams. I dream I'll find a real treasure, but all I ever find is a bunch of little bottles and stuff like that. Of course, some people don't appreciate these little things and being ignorant they just smash them up because they're disappointed at not finding real treasure. Me, I'm experienced, so when I excavate I can judge how many layers of tombs there are. There can be as many as seven or eight, one on top of the other. Of course, when you get down in there real deep, a lot of things can happen. You dig and the whole thing can cave in and you're stuck in the bowels of the earth. When the ground starts to go from under you the fear is worse than death. It takes real guts to stay there with the earth caving in, you have no idea how deep it is. You get terrified but have to say to yourself, "No, there's no such thing as black magic." As much experience as you've had, you get frightened just the same, but then you can really discover things. Digging ten to fifteen yards deep you'll find the lowest room. That's for the first one that died. Then you start back up seeing how they buried the rest of them in layers, a half-a-dozen or so more, till you get back to six feet under.

You work with iron crowbars, the steel-tipped kind. The slabs are real thick. The first hole you make through the top slab takes a good bit of tapping, so when you get to the first body it's been rattled around from the force of the blows. The bodies get so shook up sometimes, you'd think they were coming back to life. Still, I've found skeletons in one piece, but always naked.

For ten years now people around here've been making a living this way. It's hard work, though, going down there. It gets so hot you could suffocate. It must be being closed up so long that does it. Sometimes a few of us work together, and when we open up a tomb the smell's so strong we have to take a five-minute breather—even before going down. Of course, all it takes is one hole. Then you check how deep it is with the flashlight and let yourself drop down in.

As I'm going down into a tomb, I say to myself, "What am I robbing this guy for? I don't even know who he is." Of course, you know when it's a woman. I don't need my wife to tell me what it means when you find needles and thimbles. "Poor woman," I think to myself. I really know I'm in a grave. "What if her husband shows up? What would he do if he caught me robbing his wife? Don't worry, he's dead. But what about his spirit?" He'd dig my grave for me, no doubt.

Scared as we are, we don't really believe that the husband'll ever come back. We're much more worried about our companions getting to a good tomb first. It's first come, first serve. Find it, and it's yours. Of course, if you're down in there working and another guy suddenly appears, that's what really makes you jump. It gives you the creeps, scares you half to death. You've got to stop and remember he's human like you, on the same job. Still, we all work on our own. Four or five hours of digging and you can fill a whole sack. Like fishing, it's all a matter of luck.

A lot of times they have tractors turn the earth over. But being experts in tombs, we don't even need that. All we need is crowbars. The authorities go excavating too, but they never find the good things. In fact, they hardly find anything. We know more than the authorities and we always get there first. Besides, they don't really give a good goddamn about us, not the dead or the living. Us, we have to feed our children, buy new nets, repair our boats.

I do this work at night. I'd prefer doing it daytime. I'm good at it now and I'd like to give the things I find to the government. Instead of selling it for next to nothing to the Americans, the French, the Germans, or the English, I'd like to give it to Italy. They could pay me by the day and both of us would profit. It's as simple as that.

30. UNCLE FELICE

*This seventy-year-old illiterate peasant now lives on the edge of
Sambuca, a town overlooking the lake formed by the Carboi Dam.*

I lived there all my life. I had animals too, with twelve acres
of land and a little vineyard. I planted trees. They grew tall.
I had every kind, even hazelnut. Walnut, poplar, plenty of
willows, and I had a four-room farmhouse with stables and a
barn (big as from where we're sitting to that fire over there) and
it had a cellar with a big vat for crushing grapes. There was a
courtyard and we even had a shed. Baron Planeta owned this
farm at first. Then he sold it cause it was just a nuisance to him,
and being we liked the place, we paid him the price he wanted.
About forty years I spent there, with my brother. We bought
cows and settled right in. There wasn't much growing except
weeds and I did all the planting. I'd hunt up saplings and replant
em, and keep the ground around em hoed and weeded. That
helps em grow. There was fig trees too, and each year I'd pick
almost five hundred pounds. The river was nearby and it kept
things nice and cool so the trees did just fine, they were no
trouble at all. And we always had chickens.

One day some surveyors came by. They were talking up a
storm as they got to my farm. They told us they were surveying
the land, O.K.? How're we supposed to know it was for this here
lake? Then I heard the word spreading around town. "They're
going to make this lake." There was all this gossip. Not having
any way to put up a fight, we started to get a bit wary. The
word kept getting passed around, but we just couldn't believe
it. We never seen anything like it before. Folks with land wanted
to go and get out the shotgun, but somehow we just couldn't
muster it. You understand, we never seen such a thing. Why
would anybody want to just swallow up all this land?

Well, they show up with papers to expropriate all the property
in these parts that are supposed to be under water from now on

in. They had this paper all printed, they called it a "settlement contract," and we just had to sign. But it didn't have no facts or figures. "Whether you sign or not, the reservoir's going through." We complained. We suspected we'd have to pay through the nose. "Whether you sign or not, this land belongs to the State now." Almost everybody signed. I was one of the last. They gave me a statement of accounts and I signed. But money? Not a cent. They just pushed you into signing.

When they came to build the utility road, we all went out to the highway and sort of sat around. If they didn't have a utility road, they couldn't start building the dam. That's what we were thinking. Once you have a road you can deliver the materials you need to build the dam. That's what we didn't want happening. But then the cops came and we couldn't budge or else they'd of jumped us and they were armed. We had to be careful or they'd of killed us, that's their job. They had a paddy wagon full of men and some squad cars too. The whole force came along, even the chief. So we had to stay out of their way. They outnumbered us. "All right now, stand back. Make way. Beat it." They had pistols, rifles. You couldn't even count them, all those workers and trucks and officials on the job. There was hundreds of em making this wall. It was so wide a truck could cross it. What could one man do about it? Kill them all? They were draining our lifeblood and we couldn't think straight. Deep down inside we all had this uneasy feeling.

The machines did everything, mixed cement and poured it out, in that dam. All those machines, busy doing this that and the other thing, day and night, mixing and pouring. And the wall kept rising, wide like it was, a hundred yards long, even longer. Every day we came and watched, they went higher and higher, way up there. They'd set charges and blow all the stones to smithereens, but day by day the wall got higher. From our house you could always see across the valley as far as the big crack in the mountain, but bit by bit all you could see was wall.

Then one day water started to collect around the base of the wall. It was wintertime. The water kept spreading, rising. The people closest to it were losing land every day. They had to start moving off a bit. Little by little, this puddle got bigger. With every rain, the water rose and as it kept coming, people'd cut their trees down and cart em off, at least the ones they could get to. They lost quite a few, though, cause the water'd rise so quick. One night they'd go to bed with trees and next morning they'd be gone, under water. We couldn't believe it'd happen so fast, so we planted grain that year and it all went under and got washed away. It would of made real good bread, we even used a tractor to plow.

Before we knew it, the water was a lake. We could of worked that land at least twice a year and . . . well, I guess I was just too tied to the land and the place, so I hung on. But the water got so high that my nephews had to come and get me, or else I'd of been stranded. See, the house sat on top of a little hill and you could look down at the water all around you. It was becoming a little island with the water swirling around. Other folks watched it rising and kept saying, "Someday soon Uncle Felice will be under water for good." So they came to get me, but I held my ground. I was worried about the cows, you understand. So my nephews herded em up and drove em off, and I decided to go too. What else could I do? Just sit and watch the house?

Well, I kept watching it, but from here, where you and me are sitting. You could still see how it was if there wasn't so much water. Day by day it kept rising, a yard or two, always rising, till you didn't see nothing but the roof.

Then all you could see was the tops of the olive trees, and one lone walnut. Then it was all water. The more it rains, the more there is.

We were stuck, no land and no money. If and when they paid you at all, they gave you the price of second-grade land, about $225 an acre. Or else they decided it was third-grade, $190 per acre. One year they paid us the interest, five percent of the expropriation price. We're still running all over the place trying to collect, but they keep telling us we need this or that document. That way they've worn us down and broke our spirit. Of course, when they took the land, they didn't have to hunt up the deeds, but now they send us to Agrigento, Palermo, Sciacca. It's four years we've been fighting this battle. Last year they gave us seventy-five percent on half the value of the land. But the lawyer we had got fed up with the whole business, all that running around in search of papers. He dropped our case.

All in all there was 760 acres. More than two hundred families had their land buried by this lake. And we're just stuck. We don't have land, that's what we need to live. But nowadays for land close to town they're asking five thousand dollars an acre. If it's got trees on it they want two thousand for a quarter of an acre, that comes to eight thousand the acre. Sure, everybody who got their money quick went out and bought new land. They saw how much we needed it, so they went and hiked up the prices.

Now, whenever it strikes their fancy, they send us tax bills on the land and the houses under water. And we fork the money over, unless we're flat broke. Then they send the bailiff to take possession of all your belongings. They tried it on me once, they were going to take everything, so I scraped up the cash, God knows where. They've been forcing people to pay taxes on the land under water for about ten years now.

I did have half an acre left above water but they cut a new road right through. And they haven't given me a nickel. Then there's this other piece of land my father and mother left me, but I have to show proof of ownership to the authorities before I can use it. Our family's had it for more than a century and we don't have the papers on us, so we go to all the records offices and they take their sweet time and never find a blessed thing. You go to Agrigento, they tell you, "The deed must be in Palermo." You go to Palermo: "But they should have it in Sciacca." You go to Sciacca: "It's got to be in Agrigento." Or go to collect: "We're out of funds." They want me to produce papers a hundred, maybe two hundred years old. And I can't even read and write. Me and my brother, we were always close, we always worked together helping each other out as best we could. But this time he up and died of grief. When they grabbed up our property and drowned it, he couldn't bear it. Now there's my nephew who looks after things for us.

One day about a hundred of us met in Sambuca and decided to go see the chief of police. He told us to stay put, he'd send off a telegram. A few days later a lawyer and a surveyor came and handed out some checks. So we had a little cash.

But without land we had to sell the cows. Now we work as tenant farmers right on this land you see here. We divide everything we produce with the boss . . .

We had a well and our water was a joy to drink. All the neighbors came by for a drink. It was beautiful, spring water. We had enough for everybody. They came from all over just to taste it.

We had nut trees. I transplanted them all. I'd find saplings all over and ask the owners' permission, then dig them up. We had cherry trees, sweet and sour.

Down the road there was a mill with three grindstones. The surveyor told the miller he'd get a special deal. The miller and his family had put a lot of work into the place. They made the house bigger and added a loft and an attic and a barn with fourteen stalls so that when you came to grind you could leave your animals protected. All the time they were doing tests, those technicians would joke with him: "We can't wait to see Serafino propping his feet up on the desk and puffing a big cigar," meaning he'd be getting a bunch of money. Well he did, about as much as he spent for the lawyer: $750. Anyway, as the water kept on rising and finally reached the front door, those wheels kept grinding. It's not that they were making flour, they just didn't have it in them to leave the place. Then the whole mill caved in and nothing was left standing but the bridge. I mean the one with five arches where you used to cross to get to the mill. Now down there under water the wheel just keeps on turning, and when the miller's wife goes to work in the fields she turns her back so as not to see it. Fifty years she was there. When they had to leave she was shrieking so bad you'd of thought they killed her husband. Fifty years back they found it all in a shambles and bought it from the prince of Camporeale and put it into shape and smooth-running order with their very own hands. They wouldn't leave it till it was halfway under. She kept crying and throwing herself in the mud. They were up to their knees in water. There was only two ways to go, down or out. To this day they have dreams that the stone's still grinding.

Well, by now the dam's a hard cold fact. There's no way to get rid of it. When the water gets low in summer, an olive branch appears. It's like my landmark, but you can't see the roof, it's all caved in. I didn't want to cut that olive tree down. It was my favorite, and we thought maybe if the water went down, we'd have some fruit to pick. We even left the doors on the house, in case . . . Of course now, down there on the bottom . . . All you can see is a pile of stones.

We stayed till the last minute. When I was knee-deep in water, my nephew hauled me out with the mules. There was so much water the doors could hardly open. Later the roof beams floated to the surface but they didn't drift away. Two or three days later the water dropped a bit and we were hoping that . . . But the earth was a sea of mud, there was nothing you could do to prop anything back up and it started to rain again. A real storm burst and there was nothing else to do.

We don't have land. It's all taken up and nobody wants to rent. We don't have money to buy. Baron Tumminelli was selling some land, but we didn't have a red cent.

They say you can see houses some days, but my eyesight's going on me.

ENDURANCE

31. AN INDUSTRIALIST

Giuseppe Gulì, forty-five, comes from an old artisan family in Palermo that still tries to do good work and honest business.

Our grandfather was a dynamo. He gave birth to our enterprise. He was an artisan, a silk-weaver. He wove a lot of the tapestries and damasks of Mazzarino Palace. In fact, the Countess Mazzarino had him summoned. When he finished the job she was so pleased she not only paid him but gave him the loom. That's how the industry got started. With a loom, my grandfather could work on his own. Then he started to commission other weavers to do piecework. That way he created a nucleus of artisans on High Wall Street near Carini Gate.

In 1891, when the International Artisans' Fair came to Palermo for the first time, my grandfather got his first look at mechanized looms. He ordered one right away, the first in Palermo. From that moment on, the industry grew steadily. Even though he gave up silk for cotton—you see, he thought cotton, instead of being imported from Arab countries, could be grown in Sicily—he never compromised his art. In fact, he created a fabric that's still the trademark of our industry today. His sons and grandsons have carried on the tradition. The art is handed down from father to son.

Today, you can't do business the way my grandfather did. In an era of large trusts and industrial mergers, you have to operate on a vast scale. The small family unit with limited capital is helpless. They can't compete with big industry. The capitalists have enormous sums at their disposal. You need bank loans, so costs of production skyrocket.

Living in a closed circle, you can't have much initiative. In the north, when a new industry is operating, it generates other small affiliated enterprises. But there are no ventures like that here. We have no trust in the initiative of others. Instead we want to collect a day's pay—forget about collective enterprise. Maybe this is changing, though, what with new ideas germinating in our cities.

There's not much entrepreneurial activity here, so the workers have no chance to develop. They have no incentive to get better professional skills and qualifications. So every industry has to develop its own labor force. We need technical schools. Otherwise, if there's no incentive or training, workers who want to relocate in Sicily just won't come.

Unfortunately most of us are still bound by a certain mentality. You make do with what you have, be shrewd, take what you can get without paying.

In this region, generally speaking, entrepreneurs and workers have an absolute mistrust of the ruling classes. We're convinced— and unfortunately I think we're right—that most politicians aren't interested in the collective good but only in their own skin. In Sicily especially, politics is a private concern and political organization is a sewer. The wheeler-dealers run the show, and fair practice is near impossible. There are times you have the law on your side, but it takes too long to put it into effect. How can you afford the time and money to decipher all the politicians' and bureaucrats' mysteries?

The sickness is contagious. Instead of democracy, we have a client relationship between the majority of people and their elected officials. Right-thinking people give up, tolerate corruption, and get dragged into the slime. And the politicians wind up making deals with the Mafia, which in many areas of western Sicily is the electoral body *par excellence*.

Good planning creates better structures. Better technical and social structures create better planning.

But how can we have democratic programs when we still have serfs, subjects, where men can't grow free, with a sense of duty? Our strongest lever for economic planning has to be the education of people. I mean technical and moral education. We have to prepare new workers and citizens for the future. Until impoverished day laborers cast off their fetters and no longer see themselves as slaves to Mafiosi, bosses, and big-wheel politicians, no new structures will be born. Thinking about planning is absurd if you don't have men. They're the essential components of organizing and planning.

Above all, we need schools. I give priority to schools because we've wasted so much precious time. These last twenty years if we'd trained men, today we'd be able to value their resources and put them to good use.

I'm pessimistic about adults. Grown men are too conditioned, they can't root out the influences of their environment.

But I'm not too pessimistic. I dream of a better Sicily. I think a lot about how we can build it. There's a lot of sickness, but there's health and strength too. We have real values to preserve and develop. There's a lot of potential quality in us.

32. CROCIFISSA

We are in her house in Alia, a Mafia stronghold. A small woman, always dressed in black, at sixty she has learned to read and write a bit.

Sit down. It's safe. It won't kill us today. Tonight, God only knows.

Three times, we had to evacuate. Because of the landslide. They drew up a city ordinance. It all started in '35. Making cracks in the earth, in the floor. Then it hit the walls. You couldn't close the door. The walls, the whole house shifted. In one week, just before my daughter Pina was born, the floor buckled so much the wall just split. The roof kept falling in. Other houses around here had walls leaning in and out, crumbling all over the place. It was wintertime. I had three kids. We got out and went and stayed at my father's.

We complained to the City Council. They sent an inspector. He checked up on the landslide, drew up the ordinance, and had the eviction notices sent because he didn't want to be responsible. The whole neighborhood was shook up. It was all a wreck. Come the month of June we fixed up the house and moved back in September. We didn't have no way to find another house.

Nineteen-forty, the same old story. The floor buckled and split and a good piece of the wall fell down. By then I had four kids, three just wasn't enough. February they handed us another notice. The inspectors came and said they wouldn't be responsible. Come March I left and rented another house. My husband up and died on me. I was left with the four kids. So in September I scraped together what I could. I cashed in my policy, took out all my savings, and had the house repaired.

Years it rains a lot the houses are worse off. It's not so bad when it don't rain. With nowhere else to go, we're stuck here. Sure we evacuate, but we always wind up coming back. Every year the houses shift a few inches, and now it's a yard or two.

The houses up above shift all their weight down on ours. When they go, so do we. The wires tangle and break. There's no light. The landslides leave us in pitch dark. The streets are all a wreck. Where there's sewers they break open. Whole houses, whole corners crumble.

You try to plant something and the earth gives way and just like that there's no crop. It don't only break up, it all tumbles down there in the gully with the landslide. The water pipes break too. It happened to Uncle Vincenzo and lots of other folk. It doesn't all collapse at once. You see the danger coming and you evacuate. And what if it comes at night? Well, last year my son was staying with us and the plaster started to fall, but he got out in time. When the animals feel it coming they start to paw and stamp. They sense the danger right there on the floor. Once in '40, I was asleep and the mules started to kick up and the plaster came pouring down. I got out in time. When rocks start to fall the animals head for the countryside—to die before your time is rotten. Every creature gets scared.

There's no telephone wires left. You'd never get robbed. There's so many cracks, everybody can hear everybody else. To talk about your business you have to whisper or hide. But they can see you and hear you. Come night, if my lights don't work, I can see by the light through the cracks. Nighttime when you get undressed, first you turn out the light or else your neighbors'll peek in. Some nights you're dishing out the food and one jerk and down comes the plaster. So we eat rubbish.

Come wind, the houses move like they're on their last leg. They're weak. They sway, totter. Sometimes the wind's so strong you evacuate or bury your head in your arms. It's terrifying. You just try to trust in God. Nights there's wind, I'll be sitting, and the walls'll shake and we'll pray to Saint Rosalia to make the wind stop.

The smoke blows through everybody's cracks. We keep getting things fixed, but we're back where we started. They got the floor level once, but now a chair won't set straight. It's like the mountains. Two years ago I had it adjusted: kitchen, floors, walls, everything. And then another crack started, a whole side wall started to go—that was March. Now they've sent us another order to get out. Seven of us families, we've got to leave.

People leave every year. The landslide's right outside, in front. There's a big rock mountain up above—the Ilice, we call it. At first the water ran out onto Totò Battaglia's land. Then it got all dammed up and instead of draining into the fields, it backs up and ruins the whole town. It has no way to spill off. It keeps churning around. Here we are, down below, and the water keeps coming and somebody's got to pipe it off before it gets here. There's about 240 houses landsliding in our neighborhood, the Saint Rosalia district. The earth keeps right on getting sucked away. The houses keep getting weaker. The whole district is a landslide, so's the mountain. People make complaints to City Hall, but everybody minds his own business. The landslide goes on and our menfolk run around trying to fix all the cracks. There's no hope.

We go complain to City Hall, to have them fix the landslide, then our houses. "We'll get on it right away; let's see, tomorrow . . ." They'll agree it's urgent. Come election time they wave keys for new houses. Otherwise it's "you have to evacuate." "But where can we go?" "You'll just have to manage." But where, at the inn of the stars? They come by, the inspectors, the authorities, tell us how sorry they are for us. If things are dangerous, it's "you'll just have to go." But it's not like they find us shelter. It's the same old story: "We start work next Monday, or else definitely by the end of the month." So far as the landslide and things like that they tell you, "The city's got nothing but debts. We're broke." And everybody watches out for himself.

Us poor folk don't comprehend. People who can read the papers get along. Say there's important news, some kind of disaster or a special sale, some of the neighbors'll buy the paper and the news'll get around and we'll go get a paper and sit around, like you and me are doing now, and one person'll read out loud. This cousin of mine in Palermo, she'll come and tell me the latest news, like a wife-beating or a leap from a train. In town here, there's more than twenty-seven people whose brains snapped, out of being scared or plain worn out. Like last Saturday, there was this woman. First, half her wall caved in and she got terrified, pinned like she was near the window. She was so frightened her brain just went and she jumped off Ilice Mountain. One street over, there's this man keeps screaming. He'll listen to reason, then he starts up ranting and raving again: "All must die! Dead! You've eaten human flesh!" He used to be a good worker, but now he just screams and his neighbors've taken steps to have him put away.

The doorways keep on shrinking. When the doors don't shut any more you call the carpenter and he'll plane it down as much as six inches. Once I dreamed the doorway shrunk so much I had to get out through the window. Not that it's a matter of dreams. When the walls buckle they sort of screech. Say the bricks start to crumble, we wake up, turn on the lights, watch for it to stop, then shut off the lights and listen, so on and so forth, two or three times a night. Winter you don't sleep much at all. The water keeps churning. We can't rest in peace. The houses keep moving. Everything's on the move.

People make a fuss, sometimes. Mostly it's mind your business. We all paid this guy who knew how to write a few bucks and he filled us out a report. Then I made a complaint myself. But nothing ever came of it. We never found out why. We all signed our names and had it sent to the city, the region, and the State. A few months ago the Honorable F. paid us a visit and decided there was no sign of a landslide. And some of us got a letter just like the one they sent to Antonino:

CROCIFISSA

REPUBLIC OF ITALY
REGION OF SICILY
OFFICE OF THE PRESIDENT
PALERMO

October 26, 1955

Antonino Todaro
Savoia Street
Alia

Dear Mr. Todaro:

    Concerning the matter referred to below as per your request for immediate intervention, we wish to inform you that the proper officials with the specific technical competence have carried out a full investigation and have reported that certain displacements of soil observable on Gorizia Street of this Municipality have not as yet constituted the nature of a verifiable landslide. Ergo the damages recorded cannot be considered in the public domain the pretext for a state of emergency.

                                  Sincerely yours,

X Z

                                Minister of Public Works

Bureau of Complaints
Division III
ref. no. 22/589

33. SANTUZZA

*From her one-room hut shared with the domestic animals, we
enjoy one of the most magnificent panoramas in all of Sicily, a
full view of the mountains around Roccamena, the great plains
and valleys below, the sea, and the islands off the northwest coast.
Illiterate at fifty, she looks as old as this earth—yet still knows
how to smile.*

Now I can't go and pick the grain any more cause I don't have
any glasses. I can't really do any work like that cause I can't
see too far. From close up, well, I see some. I used to go
every year into the fields to gather all the grain they left
after the reaping. At three in the morning, maybe even two,
I'd head out. The earlier you get started the more you can
gather. Bent over like that all day long, my kidneys'd screw up
real tight on me, but at least I managed to get a few spikes of
wheat and that meant bread at home. And how did I manage
come winter? Well, twenty-four years now I'm a widow, and
there've been times of plenty and times of hardship. When the
spikes were plump, you could bring home twenty pounds of
wheat thereabouts. But when they were lean, you'd be lucky to
get twelve pounds. We'd do our own threshing in town with a
stick, then we'd winnow it by throwing it up in the air, when the
wind blew. Then we'd sift it with a screen to get rid of the chaff
and you'd have nice clean wheat.

I tried it this year, but I couldn't pick a thing. I went looking
for days, but I couldn't see a thing. I came home empty-handed.
I can't detect, what with all the straw and stubble. Fact is, one
day I bent all the way down to see if there was spikes among
the stalks and the stubble poked me right in the eye. It's been
some six months healing, it's taking its sweet time. Let me tell
you, it looked like the kind of black eye you get when somebody
punches you.

I can't recognize humans from far off any more. I just want

to rub my eyes real hard with my hanky, so they'll get cleaned out or clear up. I don't know, right now they're all clouded.

Around here, if you're poor, you're an outcast. You sit home alone all day long. If I could still gather wheat, I could sell some of it and buy me a pair of glasses so I could work. I used to be a good picker: wheat one month, then those pear-shaped tomatoes, the ones that are nice to dry in the sun, and I could do lots of other things too. If you work, you get the money and buy the glasses to work. See, I still got strength left in me. But if there's no money, you stay put and nothing comes your way. They tell me glasses give you your sight back. Your eyes get rested and feel stronger.

Everybody's in need around here. Where can I go for help? My daughter's married now, and her husband's gone to France cause he couldn't find any work here. If she had the money she'd help me out, but how can I ask her to do that sort of thing? She's married. It isn't fair. She has other responsibilities. The poor creature has her own burdens.

Have I talked to the priest? No, what does he understand about things like this? And what about welfare or disability? Never heard of it. And the mayor of our town? Sure, I know him, once I told him I needed medicine, but he said he was broke too.

Now then, there's the visit to the eye doctor, and the glasses you got to have made, and the bus to Palermo. That's four dollars round trip for me alone. If my daughter keeps me company, it's eight dollars. I'm not counting the price of the glasses. I don't know how much they come to. I never bought anything like that before. A neighbor of mine who had a cataract tells me they cost forty to fifty dollars. But how should I know? I'm all in a dither. When I can eat, my sight's a bit clearer. That does cheer me up.

34. SARIDDU

We meet in Roccamena. He is thirty, with black-olive skin and deep-set black eyes. Everything he does is done with concentration and intensity.

I got the notice, so I had to quit working and go to the military headquarters in Palermo. We all got there and they made us line up to wait our turn for the examination. Destination, Avellino. They handed out the first rations, seven cigarettes and seven matches. Ten-thirty at night we left on the train. I never traveled much before, so traveling all night I thought I'd be at the other end of the world by morning. But they unloaded us at Messina and our escort left us to ourselves.

Reggio to Salerno, it was boxcars. The train went like holy hell and the cars were about ready to break in two, like they couldn't take the speed. We got off at Salerno, thirty of us, destinated for Avellino. But we all got on the wrong train. When we found out, the conductor let us off, who in hell knows where. Four hours and we got the right train. Nobody was at Avellino to meet us. We waited. Then this captain appears, howling like a wolf: "You faggot punks, where the fuck you been?" One of our guys, he was from Palermo, told him to watch his language, we were still free men. "You're soldiers, you little shits! Line up!" They took us to the barracks. It was one o'clock in the morning.

Six o'clock, reveille sounds. Us newly-arriveds didn't take it personally. From under the pillow we make believe we don't hear. A corporal comes in shouting. We get up like a bunch of salamis and they escort us into this hall. All these officers start to call out our names and line us up. "You there, Seventh Company, Platoon Number . . . and you there . . . and you there . . ." and so forth. Then they assign us barracks and beds and equipment. Then haircuts. We were all shaggy and wild. They shaved our heads like we had ringworm. Next morning, reveille, coffee, and time for training.

Everybody was put in one company or another. They said they had to drill us into shipshape, make us men. This corporal lined us up by threes. "Attention! Company . . . forward march!" We moved like a flock of sheep, all at our own pace, a few in step, most not. "Company . . . halt!" One guy stops and two or three pile into him, two hundred guys in one mass collision. "All right, boys, no more of this pussyfooting. We'll get you in step—and quick!" He has three guys step forward, draws a line in the dirt, makes them toe it. One by one it's "Attention! Head up! Chin in tight! Back straight! Chest out! Body stiff! Straight as a poker, you pricks! Hands at sides! Heels together! Toes out! Goddamn you, I said heels together!" See, to come to attention you have to do a little hop, step, and click your heels together—just like that.

Then he lets us rest, but first we have to stamp our feet on the ground, make it ring out, just like this. "These are the regulations," the corporal says. It's like at Palermo where the sentries prance around and have a special box to stamp on. That way everybody hears em. "That's the beauty of guard duty," he says. "There's a real beauty in standing guard," he says. You can't look like any old slob.

Forty days! It's like training never ends. They also taught us how to salute. They gave us this funny cap to put on our heads, and to keep the corners stiff we had to insert a wooden slat. This corporal stood in the center of the courtyard and us soldiers formed a circle and kept circling around. When you got to face the corporal you raised one hand to the cap, keeping the other lined up with your leg. Hand stretched toward eye, thumb tight against hand, fingertips just over eye against cap. The corporal made believe he was a captain or something: "You there, step forward." You run up, salute, drop your hand, and freeze, chest out, just staring at the officer—remember, you're always at attention. Your eyes better not shift or else your head will too, and that's against regulations, and only they know why.

Once I had to see the captain for something, so I race up and snap to attention, saluting and freezing just the way they taught me. "All right, private, what can I do for you?" What was I supposed to do? I had something important to tell him, but I can't talk without my hands. I started to talk, but my mouth didn't make sense, moving there all alone. I just had to use my hands. You can't communicate without them. How can you stand there like a poker and talk to people? Your mouth means nothing without your hands. "Soldier, you're still at attention!" So I shut up. After a long moment of silence, he says "At ease," so I was able to finish the discussion.

They finally got down to serious drilling, teaching us how to kill men.

You start with empty hand grenades. They don't have fuses. Then you toss the real ones. The first time I almost went into a fit. Four soldiers step forward and they take these bombs from a little box like they were apples or something. Then you put on your helmet and get into this little hole and there's an officer right beside you. "Ready?" The first time I was so scared I threw it as fast as I could pull out the pin. Christ Almighty, I never saw such awful contraptions. But bit by bit I worked up the courage and it didn't bother me any more.

After that came target practice. Down at one end of the field they had six men made of wood. They'd say, "Ready, aim, fire!" and all you had to do was aim and hit the dummy. One nick meant one man down. Six bull's-eyes and you got the prize. Then it was machine-gun practice: six rounds each, forty shots per man, six dummies in all. If you didn't hit anything, the captain had a shit-fit. Meanwhile, truckloads of ammunition just disappeared. It was like kids eating Easter eggs—except it was hand grenades or machine guns eating up ammo boxes before you could even fill them, and heavy and light mortars, and pistol practice filling those poor dummies full of holes. That's the infantry.

With artillery, every shot you fire is hundreds of dollars up in smoke. Each piece of shrapnel is worth five bucks. They'd assigned me to my regiment, and it was eleven months of this kind of training, and after that I was off to war maneuvers against the enemy.

We practiced this stuff all day long. Then we were free on pass from five till nine. It was like birds getting out of a cage. Naturally we'd all go to the women. All we had was four hours. The officers would tell us to behave in ways "befitting a soldier." "Leave the nice respectable girls alone. There are ample public facilities." We got twenty-five cents a day, that makes two-fifty every ten days and it cost a buck a throw. If you just wanted a quick one in the alley, it was thirty-nine cents or two bits for the special. There were eight thousand soldiers in Avellino. Every night at least three thousand were on the loose. There were two facilities with four or five women in each. The lines were endless. We'd fight for a place up front: "You no-good whoremaster, I was first!" The MPs would make their rounds and that would clam us up. We'd all come to attention and salute and wait in line like lambs. The whole place was nothing but soldiers. Days, the girls serviced civilians. From five to nine, the whole army. After that, it was back to civilians and army men on leave.

This is life in the military—when there's no war. Attention, left and right, and whores. If they taught us a trade like mechanics, that would make some sense. But what good is it to me and my family, all this forward march and eyes right?

What did I do before the army? Let's see if I can recall everything. I picked capers, and grass to make brooms, did plumbing, cleared land for planting, made and sold candy, caught frogs and snails, picked wild greens and olives and grain, collected charcoal on the railroad tracks and lead from the firing ranges after the police was through. I sold used American clothes, ice cream, roasted nuts and seeds, spring water and aniseed, and snails. I fished for river eels and sold contrabanded cigarettes and booze and the metal I could salvage from the railroad ties and steal from hallowed ground (spikes and crosses get a good resale price), and whenever I found a real job, I was a manual laborer. And I did a lot of other things too.

Eleven months in the army and I couldn't contribute a thing to the family. Fact is, my father sent me money. It was all one big waste, for nothing. When I got back I was out of practice.

With the tools I knew how to use before, I didn't know which end was up.

Except for career men who do it for money, nobody goes of his own free will. If you don't know what else to do, you become a soldier—or a cop. Sure, there's a future in it. From private first class you go to corporal or to sergeant, drill those little bastards blue in the face, and take home your dirty paycheck every month. To a man, nobody chooses to go. Nobody with an ounce of sense goes into the army or to war with good will. We've got to tell the people, "Let's get together and round up these few nuts who want war and put them in the nuthouse where they can fight it out all between themselves."

How should the government spend its money instead? It's plain and simple. Just send the soldiers to work one year in Sicily, and hands off decent people. You don't have to buy new weapons, just give the troops a hoe or a shovel. They can plant forests or build roads, factories, houses, dams, everything we really need, and the government can write it all off on their taxes. One year in Sicily, one in Sardinia, another in Calabria, with all those thousands of men drafted every year in Italy. Ten years of work and we'd have boots—so we could start to pull ourselves up by our bootstraps. Then we would volunteer: "Today I'll work for the people, tomorrow it'll be for my family." Look, all we need is open minds and unity. Nobody could stop us, now or never. They couldn't put all the people of Italy in jail. How could they afford to feed us?

All these weapons don't produce a thing. We don't need them. We have children, they grow up, and what can we teach them? The same old story or something really beautiful? We've got to make them want to be noble when they grow up, to learn and teach more beautiful things. That's the only way they can be healthy. Can't we face the simple truth? How can you deny it? Ask the biggest idiot in the world, he'll agree. We should teach our children to be good and not kill. Except for family honor or personal money matters, you should never kill. Maybe I'm not educated, but I know what I think, especially when it's true.

I can hardly read or write but let me tell you, in Italy they waste too many men in this draft. Let them put us to good use. Let the Italian government start doing this and we won't cuss them out any more.

Instead, they called me back to fight a war. It was four years and even worse. Seven or eight days on the S.S. *Liguria* and they landed us at Tobruk. I knew the soldier's life, but I'd never seen it in wartime. That was pure hell. Three days and the war broke out and the bombs started to fall. Houses were blown sky-high. Once I was in what you call a cathouse and we heard this air-raid siren and scattered like rats. After the all-clear signal we found this woman pulverized against a wall. With every bombing more houses just disappeared. Then they sent us up to the front line.

Arms, legs, heads, shoes with feet still in them, you couldn't think straight any more. Everybody was screaming. A bomb would fall, burst, and blow everything to smithereens. That was the way it went. I'd think about my family, trust in the Blessed Mother. We'd stare at each other in those trenches and nod our heads: "Buck up." Then a companion or a friend would fall, wounded or dead, and we'd forget about wives and children. It was hard enough to remember we were still human beings.

RESISTANCE

35. A FRIEND OF MIRAGLIA'S

*(See introduction to No. 27, p. 189.) The friend, a peasant elder
from Sciacca, has been an activist most of this century in
collectivist, union, and cooperative movements. An "American"
(an emigrant to North or South America who returns to his
native village), he has had a broad range of experiences. He
knows how to read and write and how to integrate his knowledge
with that experience.*

I met Miraglia when he was fourteen or so. I saw him a lot
with this guy who had a tailor's shop. I was never sure if
Miraglia was his apprentice or just a friend. I did know he
was studying accounting. Then he disappeared from Sciacca.
They said he was in Milan or France. We ran across each
other again when he was in his early twenties. He was keeping
the books of a brick works, Gallo and Associates. Then he
managed the Rossi Opera House, but when it was demolished
he did odd jobs and finally settled down to processing and selling
fish, and that went real well for him. Soon as the war was over
in '44, the trade union got started and he was our first secretary.
We never had anything like it before. His job was to bring in
more members, issue cards, and organize a party that would
fight for justice and the people's rights. He'd say, "Organize, get
cooperatives going. If we take the first step together, we can all
have land." We agreed with him and after one year we had
eighteen hundred members. But the rich kept all the estates for
themselves, four hundred acres per person. So there we were
without land.

Nobody'd ever talked any sense to us. Nobody'd ever spoke
out and fought on our side. Other people who tried to organize
the peasants, like Bertolino and Friscia and Murnuna, they all
played their own party politics. They wanted to run for Parliament or mayor. But he wanted us people to organize to fight for
our own rights, for something we never had before. He'd say,

"Organize, and we'll have a voice in government." I thought along his lines, but I wasn't a party member. Then one day at his home he convinced me: "Look, why don't you join us? Don't you think we're really putting a good organization together?" "Yeah, it could be the first in my lifetime. But let's call a spade a spade, we've got to face the tragedy. This government's got so much power it's frightening. I'm not sure elections will solve the problem." I was judging from the past, and I'm still convinced. They'll stop at nothing so as not to give in. They've been in power so long and they'd rather kill us than yield an inch. I remember Panepinto and Verro. They came one time to hold a meeting with the League of Peasants and Workers. That was 1909, I think, before they killed them both. Panepinto first, then Verro soon after.

"Nowadays," Miraglia says, "the king doesn't run the government." See, by then Togliatti was minister of justice and Gullo was heading Agriculture. They were both on our side.

In his thinking and acting he was always for us poor people. Before the war, he fought the battle alone, hanging around the bars and sporting a goatee. I'd see him walking around with that little beard and wonder if he was man or beast. Come winter, he'd wear one of them Russian hats with earflaps. He'd fold them down so he'd look like a Turk. Yet you knew he was really decent. He had a good heart and real integrity. Maybe he looked foreign, almost suspicious, with that long overcoat and funny beard, but he talked beautifully and made you feel loved. He never ignored you or treated you like dirt.

He'd always get right to the point. He never wasted words. Another thing, in the street he always greeted you first. That never ceased to amaze me. He'd greet you by name, or if he didn't know it, he'd shout a friendly "Good morning." The people were crazy about him. He made them feel like the sun had just come out for the first time in their lives. They felt like they could really do something on their own initiative. Now, of course, we realize how much time that takes, and yet we haven't forgotten him in Sciacca, he's still on our minds all the time.

He had new ideas. They were big ideas. He wanted the world to change. He had farsighted vision. He came from a poor family too, from the land. He was precise and he never forgot a detail. Whatever he started, he finished. He'd start by talking to people, then he'd think it all out and research the best solutions. During the days of Mussolini, he got arrested and people thought, "They must be afraid of him to have to lock him up."

When he spoke, he was clear, aboveboard, down-to-earth. His words were true to our experience. He'd get all fired up wanting to help the people, but he kept a clear head. With us little guys he never played the big shot. He was always on our level. I remember once he came into a fish store and it was packed, but he took his place in line with the rest of us. Then this priest comes in, a certain Father Arena. He elbows his way to the counter and gets his fish. On his way out he notices Miraglia: "What are you doing there, still waiting?" "I may be a sheep, but that's better than being bullheaded." They did have respect for each other, though.

When he was trying to solve a problem, he'd talk to people who could help him clear it up. I remember once we had a dispute over the rent the School of Agriculture was paying for some space in the monastery. He called on me. I told him what I thought and he took notes. He'd study things in depth, take notes, and use his head. You'd talk and he'd take out his pencil and paper and it'd all go into his briefcase and his brain. Sure, lots of people criticized him. His enemies would say he was taking us for a ride, he was asking us to do the impossible, he was agitating the people just to use them and then give all the rich folks' property to his friends. They'd laugh at him. It couldn't be done, they'd say. Gossip would have it (my father said it too) that since 1860 you got excommunicated for wanting to change things, that the way the rich got everything for nothing was destiny.

He really brought the people together. We were like birds flocking to him, and he'd scatter seeds for everybody. All he'd have to say was "Tomorrow morning we'll meet at X," and they'd pack them in like sardines. Everybody'd be there. If someone came to see him, he'd stop working on the spot and go help the guy, no matter who it was. One time he was chairman of the hospital committee, and there was this goatherd who delivered milk for the patients. The contract had to be renewed, so the goatherd went to his house and he accepted the new contract right there and then. Well, the guy was so grateful for getting a fair deal that he picked out one of his best country cheeses, a nice fifteen-, maybe eighteen-pound wheel, and brought it to Miraglia as a token of appreciation. Listen to what Miraglia said: "You don't owe me anything in return. Besides, you wouldn't want to mortify me. I don't do things with ulterior motives. Nobody should work for rewards. It's a simple question of rights."

He couldn't stand people who scorned or pitied the poor. He kept telling us, "Sure, I can lend you a hand, but get organized. You've got to do it yourselves." If you worked with him, there weren't any "bonuses." You did your job right, but not for money. When we drew up the charter for the cooperative, he asked me to participate because I was the oldest in the group and had lots of past experience. And he accepted all my suggestions! I'd seen collective cooperatives fail, so we made each member individually responsible for his own investments. We had a board of directors and a chairman. They donated their time. We thought up names for it like "The Sacred Annunciation" or "Veterans of War" or "The League." His name was the best: "Mother Earth." We met twice a month, worked Sundays too, all for free.

Let me tell you, the peasants really started to learn to work together. What else could they do when he made things so clear? "If we're organized it's like being brothers. If something goes wrong, we can talk it over." See, he'd been an anarchist, and that meant organization based on this human brotherhood, to make sure everybody's rights were respected. The people weren't used to doing it like that. Their way was, "I don't want to risk it, it's up to you." Then they'd argue, "Just what do you think you're doing?" They were accustomed to getting exploited, conned, cheated, and that was the evil he was trying to root out.

Jobs were scarce at the time. There was no building going on, but the master carpenters still believed in him. Berto, Triolo, Turi Citrolo, the whole bunch, worked right along with him. Summer evenings, they'd all go down together to the fish market, talking the whole way. "We have to perfect ourselves," he'd say. "We have to be informed, aware of everything, and realize all our human potential." Seeing how many people couldn't even write their own names, he'd get sick. You know the rate of illiteracy here is hard to believe. We couldn't read up on any-thing, but when he spoke we felt good in our hearts. Maybe we didn't have the education to figure out what "perfecting" meant, but the idea made us sort of tingle inside. With all that he was doing and pushing for, we started to get convinced we could do something too. And whenever we got confused, he was there to make things clear.

The first cavalcade he rode a white horse. The guy who loaned it to him was warned not to by the opposition, but so what? The Saturday night before, all of us who needed land decided together on this cavalcade to prove we were with him. Come Sunday, I had an emergency in the countryside and I got back after things started. It all got going on time. All the peasants were with him and they passed right under my balcony. Well, I was out there hanging out my long johns and he was leading the cavalcade, way up there on that horse. So we came face to face. And he looked me in the eye and bit the knuckle on his index finger as if to say, "Where were you? Did you take me for a fool?" But he was smiling. He knew how slow I moved at the age of sixty-seven.

All the people were with him. From Menfi, Montevago, Santa Margherita, Sambuca, Burgio, Caltabellotta, Lucca, Ribera, Cala-monaci, Villafranca. All on horseback. All in high spirits, shout-ing to their friends and hissing when they ran across members of the opposition. That morning the rich stayed indoors. There were so many kids riding double with their fathers you couldn't even count them. And he looked just like Roland. It was a joy to see this mountain of a man up there on that horse. You had to admire him. Just looking at him made you love him, and he radiated that same love back. All the kids were throwing flowers.

Of course, it was just the opposite when they killed him. Sure, there was public protest at first, but then everybody got scared and disappeared and tried to make believe they never knew us. Then again, a few of us stayed. We didn't give a damn for life or death. We were still committed to digging in and building a life no matter how they threatened us.

It was an endless cavalcade, two by two, so when the last people in line passed my balcony, the ones up front must have been beyond San Michele, heading down to Palermo Gate, and coming to a halt in front of the City Hall. Can you imagine the police shouting, "Halt! Break it up!" Besides the horses, there were four or five thousand mules plus bicycles you couldn't count. They proceeded to the soccer field and he made a short speech, explaining why there was a cavalcade in the first place. He was overjoyed, praising and thanking everybody. Then he dispersed the crowd.

From that moment, it was clear he had the whole town with him and his opponents started to hate him like poison. To scare them even worse, the government agency in charge of distributing uncultivated land started to take him seriously and do its job.

We planned our first occupation for the Santa Maria estate. In those days, the whole place was run by two or three overseers. The land was mostly uncultivated and badly managed, so we had every legal right to occupy it. I mean to confiscate it and parcel it out in small holdings. As you know, that's the way it's supposed to be done nowadays too. In the early days of the Socialist League, we'd had cavalcades to occupy the land, but this time it was Miraglia's idea to take over the land through the cooperative. He said he would lead the procession. The people behind him didn't have horses. They were just day laborers on foot or bicycles, so they joined up with the farmers and peasants who had mules, carts, and wagons, and this whole mass of people got ready and set out. If you got tired, you hopped on a bicycle fender and followed Miraglia on his dapple-grey horse. What with all the day laborers and small landowners of Sciacca, we amounted to more than fifteen hundred. We were all in high spirits, full of joy. We were occupying the land. There was no thought of violence, but on the average we didn't have any foresight. We thought if everybody got his little piece of land he could produce enough to survive. When people got a plot of ground they felt strong. It gave them courage to organize more cavalcades.

Miraglia wanted to improve the people's living conditions. So he had to attack the haves. There was no other way to do it but keep on fighting them. That way their hatred for him grew like cancer. He fought to cut the rents tenant farmers had to pay the landowners, and he tried to enforce the law that gave sixty percent of the product to the farmer. So that hatred just kept on brewing, and they started to cook up their plot. I can swear to the whole thing. The last few months of his life, they started to court his favor, to "come to an understanding." That's their method. Then in case something happens to you, they'll be known as your friend. You could have guessed the evil deed was already in the making.

At a public meeting in City Hall he made an announcement: he'd been warned to back off and refrain from what he was doing. He never carried a gun before that. Fact is, he was against violence and killing. After that, though, he started to carry a pistol in his briefcase or tucked in his belt. Can you imagine that sly little threat? "Look, my friend, think first about your family. You're in good shape. All these other matters could get too complicated. Forget about them, they're not important." Some shady characters kept dropping by right up until the last night. We only realized later what that meant. If only he'd denounced them right off, in public . . . But he couldn't be one hundred percent sure of being threatened. They didn't say it right to his face. Let's say they were too diplomatic. Maybe he thought they wouldn't dare kill him. They threatened me once too: "Look, my friend, you're an old man. Your place is at home with the family." Yeah, diplomatic is what they are. "What do you think you're doing? Forget about politics, it's not for you. These people are just using you anyway."

How did they do the job? They set him up. This guy made believe he was a Communist, but he was really a friend of the Mafia. The night of January fourth, it was mean. The wind from the mountains was freezing. We had a meeting at the trade union, then two guys went with him up Rome Street, up to the streetlight near his house. He decided to go alone from that point: "Go on home now, it's too damn cold." The street was empty, but they were waiting in ambush. He got to his front door, took out his key, and they opened fire with machine guns. The first volley missed him. You can still see the bullet-holes in the wall. Then they got him in the neck and he fell against his door. They ran off, still blasting away, up toward Santa Caterina. It's easy to hide in those back streets. They were afraid of being seen.

It was like the end of the world. Pure terror was all over town. People filled the square right away. A few days later we held the funeral. You can't imagine. Even the rich folk joined in the procession. But of course after that most people just minded their own business.

In these kind of cases, the police inspectors hush everything up. The Ministry of Justice imposes silence. It always happens that way, I know from lifelong experience. But I was a good friend of Miraglia's, and Commissioner Zingone was scared enough of the public indignation, so he tried to be my friend— at least as much as a cop could be in 1947. We talked and they made some arrests. When they apprehended one of the suspects, he messed right in his pants. Before questioning, he had to change. We were all hoping this case would be solved. Word had it they got a full confession and that charges were pressed by headquarters at Agrigento. Then they released the suspects: circumstantial evidence. Later they arrested the same guys and released them again. Word had it they'd found an alibi.

Instead of promoting the cops who did some real investigating, they got rid of them. They call it relocating. The forces of reaction won out. When it comes down to the vital issues, it's always happened that way around here. They even charged these cops with using torture to get the confessions. Then, just as a formality, they had an inquest—naturally, behind closed doors. It's always hush-hush. Nothing's ever made public. They're sly and they have big-shot lawyers. After the inquest, which came to nothing, the commissioner and his men were cleared of the charges of torture . . . Think about that for a minute. That means what those guys confessed to was really true. But violence is violence. When they're in danger, they're like squid. They squirt all their ink at you and you can't see anything clear. A case may be full of contradictions, but they'll just file it and put their feet back up on the desk.

Sure, if some rich guy got killed, they'd search high and low. But in cases like Miraglia's they abuse their power and do what they damn well please—nothing. Take last year, they stole all the chickens belonging to forty or fifty farmers. Of course, they'd stole plenty of cows, mules, and sheep before. But that's normal. There's not a farm that hasn't been sacked. Anyway, the cops didn't find a feather, not to speak of the culprits. But then somebody scaled the fence of this big landowner's place and pulled off a big robbery. The watchmen were so scared they just hid, but the owner's wolf-dog wouldn't stop barking, so they shot it dead. Next day the boss goes to the authorities and they take up the matter. They set up roadblocks where they think the thieves might be traveling. Along comes this pickup truck and they flag it down and find a bunch of chickens from another "job." So they prosecute and the boss gets some poor farmers' chickens. When the interests of the rich are at stake, bingo, you've got your truck, chickens, crooks, and all.

We see it happen like this all the time. I've seen a lot in my day, but every time the Mafia commits a murder the same thing happens. In this area alone, they killed Montalbano's son and Spagnolo, the trade unionist. And the people in power kill each other all the time over one dispute or another. They got Counselor Campo from Agrigento. Then they shot and stabbed Leonardo Renda and put a rock in his mouth, because you're supposed to keep your mouth shut and be stone-faced. If your tongue wags, they'll shoot you in the mouth to let people know why. There was Almerigo too, he was the mayor of Camporeale. And Giglio, the mayor of Alessandria della Rocca, and Vito Montaperto, the mayor of Campobello di Licata. Just in our province alone. You can't keep track of them all. They shoot the people who dare to challenge their power, and figure everybody else will get scared and go on home. Nobody ever gets caught. It's always "under investigation," "no suspects," and all of a sudden, silence.

Same with Miraglia. Case closed. Like he didn't ever exist. Nobody risks his neck. And what does it all prove? Might makes right, I guess. They make things disappear. Everybody's in their power, and we mill around like sheep.

After Miraglia's death, the opposition came on strong. They strutted around town talking big and brave, saying they'd paint the trade union white (that is, Christian Democrat).

If you want anything, you have to fight. Or else it's hopeless. We've almost never united to demand our rights, so we've always been scorned, abused, robbed, killed. Experience has taught me that life is one long tragedy. They get us to destroy and kill each other, always over land.

Cooperatives won't work if you don't redistribute the land, and now I'm convinced they've got to be collective. But nobody trusts the other guy, so they flop. A cooperative catches on if it gives each guy his own property. People don't want to work the land collectively. Miraglia proposed that we work the estate together and share all the produce equally, but the members were all against it. For once they wouldn't listen to him, and he didn't push it. We lack trust, a real basis for group action. It's because we've never had any justice.

The days of cavalcades are over. We've got to organize to demand our rights and get our exploiters off our backs. We've got to stick together, be disciplined, fight for justice, keep working hard. I want to come home from work and have a bowl of soup with my family and know I'll have work tomorrow. You know, when a man has good work, he has peace of mind. There's no despair at home. If I'm sure of eating every day, I can really raise my family. I was in America three years. Monday till Saturday noon I'd work, and Sundays we'd all go out and enjoy ourselves. The family would go out into the woods. They were called Central Park, I think. There'd be music and we'd go picking greens in the fields. It made us feel good. It was like fun, not like here where you go out picking so you won't starve to death. There, life is much better.

Everything I'm telling you, I've seen with my own two eyes. Seeing what I saw in America, I started to understand things better. When I left for America I was twenty-four. Before that I lived way out in the country and didn't know what life was all about. When I got back to Sicily, I saw how much we needed a government that would care about poor people and give them work. That's why ever since I've always fought on the side of the have-nots.

36. GAETANO

He is a forty-year-old worker from Palermo. Small, thin, alert, he is full of energy and enthusiasm. Having traveled a lot and educated himself, he brings a special perspective to his work in the union.

In '45, right after the war, I went to work as a baker. My father had been a stoker. He died on the job. I chose baking because I thought that way I could bring home leftover bread with my paycheck. Then the trade union set up this work program with unemployment compensation. For every 200 pounds of flour they handled, the bakeries had to hire one worker. But let's say they handled 750 pounds and hired three men full-time and one half-timer, then the profit on those extra 50 pounds went into this compensation fund. If you were a paying member of the union but couldn't find a job, you still got a day's pay. That's how it worked till '48. The employers contributed directly to this fund, and unemployed bakers didn't have to go begging. Those times were hard, but we had real ideals.

I was only fifteen, just a kid, but it struck me to see this departure from the past. I was even hoping we could have the same kind of system for other trades. That way the union could get more bargaining power and handle our wages through its own special bank. But my dreams ground to a halt when our consortium's negotiations failed and the bosses got control of the distribution of the flour and had their way with supplies. The fund collapsed and jobs were handed out on the basis of favoritism. It got to be chaos, and to this day that's the rule.

Now bakers are paid by the hour. They're just like day laborers. The boss can tell them he doesn't need them tomorrow and they work longer hours without overtime. We're not considered skilled workers. That's because we're not united. We do our work wherever we're lucky to find a job, but we never solve our real problems because we never get together to talk them over. Bakeries, like factories, are still chaos.

I hadn't done military service yet, so I joined the navy in '49. Two years later I was discharged, and they took me on as an unskilled laborer in the shipyard. Sitting there in dry dock the ship looked like it'd run aground. I couldn't imagine how it'd get launched. The old hands had to explain to me how the whole system of pulleys and pumps worked. There was eighteen hundred men on the job.

As a kid I had an uncle who was a yard electrician. He was hired to do piecework and he'd have to finish a job in a certain amount of time, even if it meant working after hours—or else he'd be fired. See, before the war, workers didn't have any kind of contract. They didn't have the freedom to go to the toilet. My uncle told me stories. Like once they were putting up this building, this steam crane was hoisting sheet iron, and the wind came and blew one of these sheets right through the glass. Well, the superintendent was watching the whole thing and he suspended them all for three days, with a fine of a quarter per day. The workers protested, "Damn, it was the wind." "OK, it was the wind, three days isn't enough, let's make it five." He wanted to put them in their place, but they wouldn't give in.

During the war a lot of workers had gained some real skills, and knowledge, in the North. Some stayed up there for good, but enough came back so that people started to learn about other ways to work and be assured of something like fair treatment. Well, it took us more than a few riots, but we started to create a real movement in the yard. Of course, the Mafia popped up again right after the war and tried to control the hiring, but they had to contend with a few old Fascists. The workers organized and fought, trying to get rid of the whole rotten bunch. But they had us in their dirty clutches, Fascists and Mafiosi I mean, and every time we tried to make our own decisions, our leaders got threatened, clubbed, blackmailed. It was war and the Mafia pulled all the triggers. We had to retreat. They even opened fire on one of our demonstrations, and naturally all the wounded were workers.

So I joined the mass movement. We organized meetings and the workers went back on the offensive. We believed our organizers would really fight for us. After every meeting we'd talk: "What did our man really say?" "He said a lot of good things . . . He cussed out management . . . He's got guts . . . He chewed out the super . . . We can trust him . . . He's on our side." We were glad to hear how he represented us, but we still weren't ready to take the responsibility into our own hands. We couldn't understand the real nature of our problems. We couldn't see how we were an integral part of the solution. Which meant the transformation of the whole works. The management detected our weakness, and they used the Mafia to subvert our movement. A lot of our leaders from the central committee just weren't up to their task. As soon as they got a piece of the pie, they "cooperated" and let the rest of us go to pot. It was all politics: the management saw a way to undermine the workers' strength. That way we lost hope and trust. Those of us who met the problems head-on, with ideological and political know-how, all got fired, or forced out.

By '52 a lot of organizers the workers trusted had already sold out, and just as many activists were fired. Then the management sent official letters to the workers, saying if they kept it up, the yard'd be closed down. Of course, by then the Christian Democrats' Confederation of Trade Unions was working its way into the yard and trying to convince us our jobs'd be secure with them.

By '53 the yard had six thousand men employed. A lot of oil tankers docked for repairs because costs were low—given the wages for manual labor. I said six thousand, but not too many of us actually had a steady job. We all worked when there were thirty ships in dry dock. When there were ten, it was another story. It got to be chaos again, because the guys who had jobs would strike to have our demands met and that'd make the management happy. All they had to do was call on the reserve labor force, so the yard never had to shut down. In fact, the

management made sure they didn't hire too many of us and that
way they blocked real union action. Besides, to get a job you had
to be recommended by some government big shot, some cardinal,
or a Mafioso.

What was next in their bag of tricks? The way things worked
was, a foreman assigned a particular job to a team of workers
and they'd be responsible to him, deciding themselves when to
punch in and out. But then the management dreamed up another
system. Besides punching in and out every day, each individual
worker would be timed to see how long it took to finish a
certain job. They told us that would help us be more "efficient."
What it really meant was rigid time limits were set for any given
job to be done. The foreman wasn't responsible any more; instead
we had a straw boss. "This job should take half a day. We can't
keep you at this rate." And they'd fire you. Well, the work was
hard enough in the first place, and now we had to rush the job,
so naturally there were more accidents. We worked under constant pressure and a lot of guys were at the breaking point.

The Confederation of Trade Unions didn't get a lot of members, but they made enough noise to break up our unity. The last
few years I was at the yard, that's from '53 till '55, the situation
got worse and worse. We realized that since the war, it was even
harder to push and get our demands met.

Some of us believed we could do it and make our administra-
tion really democratic because people would understand the essential thing was our right to work. But year by year the workers
got more demoralized. There was a constant shortage of jobs, and
a lot of able-bodied men just stood around idle. We had a dream
of a new society, where we could change the old ways and even
the nature of our environment. But after a while most of our
best men went looking for better opportunities—and dignity too.
I mean, they emigrated to the North, and to other countries. The
ones that stayed started to believe we'd never change a thing,
never get anywhere, so they sort of gave up and got cynical. The
firm saw they were giving in and bullied them even worse, and
the bosses came down with an iron fist on the few who still had

hope. And the workers who got promoted to positions with some power (of course, never at the top), well, they started to snub their fellow workers and friends. They wanted to make it into the middle class, so they kept their distance and even in the street they ignored their old comrades.

Things were as bad for me as they were for my fellow workers. So finally I left the yard. I needed to find out how other men lived and worked, to understand how things could change, how you could develop new ways of doing things to make society better. I wanted to learn how people lived in other places and earn enough to raise a family. So in '57 I decided to go to sea.

From '57 till '60, I sailed around as a ship mechanic. My first trip I got as far as Conakry in French Guinea, Newcastle in Scotland, and Liverpool. Another time it was Melbourne in Australia and Yokohama in Japan. Actually, I spent a whole year in the Far East: Java and Sumatra and Indonesia and back. As far as America I only got to Newfoundland—that's in Canada. Then I made it to Holland, where I ran across a lot of old comrades from the yard. Traveling like that I got some idea how Sicily compares to other countries.

Believe me, on board what goes is the laws of God and the captain. The captain's word is law and the sailor has to submit. The commander gets filet mignon and champagne, the officers get T-bone and fine wines, the warrant officers get ground round and the house wine, and the rest of the crew gets slop and what they call, off the coast of North America, plain old dago red. Sure the crew resented this system, but from on high they justified it by making you think you weren't on their level.

To double back for a minute, before going to sea, in '57, I got married. Three years and I had two kids, and I kept getting more and more homesick, so I decided to return for good. Back home I got training as a stoker and found a job at the Barbera Dairy. All us workers there lived on the hope of getting affiliated with the city. That's the way it was done in a lot of big cities to get trade-union rates for the workers—and maybe even job security. All in all it wasn't bad. There weren't too many of us, and they treated us like family. But they wouldn't take me off the night shift, so I decided to switch jobs. A laundry just recently opened hired me. I can't tell you how bad they exploited us. Just imagine in 1961, about sixty people, some of us just kids maybe fourteen or fifteen, getting a dollar-twenty-five, maybe a dollar-fifty a day. They were generous with heads of families, though: six dollars a day. It was hard to organize into a union because most of the workers were women, or just girls—they thought unions were evil, or they were just plain scared. "We need the money. We have to take what they give us. If we agitate and get fired, we'll be blacklisted." As you can see, they had no experience.

Well, I knew a maintenance super at the SELIT (that's the national electric company), and he put me in touch with a department head who gave me a psychological aptitude test and hired me on the spot. The factory'd been in operation since '57, and by the time I came on the job they had three hundred workers. It was a far cry from the shipyard. With the strangest mixture of people from all walks of life, they didn't get divisive or cynical. Tailors, fruit peddlers, shoemakers, and peasants: they really started to organize, debate, develop. Our movement got so strong, it was a complete surprise.

At first the workers had accepted real low wages, and the archbishop's Curia and Don Paolino Bontade did the hiring. One word from the don and you were taken in. Of course, if you talked about changing things and took action, you were warned by the Mafia and finally forced out. That happened to this real sharp young fellow name of Puleo. In fact, all the workers felt pressured, what with the low wages and backbreaking pace and this Don Paolino intimidating them on the job. There was a certain Don Tricomi too, he acted as go-between to keep the peace between the workers and the management.

But you see, nowadays we're organized in the union and don't tolerate this sort of thing. It all started after the Ciacculli disaster, when that truck full of explosives blew sky-high and killed, as far as I estimated, seven cops. After that, Paolino Bontade threatened 150 workers with dismissal, but then he retired and went into hiding. And we rose to the occasion, united to a man, joining up with the other guys in the factory who worked for the Electronics Company of Sicily. When we got Bontade off our backs and weren't afraid of being fired, we all united. See, the economic situation was bad all over and there was a large unskilled labor force beating down the factory doors. So we decided on a general strike. To the management's great surprise, we shut down the whole operation, even after they canvassed door-to-door to bribe us into not striking. After three days of inactivity we managed to get a ten-percent raise, all dismissals revoked, and a bonus of $125 for all employees, including clerical staff.

Remember, I said at first the only union powerful enough to organize was the Confederation of Trade Unions. They were more or less free of Don Bontade and Don Tricomi and the Curia (who were all in it together). But the supers still had absolute power over the workers, and the leftist Labor Federation wasn't strong enough to take action yet because the workers were afraid to join them for fear of getting fired. See, the Mafiosi would have seen it as a double-cross. And the Workers' Union of Catholics and Democratic Socialists was yet to come, while the National Federation of Labor Unions just dealt with clerical help. So there wasn't much choice.

I remember when Filippo Mingoia was taken on, they called him into the boss's office: "So you're a barber?" "Yes." "We've taken on some barbers here and they've made a bad showing, see, they didn't have the physique: they were weaklings. You understand, this is heavy work, it'd be a shame to hire you and have to let you go right off." Well, Mingoia told the boss he could take it. He couldn't earn a living and feed his family as a barber, so he promised he'd take whatever they gave him. Then the boss got around to popping the question: "Are you a member of our confederation?" "Yes, I am." Of course, it wasn't true. From '46 on he'd been a Communist and had worked his way onto the local steering committee. But to get hired you had to say you were a member of the confederation, or nonunion . . .

At first each man just looked out for himself and thought

everything would get resolved by magic—as long as you got a few breaks. But it dawned on them that to resolve individual problems, you have to work together. See, we're all in the same fix.

At that point it was like we'd all woken out of a nightmare, we all started to speak our minds and push for our rights. We demanded better ventilation, promotions, a few extras. But the bonuses didn't matter as much as the fact that we were demanding respect for our steering committee and for ourselves as workers.

Right after the strike we called for elections to have real union representatives. The Labor Federation won three seats, and the Confederation just one. It was like a load was lifted off our backs. The workers weren't afraid to say any more they were with the Labor Federation. "What's wrong with that?" And we'd say it, point-blank, to the boss.

Once word got around that in Palermo, people were taking action against the Mafia. So the factory and office workers started to feel a little braver and not just mind their own business so much, and they even supported the trade-union activities, and we all started to feel the law was on our side and that maybe we could trust it. By demanding our legal rights with the management, the workers knew they were getting right to the heart of things: I mean the connection between management and the Mafia. So the workers felt their action was even more justified. And our new hopes kept growing.

The factory's continued to grow. Counting both companies now, there's more than twelve hundred employees. From a purely technical point of view the working conditions are modern, even good. And from the standpoint of industrial relations it's better than the shipyard. There you don't have any kind of united front. The whole story is, "if you don't like it, tough luck, that's the way it goes, period"—and things just grind to a halt. But here there's an elastic front, with real confrontation between the union and the bosses. Of course, you have to wheel and deal, and negotiations can drag on forever. They've got this public relations pitch. They pay lip service to democracy, tell us that they're always willing to discuss our demands, that they have deep concern for the individual worker, his leisure time and recreation. And they talk about setting up a company store to increase the workers' buying power. But basically they still treat us like children, and the boss is still the boss. He makes all the final decisions. Sure, there's lots of talk, but the last word is his.

Why haven't the people matured? Let's use the example of the union: we still haven't been able to make the workers realize that it's them that make the union. I can talk from my own experience. I was elected to the steering committee, and guys still come to me and say, "I voted for you, you owe me at least a coffee," or "I voted for you, the least you can do is a favor for a friend." They don't understand yet what real responsibility means.

There's nights my wife'll be talking to me and I won't even be aware of it—I'm too busy thinking. She'll tell me later I was so preoccupied I didn't hear a thing. See, I've got to have a definite purpose in my life, I've got to find a real way to live. I can't stand this resignation or being led by the nose or being alone and just waiting for a lucky break. I want to pull my own weight and have my fellow workers do the same. Maybe every little step I make forward means something, but if we worked together society would take a big one. Man wasn't created just to make money, that's not what makes him mean something. It depends on how he contributes to make a better society.

Sometimes I stop and look around at the world, and at myself —like I was far away up on a hill. I see man as a tiny creature scurrying all about. Sure, if you get up close, it looks big, like something that can stand all by itself. But really, we need other people. We can't live all alone.

37. ANGELA

She is Gaetano's wife. Thirty, slightly taller than he is, she speaks
with openness and equanimity. On the outskirts of Palermo, their
home is simple, immaculate, full of light and air.

I was fifteen when I met my husband. My mother died when I was four, so I was living in my grandmother's house. I stayed there in Arenella with my grandmother and my uncle. In fact, I never went out, so I didn't know a soul. We're good people, but we're very jealous. I wasn't even supposed to show my face through the shutters. I was the second-to-the-last of seven children and our people were so proper we never got the occasion to meet anybody else. My grandmother had a general store. We sold cigarettes too. If I'd be helping her around the store and a young man approached, she'd give me the signal to run and hide. She was extra careful because I didn't have a mother and she felt burdened with all the responsibility. I only got out once a week, to go to mass, and then they'd hurry me home. I wasn't accustomed to friends, but I loved children and mothers. Almost every girl I knew of was just like me.

One day I'm peeking out the door and I hear this scooter stop and a young fellow gets off. I kind of liked the way he looked, but I had my doubts. From his walk and the way he fidgeted with his jacket, he might have been the nervous type. Well, I saw him just that once. A month went by. Then a cousin of mine got to go to the movies, and the next morning she came to visit me cause I was sick. "Listen, Angela, there was this fellow at the movies. He kept looking us over." "Did he have a motor scooter?" She described him and I said, maybe it was him. Then a few days passed by and a new bakery opened up here in Arenella and I went to buy a couple of pounds of pasta and I saw that same fellow in the bakery. He looked at me and I did likewise. From that day on he'd always be at the bakery, standing around (see, the owner was his friend), and I'd come in to pick up our packages of cookies and things and on my way out I'd get all nervous inside cause I'd feel his eyes fixed on me. Things'd fall out of my hands and I'd be so flustered I'd blush.

But one day my brother decides, this has got to stop. "This guy has no business looking at you. It's a scandal. We can't put up with it." And he made me stay indoors all the time. I was forbidden to go near that store, so nobody'd get jealous.

Then my husband made his intentions known to my family—marriage. We'd never even spoken to each other. Oh, every once in a while he signaled to me, but I never could reply. I never thought it was serious till he snuck me a note through the proprietor's wife: "If you love me, write 'yes.' If not, just write 'no.'" And I wrote back "yes yes yes yes"—four times. My brother warned me to watch out for this guy: "He must be ten years older than you. That's too much." I was fifteen. I guess my brother thought I was still a child. But I looked seventeen, maybe even eighteen.

So we got engaged and right off the bat we cared for each other. When we were together we'd always talk. We were too intimate, my grandmother would say. They all were ashamed of us, she'd say. But we loved each other so much that we didn't pay them any mind and kept on talking that way for two years. He was a mechanic in the shipyard.

Of course, every now and then we'd argue, but we'd make up as soon as that. He'd always say, "In married life, you've got to take the thorns with the roses. It isn't easy. You've got to suffer too." But I loved him and it seemed silly to think about unhappiness. I'd say to myself, "Come rain or shine, I'll always be by his side." My family thought I was too young. I fooled them.

Sometimes him and my aunt would argue. He was a Socialist and she was very Catholic—a Christian Democrat, you know. He tried very hard to explain things to her. My aunt was afraid if Socialism won out they'd kill all the priests, shut down the churches, and wipe out religion. I didn't want to contradict him, but deep down inside I agreed with my aunt. Besides, seeing how hard they fought gave me a fright.

We got married, and he stayed on at the yard a bit longer. Then one night he comes to me and says, "I have to go to sea. You understand." "But why?" I cried. I guess I'm just that way. I didn't want my husband to go off and leave me all by myself. But he didn't make much at the yard and he figured what with kids coming, we needed a house. "You have to think of the future," he said, but I couldn't stop crying: "What you bring home's enough for me. We're fine in this little place. Please, don't leave." He didn't listen because he was set on leaving.

"And you're just going to leave me here like this? At least take me back to my grandmother's." So he did. Then I decided to rent a room nearby. Every time he'd send money home I'd buy some furniture.

He came back ten months later from that Persian Gulf. By then we had a baby girl. The whole time he was gone I didn't turn on the gas, I didn't feel like cooking. Mostly I'd eat what my grandmother sent over. Getting up a meal would have been like celebrating a holiday without my husband.

He came back and stayed two months. I kept telling him, "Leave well enough alone, stay home." I'd managed to pay the last installment on the furniture. "Find a job here." Well, he was just waiting to be called back to work, but he couldn't sit still. He found a job as a mechanic. As a special treat he took me to Turin to visit his brother and I got my very first chance to see upper Italy. See, I'd hardly ever been out of the house. For me it was like a honeymoon. His brother lived in these suburbs, almost out in the country, and they had flowers, and my husband showed me around and I loved it, seeing things all green, even in summer.

We got back and he was off again. Two years. Every twenty-six days he'd call or send a package, or sometimes I'd even go to Naples. His ship docked there, a day or so, before heading back for the Persian Gulf.

Then he came home to stay. I was overjoyed. But he'd never spend enough time in the house. He'd always have union or party things to do and I didn't want to get involved. I thought I was too stupid and couldn't comprehend. He'd say to me, "Honey, you know a lot about housekeeping, but you're innocent of the world out there." And I'd sort of scold him, "Watch out for yourself. Let things be. You're sticking your own neck out too much. Why do you have to do it all yourself? People don't even appreciate all the good you're doing for them." But that wouldn't stop him. "The day has to come when they understand. If everybody just cared about himself, we'd never push things ahead."

By now I was sort of resigned and I had my children to tend to. He'd come home at night so exhausted he'd just drop into bed. Or he'd have so much on his mind that I'd try to talk to him and he could hardly listen. I'd get mad: "Where's your mind wandering? You come home like this and hardly say a word." Sometimes he'd try to explain things, but it was hard to understand and my mind would wander to my housework. There were times he was so wrapped up in his work he didn't seem to care for me any more and it made me want to cry. I'd say to myself, "What's the use of living if it's nothing but work, unions, politics?" I wanted him home with me, at least after he finished work.

It's always the same story. Why, just last night the telephone rings and off he goes to the union, and who knows when I'll get a chance to talk to him again?

Still, I'm glad I married him. With all that union work, he does real good. Only trouble is, he wears himself out because he puts too much into it. It's not good when he doesn't take care of himself and comes home with his head pounding. I can't help thinking all the time, "Why on earth doesn't he stay home and settle down?" Sometimes I just say to him, "All right, I don't comprehend. No, you're not like the rest of them. They all look out for themselves. But then why do you have to worry about them?" He's driving himself into the ground for the workers, and some of them criticize him for not minding his own business. Many a time I expect them to fire him, but to tell the honest truth, I'm not too worried. I have faith in my husband. Then again, it upsets me. Somebody might do him real harm out of spite.

What worries me most is this: when he's upset he doesn't eat. There's lots of troubles on the job and he gets so mad he won't eat. It's fine to be concerned about others, but there must be ways to do it and still have some peace and quiet. Sure, I'm proud of him, but to tell you the God's honest truth, I never told him so.

My dream'd be to have my husband find me my own home on the outskirts of town, with fields and mountains all around, where we could grow flowers and live in peace. The way I lived my life as a girl was hard. I was unhappy, cramped up. Now that I'm married my life is still a burden. Sure, I'm freer. I can take the kids out all by myself to pick flowers in Favorita Park and eat ice cream and just have a good time. In Palermo, though, all us women mind our own business. Oh, we say hello real friendly, and I'm glad to loan my neighbors anything they need, but each one stays shut up in her own house. I'd really like to see something I don't see around here. What I mean is serious people with real integrity and parents that really understand their children. Around here everybody takes liberties and lives a very loose life, always looking for excitement.

Nobody should waste his life like that. I'd like to see men be brothers, be healthy, work and enjoy their peace and quiet, feel real good about just living. That's the way the body wants it too. Naturally we should all be united as brothers—as long as my husband can be with me more at home.

38. GINO ORLANDO

My Marxist-barber-poet friend gave me so many keys to his city.
To do his story we met at least ten times in various hubs of
activity—bars, restaurants, parks, squares, back alleys—that in and
of themselves were an education. When we reread the final
version together, Gino burst into tears. His story speaks for itself.

How did I come into this world? After my mother's husband died—he was a shoemaker—to survive she ran errands for other people. She was what you call a gofer. You know, someone who waits in all those endless lines at City Hall. That's the trick of their trade. And that's where she met my father. He was a civil servant. My mother was a beautiful woman and he began to play up to her. Of course, he didn't tell her he was married —never. He even made a few promises. So my mother gave in.

When I was born in 1912, I couldn't go by his name. My mother wouldn't ever put me up for adoption. Instead, she gave me her name. All I remember is she'd go to work and I'd play alone in the street, or sometimes she'd find a neighbor to sort of watch me.

Then my mother caught the Spanish flu and died. Nobody showed their face at the funeral. They all thought she was a . . . So there I was, a child of sin, and nobody gave a damn.

Well, I had this brother. He was legitimate—and engaged. His girl's family took me in. There was this young guy staying with them who'd go around picking pockets, and he started to teach me the trade. In thieves' language it's called filching. Starting on this innocent young lady, he taught me the method himself, the frontal attack. What's that? Well, I'd walk five or six yards ahead of our target. Then quick I'd wheel around and move in on her. Face to face with the purse, I'd decoy with my left arm, slip my right hand in under her elbow, and undo the button. In those days they made purses with buttons. Of course, some purses had hooks or zippers like suitcases, so you had to be a specialist in all kinds of openings. OK, first you get it open, then do a half-turn, slip your hand into the purse, and snatch the wallet or whatever.

When your career was launched there was one big issue: before they'd even think of giving you steady jobs, they'd put you to the test to see if you'd ever squeal. Then all it took was the recommendation of an old pro who'd been in the business for years: "This here's a good boy. He never talks." And off you'd go touring all the cities of Italy.

My first hitch was with this guy B. The first time I got gunshy—I had this tremendous urge to go to the toilet. It was awful. I was scared the woman would detect something and beat the shit out of me. I knew kids who'd get drunk or drugged first, to work up the guts. Me, I couldn't pull it off alone, but being with the other guy always made you brave. Nobody wants to look like a chicken, a coward. Besides, I needed a job. My partner had donated our earnings to the family (well, at least a share) cause that's where we ate and slept. He'd never give me the satisfaction of knowing what was in the wallets. He'd open them by himself. I'd make two or three filches a day. He was the shield and the fence.

On my street almost every family had a child launched on this career. Saint Augustine Street, Catarro Alley, Salaro Alley, up The Steps, on almost every street in the neighborhood, you'd find a master pickpocket or a school for apprentices. And it's still that way nowadays, business as usual, here and at Ballarò and other places. Just counting little kids, there's hundreds of them. Montalbo Street, Castro Street, the Borgo District, almost half of Palermo. With this expert training, people make it to America, even as far as Guinea. The old pros, once they're too famous, move on to Turin, Milan, Genoa. Up north it's easier. They don't know the tricks of our trade. They're sitting ducks. In Rome women act as the decoy: they rub up against you to distract your attention. But I better not go into detail, otherwise the authorities'll round everybody up. That's easier than helping people and giving them jobs. Things haven't changed since the landing of the

Turks. It always happens that way. They thought they could keep the peace by putting God in jail. Of course, store owners and anybody else informed about neighborhood operations would never squeal. When the cops were up to something fishy, you always knew ahead of time and made your getaway.

Nowadays they still have special trained forces, so-called agents, to hunt down the pickpockets. But let me tell you, they're just amateurs. In those days the notorious gangs of Sciabbica the Terrible put the fear of God into every crook. Fact is, he's retired now but it's still in his blood and he patrols as a hobby. Yeah, he was as quick as a fox.

I still remember how I'd go shop around. We'd go in teams of two and not just for sport. No, downtown it was all work and no play. At the hub of activity for all these crews, corner of Saint Augustine and Maqueda, we'd start to mobilize in front of the showcases and a gang would show up on the spot. I'd see it was Sciabbica coming, warn my buddies right off the bat, and we'd make a quick retreat up the alley. I'd run like hell and wouldn't stop till I got home, no matter how hard I'd be gasping for breath. All it took was being stopped and that meant three days in jail. I'd get home terrorized, thinking all the time maybe they'd identified me. You get back panting so heavy, your buddies can hardly wait for you to fork over the goods or to hear if they got the goods on you. You just got to catch your breath before you tell the whole story. This is still the way life is for these teams: alarm, panic, thrill, terror if you run across a gang. The two groups keep the same hours.

There are experts in snatching purses from women, "those poor little fish in the cruel sea." Then there are crews specializing in "fair game": men. They use the "baby hawk," a young boy around twelve, at most fifteen. He just has to be tall enough so his elbow can hit the target, depending where they carry their wallets. The baby hawk passes by the chosen prey and bumps into him so the breast pocket is revealed and the hawk's nestmate can see if there's any feed. If there is, the mate nudges the hawk in the same place where the prey's wallet is, and the hawk swoops down and nudges the coat open while his mate slips a hand in and snatches the feed.

It's easy to pull it off when there's a crowd or a traffic jam: your man has to dodge a carriage, a bike, a group of people. A lot of times the crews have to stage it all. But then it takes four or five guys. Prostitutes go in on it with you, too—see, once they're over the hill they have to find another job, like scrubbing floors, maybe even in the place where they sold their bodies for twenty years. Anyway, they're tired of going in and out of jail and they'll look for work that's not so risky. That's your labor force for what we call middlewomen. It's a matter of business angles. Then you need the shields, the wheeler-dealers, who'll push and shove and act like they have to get by.

If you pull it off, you have to divvy up the profits. To each according to his role. Actually the hawk and the mate split the pot. The shields and the whores, who are always employed part-time, take whatever crumbs you sweep their way.

Most of the victims are peasants in from the provinces. They come to the hospital or for work or supplies. As usual, they take along all their life's savings. Then there's the immigrants back from America who've worked all those years and wrapped their earnings up in a kerchief. That's a real sack of chicken feed. And it's not like they just have pickpockets preying on them. No, here like in Rome you have the shysters, trying to rake it all in. These guys'll dress up like they're just off the boat, cut out like a Yank, sailor hat, navy-blue jersey, the works, and they'll go looking for some sucker to unload the crap ("Made in America") that they carry in a suitcase: " 'Scuse me, Amurrican Consulate?"

It was the same old story till I was twelve. Usually to get us punks to work harder, they promised us a trip to the cathouse. One time they took four of us into this hellhole where there was a specialist in breaking in little kids. She just got on the bed and spread her legs and . . . Let's forget about all that filth. I'll also spare you the details about how you screw back the stool pigeon who's screwed you. That's enough of that.

By the time I was twelve it was like I was a special on the market. This guy found out I was a well-schooled thief, so he came to talk to my family and arrange for me to travel with him. My real career was launched—in the higher echelons. We even went to the Continent. What were our travel plans? The same bit. Just thinking about it hurts. We'd do the real tear-jerker routine. I'd make believe I was running away from home, and my boss, strap in hand, would act like he'd been searching high and low three days in desperation. Then he'd spot me and wave the strap like it was my scourge, and I'd fall on my knees and hug the first legs I could find for shelter. Of course, we'd already spotted the sucker as being loaded with feed. I'd shriek, cling, keep shrieking "I didn't mean it," begging the man for help. Naturally he'd have some pity and lean over to protect me from the blows, and that way my "father" could lift his wallet. Then he'd give the signal we agreed on, "Harrumpf," and I'd know we'd done our job and let go.

A lot of times we'd hire out a carriage and have the driver be our lookout. One day we were out on the Boulevard of the Thousand up near Mulino Pecoraro (I mean here in Palermo) and I spot this guy coming along with a dozen or so empty bottles. We go right to work. But as my boss gets to the wallet, the guy happens to notice. So he asks this stranger passing by to please hold his bottles cause his socks are falling down, and he takes out a gun and starts blasting away. We jumped into the cart like scared rabbits and took off. Of course, most people thought it was just one of those old-fashioned abductions of a pretty miss.

We traveled around, Palermo, Naples. Stayed in hotels. You had to get all decked out, say you were there on business. Then Milan, Turin. I got to see half of Italy. My partner got hold of a press pass once and it was easy going. But home base was always Palermo.

One time in a certain city, three of us met this woman and she showed us to this hotel. I was about fourteen. The other two were full-grown. They went about their business and I spent the night with her. She got me to soften up and tell her what we were up to. Next morning, she was gone without even collecting. When we got arrested, the cops knew the whole story from guess-who. Do you follow me? She was a double agent. So the police gave us the third degree and wanted to know if a certain sergeant, one of our benefactors from Palermo, had been working after hours like me. I played dumb and they released me. Later they promoted him to captain.

When I was fifteen, I was sent to the home of Santa Maria Capo at Vetere, Naples Province. One of my partners wasn't too happy about seeing me get locked up so he went incognito on the boat. My escort never suspected a thing. Then on the train he slipped me this medicine to rub in my eyes so they'd think I'd have contagious trachoma at the entrance exam and send me back into the streets. I wanted to be free. I was getting to like traveling around Italy so I took it. After eight days, I was declared unfit. But to this day, I still have a touch of chronic conjunctivitis.

I wasn't back in Palermo long before I hit the road again. During that swing I was sentenced twice, once for twenty days, another time for thirty. Being I was a minor, they suspended the sentences, but kept them on my record. Then one day I was arrested in Rome. They did everything they could to lock me up and throw away the key. I was shipped to Victor Emmanuel III Institute, Mantua Province.

That's where I had my first revolutionary experience. They'd beat the living shit out of us. The director did things to us I'd rather not mention. Raise a little hell when he was taking his nap and he'd land you with two or three days in solitary. Nights, we'd sneak into the kitchen and break into the cupboards for a little extra bread or we'd scale the garden wall for melons or tomatoes. Finally we decided to denounce him. We wrote a letter to the mayor with a list of all our grievances. It was signed by all the older boys and we drew straws to see who'd deliver it in person. I won. Well, when I got back, the director put a pistol to my head. But it wound up that he was asked to resign.

I was in there three years. It was the hermit's life, you can imagine. There were times you'd trade your food with the peasants for a cigarette. We had to walk miles to get to school and people would say to us, "You poor things, here, have some bread, a sip of wine." Whatever in hell they taught us I can't tell you. One teacher would let pure anarchy reign, another'd set us straight and that'd be all screwed up. From start to finish it was always a mess.

I got as far as sixth grade there. They started me in the third because I could read a bit myself. I was about ready to shave and felt like the father of the kids from town. We were all "integrated" in the classes. I still remember my first day at school. This teacher drew a triangle on the board: "Multiplying the base by the height and dividing by . . . you find the area of the triangle . . . You there, boy, do you understand?" "Yes, sir." I didn't, not a wooden nickel's worth. And he'd dictate, "This is the way the pony trots comma," and I'd write "c-o-m-m-a." "All good men come to the aid of their country period," and I'd write "p-e-r-i-o-d."

By sixth grade I was eighteen. But I went petting in the bushes with the mayor's daughter and it was a bit too close to school, so they kicked me out of the home. They'd had me dabble in agriculture, but never taught me a trade. Me, a city slicker, they wanted to make a hick. What was I going to do when I grew up —plant cucumbers in Saint Peter's Square?

Then it was three years in Rome, where I learned to be a barber. My old pals were always around, but I began to search for a new way of life. Now the court had given me a foster mother in Rome and I was determined to make a go of it there, but the police decided to ship me back to Palermo. And the police here, to solve me as a problem, past, present, and future, sent me into internment on the island of Pantelleria.

It's better not to talk too much about this either. It was one corruption after another. How does a human being lead a decent life? Tell me how. Even the little kids in town come up and say, "I'll beat your meat for a nickel." I'm ashamed to say certain things. The whorehouse was off limits to us, so people would be jealous, even of their bitches. You wouldn't believe it unless you went through it. And this is what they called rehabilitation.

I was twenty-two when I was released. I didn't have to worry about military service. My conjunctivitis kept me out. I went right back to Rome and started working as a barber: work, home, friends, a normal life. At this point I realized I had to break completely from my past. I felt a real need to raise a family of my own, to have love, affection, responsibilities. If you don't feel responsible to others, you wind up nowhere.

So I came back to Palermo. It made me sort of nostalgic seeing my old turf. Except now I was a barber, I could go to the Rose Café or walk under the clock of the Massimo Theater where all the fancy-pants (and skirts) had their little rendezvous. I went back to the Capo slums too—and felt like a foreigner. Seeing old friends, I'd tell them, "Look, all you rake in from one day, you pay back with years in jail. Instead of going to bed pissing in your pants that Sciabbica'll come knocking, earn your bread with an honest day's work and you sleep in peace." I kept saying it, but it still wasn't clear enough in my own mind for me to do much about it. Mostly I was sick and tired of what I'd had to endure in my life.

Well, I felt this real need to raise a family of my own, but as a barber I hardly earned enough to survive, so I asked this acquaintance of mine if he could find me a better-paying job. He talked to this fat cat, a real crooked gimp who pulled all the strings at this cement factory, hiring and firing as he goddamn pleased. They took me on as a "menial." That means a beast of burden. One minute I'd be at the furnace, the next I'd be carrying hot bricks with an iron hod. I just couldn't do it. To take a break, I'd go to the john three, four, five times a day. When the matter was called to the boss's attention he called me a lazy bum and told me to get my ass on out.

I was determined to earn enough money to get married. I pounded the pavements, drumming up orders for candles and other wax items. I sold figurines, cloth, fool's-gold watches, etc., etc., etc. I was even a gofer for a bit, and the worst damn hairdresser you ever saw. Jobs and all, I could never save up enough money to get married. My fiancée thought all our problems, economic and romantic, would be solved at the altar. Then she started talking about breaking it off. To me that meant all my sacrifices would be in vain, so I proposed that we elope. We snuck off and went to Rome. We got there homeless and me without a job. You bet back in Palermo they were talking: "Poor thing, she's ruined her life. Landed herself a nobody without a job."

We went to live with my foster mother. My whole life she'd been the only person I could trust. Poor as she was she still fed us. Our wedding was simple, the way the poor do it. Then my wife got sick, we had to take her to the hospital. I was still unemployed and our troubles kept multiplying. I'd have to go to bed on an empty stomach or go visit my wife empty-handed. I felt humiliated, not like a man or a husband. The day I managed to bring her an orange, it felt like a special celebration. An orange. What the hell is that? For me, it was the world.

It felt like I was all alone. I went from barber to barber looking for work. I was tempted to look up some of my old buddies in that other branch of work. The only thing that held me back was fear that my wife would leave me. One day I ran into an old pickpocket friend and he gave me a buck. That meant I could eat for two days straight and bring my wife a special treat. One evening I was eating some soup and my mother, who understood the battle raging inside of me, said, "Hey, Gino, watch out what you're doing. Remember you got a wife now, and she's just a kid. That's like a duty." Well, that brightened my outlook up a bit. Maybe it brought me some luck. A few days later a Neapolitan barber took me on for five dollars a week, plus tips. Otherwise it would have been seven. Finally, I felt happy.

My wife came out of the hospital, and we went to live in Marinella with a cousin of mine. Once in a while I'd go see my foster mother. Now that I was taking home some pay, I tried to help her out. Her husband had been one of those thousands of porters at the station, but now he lived off his former co-workers' charity. He could hardly afford a cigar or a glass of wine. Life was pure torture. Remembering how much they'd helped me out, I tried to do the same and be the peacemaker when they'd fight because he'd treat himself to something extra. Seventy years old and still up to mischief. For a whole week he'd save what he could scrape from his pipe and then chew it just for the taste of tobacco. Saturday nights he'd come home a bit drunk and lean over me so his moustache would be wet against my face, and he'd say, "Poor child."

Then we had a big blow-up with my cousin and came back to Palermo. Palermo, with nothing but our linen. Somebody'd pointed out my father to me and I knew my grandfather already. In fact, I would see him around town and ask him for two bits. Well, I had no choice but to look up my father. I'd never had much contact with him, so I felt no natural affection. It was necessity made me go see him. He decided my wife and me could live with him. He was still married, with kids, and his wife didn't exactly welcome us with open arms. But the man's word is law, so she had to grin and bear it.

My father was living in real misery. Being a Constitutional Socialist, he got fired from his job at City Hall. The first few days we were there it was me who fed the family with what little I'd saved up in Rome. It was touch and go for him, but with some friends left in City Hall, he could do a bit of gofering.

One evening before I got home, my sisters came in grumbling there was nothing to eat. Then I came in and one of them said, "Gino, Poppa's loaded but he won't give us no money for food." I looked at him to see if she was telling the truth. He nodded and said, "Yes, but it's all to pay for a client's papers." His honesty amazed me. See, I knew what most Palermo gofers were like: double-dealers and double-crossers making shady deals in front offices, law courts, police courts, all over the place. If you want forged documents, for them it's a cinch.

We finally had to move out of my father's house because every night when we were asleep on two mattresses laid out on the floor, his wife would throw pebbles at us. She wanted to make us think the house was haunted. One time my wife wanted to go to the toilet but she was trembling in her stockings: "Gino, there's spirits in this joint" (I guess the pebbles were getting to her). So I decided to turn the spirits on his wife. She and my father slept in a room with a little altar and it had a candle that gave off light into our room too. One night when the stones were flying, I grabbed a shoe, took aim on the altar, and hit the target so everything went pitch-black. Then I wrapped myself all up in a sheet and ran around screaming, "Ghosts! Spirits!" and I jumped on the queen mother's bed and pummeled the living daylights out of her. Next morning I put on a poker face: "You mean to tell me there's spirits? Then we're leaving." And we left.

I rented out a barber shop. It was tough. You could lose a customer just for forgetting to brush off his lapel or help him on with his coat. They'd come to set up regular appointments and I'd write it all down on my calendar: "Your name, please, sir," or "May I have your name, sir?" One false move and you lose a customer. Miss a hair or don't bow deep and kiss ass like your competitor down the block, and that's it. Tough stuff. The barber in Rome gave me regular hours, but with the Neapolitan, a real Southerner, I had to work till the guy across the street shut down for the night. He pulled the same trick, so nobody'd get home till ten.

I remember seeing in my father's house a picture of a young woman dressed like a real lady. "Who's that there?" "It's your sister; she lives with your uncle." It turns out she was also my mother's daughter, seven years older than me. And I happened to find out where she lived. But to see her at first I had to disguise my identity, making believe I was bringing word from an uncle of hers in Rome. Bourgeois society, let me tell you, there's so much pettiness they can't work up the courage to say, "Yes, I'm responsible." But they'll stop at nothing to sidestep their own filth, to avoid real love and affection. If my father'd had the guts to say right off, "He's my son" (the way my mother did), I wouldn't have had to plow through all that garbage . . .

OK, I had to make a special date to see my sister on the sly, not at this uncle's house. We met at my cousin's—I'd never met him either. I came in nervous and all choked up. Everybody sat down on this couch. Moments of silence, just waiting to see who would start up the conversation. I tried my luck: "How come you're living with Uncle . . . and not with Poppa?" "Uncle loves me dearly and doesn't have any children. Besides, he's furthering my education just like a father should. But where have you been all this time? Poppa told me I had a brother but he never told me where you were." "Look, I didn't know I had a sister till just recently." Then she asked for all the details: degree, religion, ideology (it was during Fascism). I told her I'd gotten up to sixth grade but never studied much religion or politics. Well, she launched into this disquisition on good Catholics and Fascists, and was amazed to hear that I wasn't either. She had a degree in liberal arts. To further her amazement I told her that if I'd had her education, I'd probably have the good fortune to be Fascist, Catholic, and Degreed like her.

How could I feel love for a sister like that? In bourgeois lingo, you say it's the blood. Well, mine's got to be different. I said, "Sure, we'll get together," and left.

Our paths crossed again: she needed somebody to escort her to renew her party membership. Lucky me, we're on our way to Bologni Square (where they'd set up the Fascist headquarters) and she warns me that if we run across a very short man, I should get out of sight. See, being her fiancé he might get jealous. (Incidentally, she didn't want him to know we were related.)

Then we lost contact till after the war, when my father died. I'd visit her now and then. At that point I was a Communist. She invited me over once on Christmas—for supper. I showed up right on time. They were getting things ready and the doorbell rang: it was his relatives (by then he was my "brother-in-law"). My sister got flustered and asked me to wait in another room. I walked out. I've never seen her since.

Why did I become a Communist? First off, with the hell I'd been through, something was all built up inside. Communism meant a new life for me and everybody, work for everybody, redemption, no more Sciabbicas, because if there's work, there's no crooks, except the kleptos. That's the theory. Now let me tell you about the practice.

To keep a barber shop going, you had to deal with the black

market. I sold contraband cigarettes supplied by a Customs guard. I did it without any scruples, because to tell the truth all us barbers did it. So we ate well while everybody else went hungry.

One day I decided to demonstrate against hunger. I organized the whole thing. In the back room of the shop I wrote a manifesto. It ended with "Long live Stalin, long live Roosevelt, long live Sicilian Communism." I asked for contributions and got it printed, bought the paste myself, and we formed our own Anti-Fascist Action Party. One item on our agenda was to kick the Fascists' ass. Some of my comrades went with me to post our manifesto all over the place and pass it out to people downtown.

One day I was giving a shave when this deluxe American car stopped in front of the shop. I thought it had to be an important customer so I told my wife to get out a clean towel. Instead it was some officers of the American armed forces. They'd come to arrest me for disobeying Alexander's orders. "Aren't you familiar with the Alexander Directive?" "The only thing I know is people are dying of hunger." So I had to stand before a military tribunal. They gave me a year, sentence commuted.

A few days later, seeing what I'd done, this schoolteacher came into the shop and invited me to stop by the Socialist headquarters. They still couldn't organize out in the open, but I went to some of their private meetings. Once I dissented when we voted on the agenda, and they reprimanded me for the way I expressed myself. I applied for party membership. But I got fed up with all the debates on pros and cons. I wanted to see some action, so I stopped going to meetings.

Then they were authorized to go public. I organized a barbers' demonstration with them, but I met a Communist there who convinced me that my place was with his party. I joined the Party in 1943. Right away they made me responsible for a street cell. Later I headed a section. Reading really started to mean something to me. Besides teaching me what the Party believed, it satisfied that thirst for knowledge I had all along. I organized collective readings with the workers. We began with *Historical and Dialectical Materialism* by Marx. For months on end, we racked our brains to understand. Then there was the history of the Bolshevik Party. And *The City of Socialism* by Gramsci: I learned a lot from this book and it's always served me well. See, society's like a train with a whole lot of cars. In front there's a new streamlined engine and the cars hooked up to it represent the various stages of development of society in the past, all its different structures with all their defects. It's a rough ride because the cars are in bad shape—bolts keep jarring loose, doors fall off. To repair things you need everybody working together. When everything's straightened out, you travel smoothly toward the City of Socialism.

I got a Marxist education and kept working as a barber. But this trade, especially in Palermo, is no way to earn a decent living. Besides, by then I was the father of four kids, so I tried to get into something else. One day I spoke with a qualified comrade who proposed that I clerk at the Agricultural Workers' Federation. I accepted. Meanwhile the party leaders had started up a correspondence course in politics. I took part.

Believe me, I worked damn hard. I was committed to my studies because I knew that the more political education I got, the more I could contribute to the Party. I remembered something else Gramsci said: "Educate yourself because the revolution is made with human resources. Society needs new men, men who are aware." I read by candlelight to save on electricity. But one day I got depressed, I kept thinking maybe I wasn't good at anything. It was partly from all that studying that I started to suffer from nervous exhaustion. I wrote the school, the Party in Rome, asking them if it was worth it for me to continue. I started to doubt that revolution would ever come in my lifetime. They wrote back saying the mere fact that I could study under such conditions was a hopeful sign, and besides, history couldn't be measured in terms of one man's life. Well, I wrote the final essay for the course and a comrade told me it was excellent: sixteenth best out of four thousand. I really felt appreciated, and I started to work for the local steering committee with coresponsibility to organize the peasants.

My first meeting in the provinces, the peasants were expecting my comrade in person. The hall was decorated for a gala celebration. When they saw me instead they asked, "What's up? Who are you? Where's P.?" Well, I saw this P. was their hero, so I tried extra hard to convince them that the class struggle has nothing to do with private interests and that the individual has to be one with the masses. There were no heroes, I said, just people who understood and expressed our vital needs. I was pleased when I got back home. I'd gained their attention and trust, felt their genuine warmth, and even though I still couldn't express myself well, I'd found a way to make myself understood among human beings who were struggling for the right to live. At first, I'd struggled just for myself alone. Now it was a real redemption.

In '49 I was invited to the National Congress of the Agricultural Workers' Federation at Mantua, and I realized that those desperate Sicilian peasants, who were digging in and getting ready to occupy the barons' lands, were one with the whole working-class struggle in Italy. It choked me up when this poor woman from Lecce got up on the platform and said, "I'm sorry. I don't speak Italian good, but up till when they give us land and my babies got shoes, me, I'll never wear out. Not ever. I'll fight with my comrades. I don't give a damn, not even about billy clubs."

When I got back, I went right to Marineo where the struggle for occupation was in full swing. I replaced this comrade who'd let anarchy reign, and next day I organized the peasants in a march to occupy the estate. That was when I learned a hard lesson in practice. See, I'd read about semicollective experiments in Russia so I urged the peasants to do total collective farming. Instead they ran around trying to divide the land into small plots. Each one to his own little acre. They all wanted to stake their claim, with fences, stones, even harness straps. It was like people on a train plunking down hats, purses, newspapers just to save a seat.

I was so amazed I called a peasant aside and said it just wasn't fair. "Sorry, Comrade Gino, it's tough. Let that guy work his fingers to the bone, I'll work hard and have the best crop and everybody'll envy me."

I can't exactly say how things worked out because soon I left for Montelepre. I made stops in Terrasini and Partinico before I moved on to Montelepre. Wherever I went, I'd see it in peasants' faces, real joy in making their dream on earth a reality—"a chunk of land." It's hard to describe what I was feeling and thinking in those moments. Montelepre, thanks to Giuliano, was in the limelight internationally—and here I was in the heart of that bandit country. Sure, I'd think about how thirty-six peasant organizers had been riddled with the bullets of hired assassins right here in this part of Sicily. I guess I took chances. This peasant showed me the short cut from Montelepre back to Carini. Another time we went from Partinico to Montelepre, same kind of road. Do you follow me? I never worried about things like that before, not even during the War of Liberation, when the enemy was always staring you in the face. But here you never knew: one blast from behind a prickly pear bush and . . .

One evening I was speaking at the Montelepre trade union and a cop came in. He invited me down to the station. The captain wanted to talk. I told him to wait till I was finished. As we were leaving, about twenty peasants decided to come along. The captain was waiting, trying too hard to keep cool. "Please sit down. Sorry to put you out of your way, but you must know about the area and it's our duty to notice strangers here in town. Of course, I don't mean to intrude but tell me, what is it you're doing here in Montelepre? Now don't think I have anything against trade unions. I'm a worker like you. Look, in Turin I made the personal acquaintance of Togliatti's wife . . ." When they ushered me out, I found the peasant workers still waiting.

From another experience I became aware of the gap between the thinking of an overwhelming majority of the peasants and the real function of the union. It was like the union was a welfare or charity organization. Not many peasants understood that it wasn't just a struggle to survive economically, but that it was a vital necessity to join in the political struggle and transform the whole of Italy.

I went to Carini to help coordinate things. The whole area was patrolled by police, so we had to figure out how to get to the estate. We couldn't all go as a group. Otherwise they'd spot us and that'd mean jail. We talked it over with the local organizers, trying to think of all the shortcuts, whatever way to go so we wouldn't be spotted. I was new to the area so I just listened. Finally everybody agreed that we'd start out in groups of four or five, making believe we were on our way to hoe, and that we'd meet at a given time at Case Nuove, unfurl our banners, head for Sagana, and all descend from there to the estate on the Plain of the Oranges.

People had to come from towns nearby, so some of the organizers went to tell them we were on the way. I stayed in Carini and next day at dawn we went knocking on everybody's door: "Turi, wake up, we're going to the land. Land, don't you want none? . . . Land!" Then we left in small groups. We came across a squad of cops, but they were fooled. The road through the mountains was hell and my shrapneled leg kept acting up. I got wounded as a volunteer in the War of Liberation. Somehow I kept going by hanging on to the mule's tail. Once I just sprawled out on the ground, sure that I'd never make it.

We got there around seven. The groups arrived one by one. All in all there were about thirty of us. We rolled out the banners and headed for Sagana. At the edge of town we saw in the distance another group of peasants with banners, the Partinico comrades. We joined forces, hugging and kissing. But meanwhile the Commando Militia for the Elimination of Banditry had formed their wedge in our path. An officer marched up and asked us our business. We told him the truth: we'd come to occupy the estate. He tried to break us up with threats, "Law and order, prison, etc." At the same time, a captain was intimidating a group of peasants. They were carrying the Italian and the Red flags. "You there, down with those banners. Around here

we're not Communists. Ditch that Red flag, we're in Italy."
There was a real danger that we'd react and fall into their trap.
In fact, I found out later that's what happened at Bisacquino.
Over the issue of flags all hell broke loose. People and police had
been seriously wounded.

But they couldn't scare us, not even with all their Tommy
guns. We came to an agreement. The flags would be leaned up
against the wall, but left unfurled. Meanwhile the officers tried
to stall for time. They told us the prefect was meeting with
peasants at Montelepre to make a pact. The land would be distributed and no occupations would be necessary.

Since we were waiting for the peasants from Montelepre anyway, we started to play a little tiddlywinks. We waited and
waited. They didn't show up. Somebody suggested we should
keep going and occupy the land. We sent a comrade to see what
was happening in Montelepre. Meanwhile, way off in the distance, we detected some movement along the road. "The comrades! Here come the comrades!" No such luck. We finally
realized it was the police, with gold braids and guns glittering.
You bet your sweet ass they were armed to the teeth. To them we
were a gang of bandits, and maybe the real bandits were watching from their hideouts and enjoying the whole show.

They came with armored cars, rounded us up, and herded us
into a courtyard. Then they ushered us into their headquarters,
a dungeon from the days of the Bourbons. The captain sat down
at a desk and they had us all line up according to our hometowns.
He sees me standing out of line: "You there, where you from?"
"I'm an organizer. I represent all of us." They begin by taking
down our names and addresses. "This is a warning. You're on
record." Then they escort us to the square opposite headquarters
and the officer launches into this diatribe: we better watch out,
the law won't tolerate such things. We cut him short: "You're
a cop, not a lawmaker."

Seeing that the organizers had been detained, the peasants
decided to stay put. To them we were as good as sentenced. The
police trained Tommy guns on them: "All right, break it up.

Move along, all of you." To avoid any confrontation, we told them to go home to their families.

Well, it turns out that as they're moving along, our comrade arrives and says Montelepre's surrounded and that's why nobody showed up. But being a Northerner he knows his way around and isn't afraid of bandits or cops. So he gets the peasants charged up and leads them to the estate. Later, of course, the cops ran them off.

Meanwhile they've escorted all us organizers to the paddy wagons parked on the state road. A limousine arrives and the officer rushes up and makes a big salute. It must have been the prefect, because when the car takes off they hustle us into two wagons and take us down to the station. When they get news that our comrades have occupied the estate, they take us to the Ucciardone Prison in Palermo. That's where they gave the bandit Pisciotta* a cup of poisoned coffee and nobody breathed a word. Get these charges: "Inciting to riot, criminal conspiracy, and attempted occupation of land."

We were packed so tight in this four-man cell that we could hardly budge. What with the shit-bucket and the soup, there was this combination of stinks . . . I was in jail for six months. So I could study serious social problems firsthand, and we set up the Sagana Cell and even enrolled a few members. Then I was released and went back to my normal activities with the Agricultural Workers' Federation.

When Eisenhower came to inspect the troops in Italy, the people staged a mass demonstration against the war. I made it a point to be in Massimo Square. I had to participate. I don't know how it happened but confusion broke out. I saw a woman getting shoved up against a paddy wagon and the Honorable Colaianni, introducing himself as a deputy, was trying to talk the cops out of arresting her. Somebody thought it was Colaianni being arrested and they all started shouting, "Long live Sicily! Long live the Sicilian Parliament!" There was insurrection in the air, and as usual, the riot squad ran around like chickens with their heads

* Giuliano's second-in-command, who finally betrayed him.

chopped off, and I found myself in a headlock of this chief blood-
hound. Well, I showed him my disabled veteran's card, but they
billy-clubbed me anyway and threw me in the wagon and took
us all to Faletta Prison, where I met men and women arrested
after the demonstration on the Plain of the Greeks—the same
place they killed Damiano Lo Greco, a peasant who was also
demonstrating for peace.

I was in custody eleven days. Then I was jailed officially and
brought to trial before the Commission for Internment. In prison
I realized how valuable our party paper was, keeping me in contact with what was going on. One day I open *Unity* and see this
article in the form of a letter signed by all the groups in our
movement and also by some of our representatives. "Who is
Gino Orlando?" was the title, and right there in print was my
life, how I'd evolved and managed to redeem myself on the
front lines of the struggle for peace and freedom. If it wasn't
for the comrades who defended me, I'd of been sent up for five
years.

Well, the prefect was working with this commission and he
wanted to know exactly what I was doing in that crowd: "We
have reports of missing wallets." I felt humiliated, rotten. There
I was in that room smelling of deluxe cigarettes and perfumed
overcoats on velvet couches. He keeps prying: "That's a very
fancy coat you've got on." I'd bought it at the flea market where
they sell surplus American goods.

I was put on probation for two years and barred from any
political activity. I had to stay within city limits. How could I
ask the police for special permission to go and organize a peasant
meeting? But the Party kept my position open the whole time.
Their expression of solidarity kept me from going over the deep
end. From one minute to the next I was trying to overcome my
past, but the authorities kept nailing me down to it. You report
to them and they do everything they can to enlist you as one of
their spies, their stoolies.

They'd call me down to the station on any poor excuse. One
time the chief inspector said, "You, boy"—I had five kids—"have

you ever been in jail?" "No." So he promised to suspend my probation. Then he summoned me again. My record was out on his desk. "You told me you'd never been in jail, but look here . . ." "Your Honor, I've never been a *political* prisoner before." Well, he got fatherly. "Listen, my boy, look out for yourself. You weren't born for politics. To each his own. Find an honest job, let's say . . ." "Sir, I'd be glad to . . ." "Let's say, selling fruit, or . . ." "But, sir, I have a record. I can't go beyond city limits. It's you who've put me under surveillance." "But it's you who've asked for it. What do you say? Keep out of trouble, bring me some news every now and then . . . to me, personally . . . nobody else, and. . . ."

Here they say, "You're my sweet tooth." Before being what we call in Palermo a "chocolate peddler"—that means a spy—I'd have killed myself. These chocolate peddlers have an organization, a network of gangs, made up of four or five guys with a record. They take about a hundred of those hollow chocolate candies and insert slips of paper with numbers, ranging from one up to five hundred. All these chocolates are mixed in with the thousands of regular candies.

The high-numbered chocolates are marked. They put little dots on the wrappers so you don't see anything unless you're wise to it. It's only the associates who know about the system. Just like the guys who are in the numbers, these peddlers sell their chocolates. First, they put on a show to attract a crowd. They clown around, do Punch-and-Judy stunts, pull eggs out of hats. Pay your money, you get a chance to draw, just like in a raffle. If business is slow, the associates bid high. Of course, the man in the street picks a candy worth one or two bucks—or nothing. It's the associates who get the high numbers, but if a person in the crowd picks a lucky candy the peddler pulls a chocolate with a lower number out of his pocket (he's got them there on reserve), and with a sleight-of-hand he does an exchange.

There must be about two hundred chocolate peddlers in Palermo. Technically, it's gambling, swindle, old-fashioned American style. So if they weren't stool pigeons, they could never do it in public. They also do card tricks ("now you see it, now you don't") and the "guess-where-the-little-ball-is" with thimbles.

Just about every neighborhood has its chocolate peddlers. A lot of them are retired killers who used to terrorize the Capo or the Albergheria. Nowadays they're lucratively employed by the cops. The authorities wouldn't think of helping them find work, something they could be proud of. Instead they see them down-and-out and take advantage, playing on their guilt complexes for their past and letting them sink even deeper. Maybe it's better when they're so-called men of honor in the underworld. At least they have some kind of respect. But when they become double-crossers, their old buddies won't give them the time of day. Everybody treats them like scum.

The relationship between the authorities and people struggling to survive is based on charity, paternalism, if anything. People need connections. Take the brain and tripe hawkers. The stuff is hard to come by. They have to kiss ass to get their goods. They look up to the authorities like they were gods. If their supply gets shut off, they starve to death. Naturally these poor bastards vote for the Man and his boys. Generally speaking, they don't give a damn about politics so they vote for you-know-who. Yeah, the Mafiosi get their greasy paws in there to control the votes for the Man. Or when there's a breaking-and-entering, they get busy all over town and get the stuff back for their clients. That way, the merchants will be sure to tip them off. Little folk have to eat.

Well, I go back to being a traveling barber, six kids by now, and the Party's broke and can't manage to put me on salary. I visit my regular customers right on schedule, but it's not enough to make ends meet. So I pound the pavements of the Capo and people recognize me passing by with my sack and call "Gino!" and bring a chair out into the street and put a bowl of water on the stoop. Somehow we survive.

Here's the real torment. Mornings when I leave for work, I start doing the arithmetic in my head. How much will I have to take home? I shave a guy all the time thinking about that quarter I have coming to me. When I'm through he might say, "Hey,

Gino, how about if I pay you tomorrow?" That happens a lot. And how can I collect if a guy is sick? Sixteen years of marriage and we still don't have enough furniture. Till just a few days ago we were renting one room, third floor. Eight people in a space eight by twelve. Then the house just fell to pieces and they evacuated us here to the school, with eighteen other families. The rest went to Feliciuzza Hospital. School starts again in five days and we don't know where we'll wind up.

Once a month I go down to the disabled veterans' placement office to have my little book restamped. See, there's a law that promises us a job. In nine years almost to the day, they've never found me a single day's work. Yesterday I went there to update my dossier. It was the same old story. I hand my book to this servant of the public. The poor bastard is at the end of his rope. By any stretch of the imagination he has to do the work of five or six employees. It's backbreaking. He's on edge. He's nothing but a bundle of nerves. (When I was a kid I was considered a public enemy and the boys down at the station harassed me, hunted me down like I was an animal. Now that I'm older I realize that I have to understand the tragedy of their lives. They're nothing but workers exploited by this state too. As a kid I'd see a cop and get like a rabbit caught in the glare of a car's headlights. Today when I see a cop, I feel for him. As a group they've gone nowhere. They still have the same mentality.)

It's one big chaos, people packed so tight they're crushing each other. "Quiet, please . . . Mazzola, Ganci, DiMaggio." "Here!" "No, he's not." "Here, pass it down." "Sorry, that's not my book." "Yes it is." Meanwhile everybody's grumbling: "What in God's name are they doing? It's a disgrace." "What we need is a bomb." "Watch out, they'll hear you. See what happened to that guy yesterday." We're all jammed together, men and women. This young guy gets in a cheap feel. He rubs up against his neighbor and plays a little pocket ball. It's raining. People outside are trying to push their way in. The people inside push back. The guard shouts, "Stand back!" That makes everybody push harder. An invalid elbows his way through. "Your papers, please. Excuse me.

Where do you think you're going?" "Minasola! Minasola!" The
main door swings shut. Somebody pushes it open. "Sorry, did
you call Geraci?" "Where's my book?" "Come back tomorrow."
"But I'm sick." "So what am I supposed to do about it?"
It's not a placement office. It's a Tower of Babel.

Sometimes I wonder how I've made it through forty-two years
of life. Maybe it's all been worthless, but I remember that I've
spent some of those years making life a little less hard for others,
so they wouldn't have to go through the same experiences I did.
Then again, I've lived for my family, my children, and the Party.
I believe it's been the struggle, the experience with the Party,
that's made me a new man. Many mornings I get out of bed
before going off to work and go to the crib where two of my
children sleep and I kiss the baby and think that at least he has
the warmth I never had. "Maybe I'm good for something after
all"—though I still keep thinking maybe . . .

You see, the kind of life I led in the past has left me with an
inferiority complex. In spite of my new idea of life, I have a hard
time dealing with others. That happens especially when I need
the strength to try to make fundamental principles of our democratic structures prevail.

If I had to keep struggling on all alone, measuring my own
strength against all the odds and all the men I work with and
against, I'd really get discouraged. But what I've learned keeps
me going. See, life is like a bottle of oil and vinegar. If you
keep shaking it, everything gets mixed up. But just stop and the
oil (that's the truth) comes to the top. That's the way nature
works.

With this faith, struggling to earn my bread, I'll never stop
working with others for the good of the community. Whenever
the chance comes to fight on behalf of the people living in a back
alley or for somebody's family, I'm ready. Here, read this letter I
just got from a comrade: "I just wanted to thank you and all the
other comrades for everything you did to make my military
service in Palermo a worthwhile experience. Thanks for all the
political education. I promise it will be put to good use. Thanks

for the unforgettable dinner you gave me just before I left. And for all the warmth and hospitality you showed me and my fellow soldiers. I'll never forget you. When I get old and take my grandchildren on my knee, instead of telling them all those fairy tales about sorcerers and hobgoblins, I'll tell them about my courageous comrades from Palermo who keep fighting to free Sicily from its exploiters and bloodsuckers, to help it evolve and make it more beautiful. I'll tell them the story of how you welcomed your fellow men who came all the way from Emilia—as brothers."

39. THE CHILDREN

This is one of the many maieutic discussions we've had with children during our seminars at the Borgo di Trappeto (formerly, the People's Free University). These children range in age from about six to fifteen.

AMICO: White horses run the best.

DANIELA: Right, they're stronger and beautifuller.

CIELO: That's because they're lighter.

DANIELA: Yep!

CHIARA: They sure are lighter.

DANILO: But why?

CIELO: They're happier.

AMICO: Their color, that makes them lighter. It's like when I run faster cause I'm all dressed in white.

CHIARA: White is lighter.

LIBERA: But there are strong dark horses and weak white ones. In the races last summer there were light and dark horses. The darkest horse won.

CIELO: But the horses that lost weren't white.

DANILO: Chiara, Amico, what do you think?

CHIARA: Hmmm, let me think . . .

AMICO: If it's the way Libera says, then dark horses run better.

CIELO: If the light horses were white, they'd of won.

LIBERA: What if the white horses were too weak to pass that dark one?

CIELO: What if the best horse was the one that got trained the best? It wouldn't matter if it was light or dark. If they train you the best, you win.

LIBERA: That's it.

AMICO: Know what? Libera and Cielo are right. If you're weak, you can't run.

CIELO: Maybe the lighter horses were slow because their shoes were too tight or too loose. Or maybe they were smaller and took smaller steps.

RUGGERO: Or maybe the jockeys weren't so good.

DANILO: So what is it that makes a horse fast or slow? How do you measure its speed?

CHIARA: What does "measure" mean?

LIBERA: How much speed there is, faster or slower.

AMICO: I don't know about horses. I can't tell. Maybe we should watch a whole bunch of them run. Then we'll see who runs the best.

CIELO: It all depends on training and how strong they are and how long their legs are and how old, too.

CHIARA: You're not so strong when you're old.

DANIELA: That white one runs the best. She's my favorite.

CHIARA: Only if she's trained the best and she has the longest and strongest legs.

LIBERA: Dad, I forgot the question you asked us.

DANILO: Does a horse run faster or slower because of its color?

LIBERA: OK, we want white horses to be the fastest and strongest because we like them the most. But like Amico says, we want to be sure what we want to be true is true, so we have to try it out.

CIELO: Yeah, it's like when we think trees are alive and really talk to each other. But you've got to see if it's really true. Maybe we don't hear everything they say to each other.

LIBERA: It's like when we want stars to talk to each other. You have to check if it's really true. Sure, they have an attraction, they communicate. But do they really talk?

BRUNA: It's like when we hope all men are brothers. Then we look around and see Mafiosi beating down the peasants and people don't have work and nobody gets together. They shoot each other and there's always wars. We got to be brothers. We can't mind our own business. We got to work together.

EPILOGUE

In spite of difficulties and contradictions that pile up every year, every day, our growth process of conscientizing never stops.

In this area, the most rural part of western Sicily, we are trying to understand the positive values and limitations of the local culture. Of course, pure objectivity is impossible. But in the uncertain light of our consciousness, we must search for valid intuitions and try to verify our findings by comparing them with other cultural values. Naturally, in a context that is always changing, the process of intuiting and testing intuitions in confrontation with reality is continual.

First, you have to scratch beneath the thin but sticky surface of the local bourgeoisie. It's a surface full of the pretty bubbles blown through the mass media by the State and by international conglomerates. Nevertheless, if you can reach the people who still live in close rapport with the earth and sea, you can discover essential values, their genius: (1) love of work: the earth, its every tree and piece of land, is conceived as part of the family; (2) a culture rooted in and nourished from head and hands, neither too intellectual/spiritual nor too materialistic: witness the high quality of the people's works of artisanry, where beauty and utility, form and matter, are perfectly balanced; (3) the need for a simple, unitary life: if they drop a piece of bread, they pick it up and kiss it; (4) a profound sense of family responsibility seen in natural concern for elders and children; (5) the need to be clean, morally: cleanliness at home is important—in fact, they scrub till the tiles are worn thin—but the very word "clean," while not used in a social context, is the key to affirmation of personal dignity; (6) the need to explore religiously the most profound questions of life and death (often at the risk of falling into superstition).

Perhaps the most serious limitations of the local culture are: (1) the absence of traditions of democratic planning and group action; (2) the lack of a progressive awareness of what nonviolence means. (Naturally, progress is a relative matter. Who can judge? And what is progress? There's a fine line between positive and negative values. And virtue, in excess, goes wrong.)

Here are some recent front-page headlines from major Italian newspapers:

—7TH VICTIM OF TERRORISM THIS MONTH

—NEW WAR ON TERRORISM: BATTLES RAGE IN STREETS: ARRESTS

—TERRORIST SENTENCED TO 10 YEARS: FILES BARS, ESCAPES

—MAXIMUM SECURITY IN ANTI-TERRORIST OPERATIONS

—TURIN AND MILAN: BLOODY AMBUSHES BY RED BRIGADES: KNEE-CAPPING, ARSON, ARMED ROBBERY

—200 TERRORISTS ARRESTED IN 5 MONTHS

—PROSECUTOR AND GUARD KILLED

—3 TERRORISTS APPREHENDED: WARRANTS OUT FOR 40 MORE

—TERRORISM AND VIOLENCE SPREAD

—JUDGES REQUEST PERSONAL PROTECTION, STRONGER MEASURES VS. TERRORISM

—JOURNALIST AND POLICEMAN CUT DOWN

—FOUND IN RED BRIGADE HIDEOUTS: BOMBS AND COMICS: MICKEY MOUSE AND POPEYE

—NEW GOVERNMENT STRATEGY: ANTI-TERRORISM PLAN UNDER MINISTERS' STUDY: FUNDS TO POLICE ESCALATE

—NEW TERRORIST LOGISTICS

—TERRORISTS SUSPECTED OF DRUG TRAFFIC: CONTROVERSY OVER NEW POLICE BRUTALITY

Once again, in Italy, violence is countered with violence. Once again the State fails to analyze and root out the profound causes of the problem. Ignoring how the crisis strikes young people first of all, the State treats the symptoms, not the disease.

Banditism has taught our leaders nothing. The chain reaction of tragic eruptions of violence has taught them nothing. They take the same old approach: shoot first, ask questions later. They never try to learn, or comprehend.

I've thought a great deal about how I might put these stories in the context of the immediate present. Thirty years have passed since I began my work in Sicily. Calò (denounced by our Center for Research and Initiatives for his Mafia connections), the cardinal (thwarted in his campaign to become pope), Salvatore Vilardo (convicted for fixing soccer games), Princess Sonia, Miraglia's friend, are dead. Rosario is still unemployed, as is Santuzza. Gino, still lucid, is chronically ill, yet insists upon remaining in his slum neighborhood across from Palermo's Cathedral. Gaetano is still struggling with trade-union problems. And the children, now young adults trained as artisans, musicians, educators, and conscientious objectors, must struggle to find jobs in a miasmic social body where the unholy alliance of the Mafia and "legal" institutions is even more insidiously powerful. In fact, chieftains like Don Genco have been replaced by technocrats, financiers, and corporate executives, on international as well as national and regional levels.

Perhaps the best way to conclude, then, is by telling another timeless and timely story. Just outside Partinico, there's a narrow country road that winds up a mountainside as far as a small mill. The road keeps washing out and getting more and more dangerous. But one spring, just beyond the cracked bridge without rails crossing a deep gully, among the almond trees, a school called Mirto is built: an experimental school conceived by the people themselves where educators, children, and parents can be midwives to one another, helping to draw out one another's creativity in an atmosphere of mutual respect and trust, growing maieutically and flowering together as creatures of this creature called the earth.

AMICO: On our walks, just like we agreed, I write down our discoveries. That way, when we go back inside we can remember every sentence, every name, every moment, in all their resonance:

"A snail's too small to make noise. But maybe it hears us cause our voices are loud."

"Onions make noise if you slam them—or else they don't."

We come across a small waterfall and stop to listen.

"The water makes noise cause it's so steep."

"The stones don't move, but the water runs."

"It makes noise cause the stones don't move and the water slides over."

"The water slams the rocks."

"If there was all water where there's stones, that wouldn't make so much noise."

"The water slams the rocks and other water and that makes noises."

"The water makes different noise up there, higher up."

"Up there it hits and jumps up, but here it hits and turns around."

"The water hits different rocks so there's different noises."

"The water makes different noises when the stones are in different places."

"Down here it's quieter cause it doesn't splash."

"There's no stones down here so the water is quiet and slow and smooth."

ELENA: Some disciplinary problems come from environments that don't stimulate children. They can be resolved by creating a new context where children can express their natural interests and develop a real ability to concentrate. If children pick up objects that can harm them, you have to take the objects away. But simultaneously you should offer an interesting alternative. I try to respect children's attention span, their rhythms of concentration. It's crucial not to distract or frustrate them.

BIANCA: On our walk today, the children filled their pockets with snails, and as soon as they got back to Mirto, they washed the snails and lined them up on the table.

"They're wet and soft."

"They see with their horns."

Sometimes the children throw themselves all over me, hugging me so tight I could suffocate: that way we feel closer, and our friendship grows deeper. Renato, the youngest child, is jealous when the others hug me. He pushes them all away.

We've planted lettuce in a patch a peasant hoed for us. The children were delighted. They came back inside with visions of green salad.

ANTONELLA: When we climb the mountain, the bigger children help the little ones. Irises grow thick among the rocks. We pick bushels of wild blackberries and share them, counting them out one by one. We try to learn to speak like lambs, dogs, cows, horses, and chickens.

On our way back we spot a fat green caterpillar, almost completely hidden in the grass. Sebastiano notices it's not moving and asks if it's dead. He decides to take a twig and see—gently. The caterpillar wiggles. The children laugh with surprise.

They all draw their faces on mirrors. Then they draw self-portraits on pieces of cardboard, and we tape the drawings to the door. All the children recognize themselves and each other.

LIBERA: We learn to listen, to intuit the children's desires, to coordinate our planning *with* them so that everybody feels expressed. In this process we try to help the children develop skills related to motor control, tasks, expressivity, observation, and exploration —in a well-balanced program.

In planning our trips, we ask the children where they want to go. And we take their wishes seriously. We've been to the sea, the airport, the dam, the railroad station, the port of Terrasini. The children feel they are discovering worlds beyond home, family, school.

All the groups* have developed well. They have points of common interest, but each is unique unto itself.

* At present there are six groups of fifteen children each (ages four to seven), with one educator and one assistant per group.

RENATA: I work with the children in the morning, but my main focus is the families. On the basis of their interests, I try to integrate their work and the school's. In fact, the development of our educational method is rooted in the family environment, its culture and potential to put its best values into practice. In spontaneous and intimate relationships, educators and parents share their knowledge. We concentrate on the children's behavior: what they do and don't like to do, how they react in different situations. In short, we try to develop a grass-roots analysis of school, home, and family.

The morning of March 22, 1977, after a night of heavy rains, the school bus (twenty-one children and two educators, besides the driver) skids in the mud on the bridge to Mirto. The tires grip inches from the edge, over the rock-bed gully.

We contact the mayor of Partinico. He is sitting in the main square. We tell him what has happened and emphasize the urgency of approving the public works project to rebuild the road and the bridge. Noticing my concern, he smirks: "But nobody was killed." (Those are his exact words.) A town councilor, sitting beside him, adds, "We've been working on the hospital ten years now, and it's still not finished. The road's been in the hopper only three or four years."

The following is part of the chronicle of initiatives to get a road to Mirto built:

DECEMBER 1972:

After numerous trips to municipal and provincial departments of public works, we are informed by the province that the city has been awarded the contract.

MARCH 1973:

Our group, the Center for Research and Initiatives (CRI), sends a letter to the minister of public works, asking him to intervene.

MAY 1973:

We send a letter to the mayor of Partinico, stating that the bridge is a hazard to public safety and requesting that he take immediate action to assure safe crossing for the children.

SEPTEMBER 1973:

The city planner in charge of the project presents an up-to-date report to the Provincial Office of Chief Surveyors and asks for the go-ahead.

JANUARY 1974:

POCS refuses to okay the project—owing to inflation. The proposal must be updated with more realistic estimates.

JUNE 3, 1974:

The mayor of Partinico goes on record in favor of doing everything in his power to get the road built.

MARCH 1975:

The mayor communicates the foregoing commitment in a letter to the Regional Ministry of Public Works.

MAY 1975:

The city planner presents the ministry with a new plan, budget included.

OCTOBER 23, 1976:

I quote from Palermo's afternoon daily, *The Hour:* "Head of Regional Government Visits Mirto, Vows Sicily's Aid. . . . The Educational Center of Mirto, built in a lovely natural setting between San Giuseppe Jato and Partinico, yesterday received the Head of the Sicilian Government, the Honorable Pancrazio de Pasquale, who, in a brief encomium, extended his warmest congratulations for the beauty and functionality of the school. The President vowed that the Region would come to the school's aid." And what about the road and the bridge? Assurances were made that it would all be arranged.

FEBRUARY 1977:

The ministry sends the new proposal back to the city planner. Approval of POCS is still pending.

CHRISTMAS, 1977:

Bad news in the headlines:

—TRAGEDY AT ILL-FATED AIRPORT
—PALERMO'S RAISI POINT: 108 VICTIMS: EMIGRANTS HOME FOR HOLIDAYS: DISASTER COULD HAVE BEEN AVERTED
—EXPERTS SAY REQUESTS FOR SAFETY EQUIPMENT IGNORED FOR YEARS
—6-YEAR AIRPORT TOLL OF RETURNING EMIGRANTS: 223
—TRAGEDY WAS PREDICTABLE
—PENINSULAR AIRPORT WITHOUT EMERGENCY COAST GUARD
—ENRAGED SEA FRUSTRATES SEARCH FOR BODIES
—LANDING GEAR OUT OF ORDER FOR 2 YEARS
—NEAR DISASTER THE NIGHT BEFORE: A FATAL REHEARSAL?
—ROSES, CARNATIONS, GLADIOLAS, FLOAT ON SWELLS

FEBRUARY 1978:

A delegation from Partinico, made up of the mayor and representatives of the political parties, the unions, and the CRI, meet with the regional minister of agriculture to request immediate approval and financing of the road-to-Mirto project (estimated costs range from $150,000 to $250,000). The minister agrees to approve the proposal, provided a few modifications in the budget and the wording be made to foresee future extension of the road.

MARCH 1978:

City planners present the responsible parties in the ministry with a modified, updated proposal and ask for official guarantees that future delays will be avoided.

APRIL 1978:

The specifics of the project regarding the reconstruction of the road and the bridge are discussed with peasants who have land to which the road is the main access.

MAY 1978:

The proposal is on the minister's desk, but clearance from the towns of Borgetto and Monreale and from the Provincial Department of Country Roads is awaited.

JUNE 1978:

To express their solidarity with the CRI, the peasants send delegations to each and every government office.

JULY 1978:

The City Council of Partinico meets to discuss the proposed extension of the road. But owing to conflicts between the political parties, all decisions are postponed. To resolve the whole problem once and for all, the CRI and the unions urge that party leaders, the mayor, and the minister confer. The mayor vows to put the question on the agenda of the next meeting of the City Council.

AUGUST 1978:

The City Council approves the road-extension project and sends it with a complete record of proceedings to the Provincial Budget Committee.

OCTOBER 1978:

The city planner meets with the chief surveyor of POCS to take stock of the situation. They are still awaiting a decision from the PBC.

NOVEMBER 1978:

Under a new law, final jurisdiction regarding such a project rests not with PBC but with POCS.

NOVEMBER 1978:

The proposal cannot be sent to POCS yet, because clearance from Monreale is still pending "owing to the negligence of no party."

1979:

With contributions from friends all over the world, we manage to repair the bridge. But every time the bus crosses it, we hold our breath. The parents are frustrated, disturbed. "It's going to take a death or two."

It's not an industrial route, so nobody can pocket any kick-backs. It's not a boulevard to the estate of a big vote-buyer. It's just a road to the healthy development of children and peasant families.

We send a telegram to the president of the Republic of Italy, the head of the Sicilian government, the minister of agriculture, and the mayor of Partinico:

PARTINICO-MIRTO ROAD INCREASINGLY HAZARDOUS STOP WALLS ALONG ROAD CRUMBLING STOP LANDSLIDES INTO GULLY STOP IMMEDIATE ACTION NEEDED TO REBUILD ROAD AVOID SERIOUS RISKS OF LOCAL PEOPLE'S LIVES . . .

Partinico, 1980
Danilo Dolci

This book was translated with the help of its composer and his co-workers. My human resources were plentiful: intellectuals who knew Italian and Sicilian, peasants and workers who were experts in Sicilian ways of surviving and expressing their *Weltanschauung*, companions who taught me quintessential nuances of Sicilian language and culture.

Dolci's comments are useful in helping all of us understand the general context: "This book is a selection of the stories told to me by people with whom I've worked these past thirty years in western Sicily. I've tried to choose the best, the most readable, without resorting to editing or embellishing. Readers should keep in mind that there is no room here for the distracting luxury of aesthetic pleasure. These stories penetrate Sicily's profoundest problems. Thus they are much too expressive, too perfect, to allow for aestheticizing. . . . We need such immediate truths, spoken by the people who live them in all their concreteness, with all their dilemmas, pain and suffering, struggle. . . . In a world where humans are becoming more and more enslaved to mass production, consumerism, stereotypes, where our alienation makes us regress to uniformity, these authentic human voices emerge, each and every one in his or her own tone and rhythm, with a unique, tragic sense of life."

To live the truth of nonviolence—in Gandhi's language, *satyagraha* means the desire for and strength of truth, the best way, the truth of being—was the impulse that not only led Dolci to compose *Sicilian Lives* but also brought him to Sicily in the first place. At the age of twenty-five, with a promising career in architecture ahead of him, an idealistic intellectual experienced a moment of existential lucidity: "I was dreaming of new skies and new earth—but only in the abstract. Violence revolted me, but I did nothing to resist it. I'd go to a Bach concert and feel his passion for a life conceived in harmony and serenity . . . but once I reached the exit I wasn't a better human being."*

That was 1949, when Dolci was about to receive his degree. Instead, he decided to shed his middle-class skin and go to work at Nomadelphia, a Christian commune in Tuscany that served as a family for war orphans and rejects. Hoeing, cleaning latrines, sharing with the poor, Dolci learned how to "burn off my dross and discover essential needs and values." Then in 1952, "more interested in how human beings could thrive and create together [than in] how with stones you could devise harmonious structures," he left for Trappeto in western Sicily—"the poorest place I had ever seen."†

Dolci still lives in Trappeto. Through his efforts and those of peasants and fishermen who joined his nonviolent protests, sitdowns, fasts, strikes-in-reverse (where the unemployed and underemployed do public works without authorization to demonstrate the need for jobs), Trappeto now has paved streets, sewers, a drugstore, and a government subsidy to improve its terrain and port. That is to say, it subsists—although roughly 25 percent of the villagers must still emigrate to find work.

But more important, Dolci, getting his own hands soiled and blistered from the first, has helped to develop in the larger territory of western Sicily a method of grass-roots consciousness- and conscience-raising as a spur to democratic action and radical, peaceful change. He has toiled with and learned from Southern Italians. Through true respect for the indigenous population and admiration for the real qualities of its culture, Dolci earned trust, and the people have let him excavate the values most deeply rooted in their ancient agrarian-artisan civilization. Realizing what could be done to put human and natural resources to best use, Dolci and his co-workers have pressed over the years for the

---

* See "What I've Learned" in the forthcoming translation of Dolci's lifelong documentary studies and essays, *Experiences and Reflections.*
† Ibid.

construction of dams to have water from winter rains for the three growing seasons; for the distribution of water for irrigation by peasant cooperatives, not by the Mafia; for the development of wine, produce, and artisan cooperatives (now the major form of healthy economic organization in western Sicily); and for the creation of schools where, because peasant children and their parents actually participate in choosing pedagogical methods and designing programs, education is authentic in serving communal needs.

It's impossible to sum up Dolci's life and work in a page or two.* But what I do want to stress is his role as a catalyst in creating an environment wherein the oppressed might take responsibility for building new sociopolitical and economic structures that eliminate oppressed and oppressors. Taking literally the idea that life should be a work of art (as a poem is an organic whole with unity in all its diversity), Dolci has struggled with the people of Sicily and "the terrestrial city" (his organic, utopian space without national or ethnic boundaries where every being is a "creature of creatures"), for a personal, cultural, structural, and cosmic revolution. Aware that "it's easier to stop hurricanes/ than make a revolution/without bosses," Dolci has tried to act as a midwife who "gently/pushes/sets free," providing occasions for creativity—as he has done in this choral work by bringing into harmony and discord, dialectically, the voices of the people of Sicily.

In spite of consumptive Newsspeak, media bombardment, and satellite and computer bleeps, I've tried to communicate these voices via American idioms. Searching for language appropriate to different socioeconomic classes and to every human within each class, I've striven to avoid slang that is too archaic, local, or hip. If there's any idea of beauty pursued here, it would approach

---

* See the introduction to my translation of Dolci's *Creature of Creatures: Selected Poems* (Saratoga, Calif.: Anma Libri, 1980) for a more comprehensive discussion. For further background, see Jerre Mangione, *The World Around Danilo Dolci: A Passion for Sicilians* (New York: William Morrow & Co., 1968).

Chekhov's "aesthetics of the dungheap": beauty based on telling a story, however bittersweet, in a form authenticated by its bittersweet content.

This kind of narrative should flow like grape juice between the toes, or dough among the calluses. Call bread bread and wine wine, but realize things are always fermenting.

In his introduction to *Creature of Creatures* Dolci says, "I've tried to get to the essentials and be as precise as possible, always keeping in mind that if the flour's too refined, the bread loses its flavor." This also describes my effort to translate.

Justin Vitiello

ABOUT THE AUTHOR

Danilo Dolci was born in Northern Italy in 1924. In 1952,
he moved to western Sicily. For more than twenty-five
years, he has lived and worked with the Sicilian people
whose voices are recorded in these stories. Mr. Dolci has
been awarded four international peace prizes for his efforts
to provide innovative, nonviolent solutions to the
economic, social, and cultural problems of Sicily. He has
also been nominated several times for the Nobel Prize.

ABOUT THE TRANSLATORS

Justin Vitiello was born in New York City in 1941. He
received his B.A. from Brown University and his Ph.D.
from the University of Michigan. At present, he teaches
Italian and English composition at Temple University.
A poet and essayist, he has long been committed to the
work of Danilo Dolci.

Madeline Polidoro, a native of Philadelphia, was
graduated from Temple University. At present, she
works for the International Business Machines corporation.

THE PANTHEON VILLAGE SERIES

"Literate social science at its best."
—*The New York Times*

TITLES NOW IN PAPERBACK IN PANTHEON'S SERIES OF REPORTS
FROM VILLAGES THROUGHOUT THE WORLD:

Akenfield: Portrait of an English Village, by Ronald Blythe
0-394-73847-0 $3.95

Amoskeag: Life and Work in an American Factory-City,
by Tamara Hareven and Randolph Langenbach
0-394-73855-1 $6.95

*Longtime Californ': A Documentary of an American
Chinatown,* by Victor G. Nee and Brett de Bary Nee
0-394-73846-2 $6.95

Report from a Chinese Village, by Jan Myrdal
0-394-74802-6 $6.95

Shinohata: A Portrait of a Japanese Village, by Ronald P. Dore
0-394-73843-8 $4.95

Sicilian Lives, by Danilo Dolci
0-394-74938-3 $6.95

Ten Mile Inn: Mass Movement in a Chinese Village, by
Isabel and David Crook
0-394-73328-2 $6.95

9 780394 749389

Printed in the United States
by Baker & Taylor Publisher Services